V. C. W.

Also by
M. M. Marberry

THE GOLDEN VOICE
Biography of I. S. Kalloch

SPLENDID POSEUR
Biography of Joaquin Miller

FOOL'S GOLD
Alaska Gold Rush Days

VICKY

A BIOGRAPHY OF

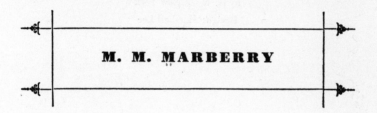

Victoria C. Woodhull

M. M. MARBERRY

FUNK & WAGNALLS

A Division of

Reader's Digest Books, Inc.

New York

Again, for Therese

Contents

The Petticoat Politician
NEW YORK: 1870-71
· 3 ·

Much Ado About Blackmail
NEW YORK: 1872
· 77 ·

The Woodhull Compromise
NEW YORK: 1873-77
· 135 ·

Operation Virtue
LONDON: 1877-87
· 199 ·

The Fruits of Respectability
ENGLAND: 1888-1927
· 253 ·

A Selected Bibliography
· 331 ·

Index
· 337 ·

The Petticoat Politician

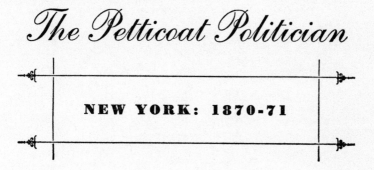

NEW YORK: 1870-71

. 1 .

Each morning people gathered expectantly, facing the curb on Broad Street, a block south of Wall in the core of New York's financial district, and promptly at ten o'clock their vigil was rewarded. The open landau, pulled spankingly by two white horses, drove up at a brisk pace. The coachman in scarlet livery jumped down from his perch, opened the door of the carriage and bowed low. The two occupants glanced with amusement at the throng as they waited for a path to be cleared, then they gathered up their Dolly Vardens and swept majestically through the doors of the banking house at 44 Broad Street. Most of the gapers soon would disperse, but there were always the overcurious who flattened their noses against the new-mode plate-glass windows to peer inside, anxious for one more peep at the first women in the land who dared invade man's private field of finance, who early in this year of 1870 were known far and wide as the "Lady Brokers," though the word *lady* never was used by the uncharitable.

The banking house (as brokerage firms were called at the time) was fitted out with elegance. Its lobby was shiny with black marble counters, and rich carpets covered the floor. The furniture of black walnut and chestnut and the huge safes lining the walls lent a note of stability and integrity to the establishment. Beyond was a receipt room where the ladies met their business friends and settled deals in stocks and gold, and farther back was a door leading to their private parlors, with the admonitory sign overhead:

ALL GENTLEMEN
WILL STATE THEIR BUSINESS
AND
RETIRE AT ONCE

but there were the skeptical who were convinced the austere injunction was not intended to be taken too seriously. Some of the gentlemen lingered to pore over the scrapbooks of clippings and pictures always open for inspection, and they noted wonderingly that, no matter whether the notices were good, bad, or indifferent, they were pasted in and shown with delight. Others less perceptive were attracted by the magnums of champagne bubbling invitingly in the silver buckets. But all the gentlemen knew that the chief allure of the establishment was the presence of the two vivacious and frankly "modern" ladies.

The favored who gained the intimacy of the private parlors saw at once that the "Fascinating Financiers," as the penny press alliteratively put it, were beautiful. They were sisters and their names were Victoria C. Woodhull and Tennie Celeste Claflin, the latter preferring to be known as Tennessee, a compounding of Tennie C.

Victoria—often called The Woodhull or Vicky by newspapers and magazines—was of medium height, with a broad
and high forehead and prominent cheekbones, lithe in appearance and elastic in step, with a tricky way of gazing, almost
staring fixedly, into the eyes of the person she was talking to.
She was free in manner, highly informal, and, the press admiringly reported, "could talk a blue streak from here to Christmas." Victoria was daring when it came to conversation and
the men liked her for it. "She is apt to call things by their right
names, speaks out boldly what she thinks, and we should infer
that she has adopted as her own the motto of the Knight of the
Garter," wrote a reporter. Like Tennessee, she always was fashionably attired, with a talma draped carelessly over her shoulder, a tea rose in her hair, a diamond ring on her right thumb,
and, unthinkable for the age, she and her sister Tennessee both
wore their curly reddish-brown hair bobbed. Victoria—she was
named after the queen who was crowned the year of her birth—
was thirty-one, seven years older than her sister. Tennessee was
ivory-skinned, blue-eyed, petite and plump, with the overripe
body so acceptable at the time, and was thought the more beautiful of the two, though all agreed she had not the compelling
charm of her sister. Some people felt that Tennessee acted a
trifle boldly for a lady (she had "the impulsive gaiety of a
gypsy," so said the New York SUN), for, no more subtle than
an aching tooth, she liked to be close to a male when she con-
versed, and this delighted the gentlemen. "She is all verve and
vivacity, full of imagination and excitability, very free in her
modes of expression," a newspaperman wrote. She was a special favorite of the dashing men about town, who liked to sere-
nade her with the song, "Oh, that Ten-Ten-Tennessee!"

The sisters were from out of the Midwest, somewhere. No
one knew exactly what state they came from, or what kind of
life they had led there, for, though they were fond of talking

about themselves they were reticent about their background. One fact in their lives, however, was known to everyone: The Lady Brokers, first of their kind in the country and world, had money, lots of it.

They had money and they spent it. For business conferences the sisters used Parlors 25 and 26 at the Hoffman House in Madison Square, an inn considered by the genteel as being out of bounds for ladies, inasmuch as Bouguereau's huge oil painting of mythological nudities was displayed there in the bar. They had a private table reserved at the Astor, and some people were puzzled to learn that they also had private apartments there. They ate at Delmonico's and Sherry's and other stylish restaurants, and more than once it was noticed they ordered the breakfast of blades—pâté de foie gras and champagne.

A New York HERALD reporter saw while interviewing Tennessee that Parlor 26 was crammed with statuary, richly upholstered chairs, a deep yielding couch, a glazed motto, "Simply To Thy Cross I Cling," and, dominating the room, an immense oil portrait.

"It is a novel sight to see a lady on the Street as a stock operator," said the newspaperman as he gazed speculatively at the oil painting, "and I presume you find it rather awkward."

"I despise what squeamy, crying girls or powdered counter-jumping dandies say of me," replied Tennessee, for she liked to use forceful language. "I think a woman is just as capable of making a living as a man, and I have seen men so vain of their personal appearance and so effeminate that I should be sorry to compare my intellect to theirs. I don't care what society thinks. I have not time to care. I don't go to balls or theatres. My mind is on my business and I attend to that solely."

Tennessee explained, as had her sister to other inquiring reporters, that the "Queens of Finance," to use the HERALD's own words, had an initial banking capital of $250,000 (with a backlog of $700,000 profits cleaned up in six weeks by a coup in railroad stocks) which they believed was ample evidence to prove their contention that women could compete with men in finance. They were willing to lose it all, Tennessee said, to prove the point.

There were others, the doubting souls, who thought that if the money were lost the old Commodore, Cornelius Vanderbilt, whose oil portrait hung on a wall of Parlor 26, would be the loser. And he could afford it.

. 2 .

Commodore Cornelius Vanderbilt, king of the mighty New York Central, was the richest, or almost the richest, man in the country. At seventy-six he was still vigorous in body, but he was becoming more and more eccentric. Grief-stricken after the death of his youngest child, he had taken up Spiritualism, Mesmerism and Clairvoyance, all in tremendous vogue in the 1870's, and had communed with various departed spirits through a variety of mediums. When the Claflin sisters arrived to take exclusive possession of the old Commodore's expeditions into the beyond, they convinced him that Mrs. Tufts, hitherto his favorite astral guide, had no genuine connections in the realm of the supernatural. As they put Vanderbilt in touch with some of the most authentic shades (though jealous rival mediums claimed no respectable phantom would ever answer their call), it was but logical that he would appreciate their unselfish interest, and reciprocate. This he did, in a more

earthly way, by lending his hand—and purse—to acquaint
them with the ways of the business world. Vanderbilt helped
the sisters to the supposed $700,000 melon when the railroad
war was at its height, and hence their journalistic nickname,
"The Princesses of Erie." Many brokers thought the sum was
less, considerably less—$700, maybe.

Many mediums were saggy-cheeked and blowsy, but not the
Claflin sisters, the beautiful Claflin sisters, and there were few
in the country as adept as they when it came to exhibitions of
levitation or table-tapping. Mrs. Tufts had set salt cellars under
the legs of Vanderbilt's bed to act as health conductors. The
sisters called this child's play. They could cause ectoplasm to
float about a darkened room in a silver smoke, dissolve into a
shadowy gray-white film, then into a shimmering vapor. As
Tennessee confided, "Jesus Christ was a medium," and she
pointed out, in strict confidence, that it was a matter of record
that Lincoln had been a Spiritualistic convert, for a message
sent by an unnamed medium had moved him to emancipate the
slaves. This revelation was gratefully received by old Vanderbilt, but it did not mean that he could be led by the nose. As
befitted a dynamic tycoon, he had a mind of his own. One day
when Victoria brought into a dimmed room the apparition of
his dead wife, Sophia, the Commodore flatly refused to com-
municate with her. "Business before pleasure," he ordered.
"Let me speak to Jim Fisk."

Vanderbilt had great faith in the advice of the murdered Jim
Fisk, but his faith in Vicky was absolute. Soon he let her solve
his most perplexing business problems. In later years a New
York TRIBUNE editor recalled that the Commodore placed
greater credence in the ability of The Woodhull to foretell rises
and falls in New York Central stock than in himself, master of
the road. "Do as I do, consult the spirits," he told a widow who
solicited a market tip. And, in advising another lady to take all

her savings out of the bank and buy Central common stock, he declared, "It's bound to go up twenty-two per cent—Mrs. Woodhull said so in a trance."

With increasing age the Commodore liked more and more to be with people who did not stand on ceremony, and the beautiful sisters were ideal companions for him. "Wake up, old boy!" Tennessee would cry as she slapped him on the back and tugged at his whiskers. Victoria, though less boisterous, was equally comforting as she assured this implicit believer that the mysterious Spiritualistic world was as real to her as it was to him. Vanderbilt had remarried soon after the death of his first wife, but that did not prevent him from seeing the sisters. "Didn't you promise to marry *me?*" Tennessee reproached him. "Yes, but the family interfered," the Commodore explained. Tennessee was so fond of the old rip that she took $2,000 from the Erie loot and presented Vanderbilt with an oil painting, "Aurora," which he displayed in his Greek Revival mansion at 10 Washington Place. The picture shocked many people, for Aurora, to use overstatement, was thinly clad. The Commodore loved to sit quietly for hours in his chair and look at it.

Vanderbilt explained to his horrified relatives that he liked the sisters because they had spirit, and he did not intend to pun. When they were denied admittance to Delmonico's because they had no escort, Tennessee had dashed out into Broadway, caught her coachman before he drove to the stables, and returned with him. The coachman, wearing his scarlet coat and leather boots, had sat down and ordered dinner for three. The old Commodore had roared at the frustration of Charles Delmonico. And when Victoria had commandeered a hotel porter to sit with her in a box to see Madame Ristori, for women could not attend the theatre unless accompanied by a gentleman, he drank an appreciative toast to her—his usual wineglass filled with gin and sugar—while out driving his trotters, and in full view of passers-by. He had guffawed at the shrewdness shown by Tennessee when first she had entered Wall Street. Tennessee deposited a check for $7,000, endorsed by Vanderbilt, with Henry Clews's banking house. She confided to Clews that she had a tip and wanted to buy one thousand shares of New York Central stock. Clews, trying hard to be astute, reasoned she was planting a bad tip to lure him into plunging. "The Commodore was then regarded as the power behind the throne, or behind the fair sex," Clews recalled in his memoirs. "If the sisters had any scheme in the background (and I have reason to believe they did) I did not get caught in it."

As Vanderbilt pointed out, however, Clews was outwitted in the end, for Tennessee immediately withdrew her account and deposited it in the Fourth National Bank. She asked Clews to identify her there, which he did, thus gaining the doubtful distinction of being with the old Commodore a secret co-sponsor of the sisters' banking house.

"The firm has been in business for three years," Victoria told a reporter, stretching the truth by some thirty-five months, "and it has made $700,000, but what do present profits amount to when it costs us over $25,000 a month to live?"

The newspaperman, noticing the glittering diamond on her thumb, the rose in her hair, found Vicky beautiful, of nervous temperament, and—probably remembering her casual reference to the millions about to be dredged from her silver mine in Nevada—sanguine.

. 3 .

Money was needed by Victoria and Tennessee, though not necessarily in such quantities as $25,000 a month. In addition to their parlors at the Hoffman House and their suite at the Astor the sisters had leased a four-story mansion, full of statuary, oil paintings, and gilt, at 15 East Thirty-eighth Street in the fashionable Murray Hill district. The place was crammed with members and allies of the Claflin clan. In this house lived their mother and father, Victoria's first and also her second (and current) husband, her two children, a well-known theosophical thinker, a sister with a husband and two children, another sister with four in the brood, and still another younger sister. Counting three servants, a coachman, a cook, and a nurse, the ménage numbered twenty-four.

No one outside the family knew anything about the father, Reuben Buckman Claflin, a one-eyed man called "Buck." Occasionally there were rumors that he had spent much of his time traveling with a medicine and fortunetelling show, selling an Elixir of Life guaranteed to cure cancer, colds, cramps, and any-and-all ailments. The sisters denied this. They described him as a rich and prominent Ohio lawyer who had retired after a long and honorable career.

The mother, Roxanna, familiarly known as Roxy, had been well-known in the West at one time as a Mesmerist and Spiritualist. This was not denied. Victoria and Tennessee were but two of the ten children she had borne, seven of whom were alive.

Another member of the household, Dr. Canning Woodhull, in 1870 at the age of forty-five was already a broken man who tended to heavy drinking or, when temperate in liquor, to the use of morphine. A physician, he had married Victoria in 1853, when she was fourteen and he exactly twice her age. They had been divorced in 1864, but now he had come to live with the family. Dr. Woodhull claimed to be the nephew of Caleb Woodhull, once Mayor of New York, but his "kin" did not acknowledge the relationship. Dr. Woodhull was staying with Victoria even though her current husband, Colonel James H. Blood, lived in the same house. This arrangement had Colonel Blood's blessing. Victoria said she carried over no physical affection whatsoever for her first spouse, but as a Christian she was helping him in time of need.

Colonel Blood, thirty-three years old, described himself as a man of many parts. He was broad-minded—a Free Lover, a Spiritualist, a Communist, an Internationalist and Cosmopolitical—the latter being a radical of extreme radicalism, he explained. His military rank of Colonel was self-adopted, but he had served with the Sixth Missouri Regiment during the Civil War and carried bullets in his body to prove it. At the end of the conflict he had been elected City Auditor of St. Louis, so he said, but authorities in that city declared Blood must have mistaken himself for a remote cousin who had held the post. He preferred not to talk about his life, particularly when people from the Midwest sometimes recognized him to be "Dr. J. H. Harvey," king of the medicine showmen. He was below average height, handsome, with dark brown hair, a flowing mustache and Dundreary side whiskers. There was only one event in his past of which he would talk freely: The first time he met Victoria. As President of the Society of Spiritualists of St. Louis, he had called on Victoria one day in his capacity as a fellow Spiritualistic physician. On seeing him, he remembered, Victoria

swooned in a trance, but was conscious enough to mutter that
destiny decreed the two be linked together. Thus, Blood gravely
stated, they were betrothed on the spot by "the powers of the
air." After two years of intimacy, physical as well as Spiritualistic, Victoria had secured a divorce from Dr. Woodhull and
married him.

Two other members of the house were Zulu, Victoria's eight-
year-old daughter, and Byron, sixteen, who seldom was seen as
he was retarded and under the care of a nurse. Dr. Woodhull
was their father. Then there were three sisters of Victoria and
Tennessee: Polly Sparr (with husband Benjamin and two children), Margaret Ann Miles (with four babies), and Utica,
aged twenty-seven, who envied her older sister Victoria and
was assuaging her chronic discontent by drinking her way to
the grave.

Another inmate was a man who had dropped in for a week-
end and stretched it out to a visit of months. He was Stephen
Pearl Andrews, a lifelong radical. Andrews, a one-time Abolitionist, was at the moment a Philosophical Anarchist, in addition to being the inventor of a universal language, *Alwato*, the
author of many books, a master of twenty languages including
Chinese, an atheist, a student of the isms of Fourier and Swe-
denborg and Marx, and the founder of a perfect society, a
socialistic cult called Pantarchy. The basis of Pantarchy was
Free Love. Andrews hoped to be Pantarch of the United States
come the Revolution, and to rule the country from a Zodiac
Palace.

Stephen Pearl Andrews had many brilliant philosophical
ideas, some of which survive today, but, being timid on a platform, he could not voice them. He found in Victoria a willing
sponge who quickly soaked up his involved notions once they
were put in writing and studied. She had begun to spread his
ideas, first gropingly, sounding out her circle of friends and

acquaintances, then organizing informal talks before small but select audiences. She may have met James Gordon Bennett on one of those occasions. As she became more and more famous —infamous, a great many people said—Bennett, who always could scent a good story, opened the columns of his New York HERALD to her.

Victoria made the best of the opportunity. Her weekly column—headlined rather derisively by the HERALD as "The Petticoat Politician" and presented under similar gaily frivolous titles—touched on many, many subjects, ranging from the equality of women to the murder of American citizens abroad by Spanish cutthroats, presumably with the blessing of President Grant. The HERALD liked that, so much so that Vicky was given great latitude in expressing her views. She was permitted to boost woman's suffrage—and to tout herself as the next President of the United States. The fact that women could not hold political office, or even vote, was no bar to Victoria's campaign. She asked that occupancy of the White House be given her "solely on the score that I have the means, courage, energy and ability necessary to contest the issue to its close."

The HERALD applauded its gingery columnist, but even it was somewhat pessimistic when considering the possibility of her election. "It is with some difficulty to see what good will come out of this particular Nazareth," the newspaper speculated. "The public mind is not yet educated to the pitch of universal women's rights." And President Grant, sitting in the White House, though almost totally devoid of executive ability, was said to be not in the least alarmed about losing his job.

· 4 ·

As Victoria's polemics began to arouse public attention she found she liked it, and so she decided to launch a weekly newspaper designed, among other things, to further her presidential ambitions. It never was learned where the money came from, but it was believed the faithful old Commodore, so stingy in many respects, was the backer.

The newspaper, an acknowledged "radical, reformatory paper," edited jointly by Victoria and Tennessee, was named WOODHULL & CLAFLIN'S WEEKLY and its first issue was published with a two-week predate on May 14, 1870. It was a sixteen-page, four-column sheet, with the inspiring motto, "Upward and Onward!" Handsomely printed on good stock, it soon obtained a tremendous circulation for the time—about twenty thousand readers. Later, that figure soared to spectacular heights.

The WEEKLY came out for less rigid divorce laws, for organized labor, Spiritualism, Free Love and a variety of other causes, and its first serial was written by the "notorious," as she then was regarded, George Sand. Free Love was euphemistically described as "a single standard of morality." "The highest order of humanity results from sexual relations in which love is the only element present," the journal asserted, and women and men from coast to coast gasped. The New York TRIBUNE queerly concluded that Victoria was in favor of prostitution, all because the newspaper deplored police "shakedown" raids on whorehouses. The WEEKLY also condemned abortion and favored birth control, and while the abortionists, far from being intimidated, continued to do business as usual, and while there was no measurable decline in the country's birthrate despite her frank suggestions for precaution—well, it made spicy reading.

The front page of the newspaper always was taken up with announcements paid for by reputable bankers and brokers in the city. The advertisements of wine and liquor dealers and keepers of billiard parlors were relegated to the inside pages. Abortionists and Madames, who publicized their trades freely in other sheets, did not patronize the WEEKLY. The journal, however, was full of other unsavory ads. There were "infallible" cures for cancer and other afflictions, and occasionally there would be personal notes such as:

"A lady in good standing having no acquaintances among gentlemen, would like to meet with one of liberal tendencies, worth from $15,000 to $20,000 . . . [he] should be mature in years and of genial nature. Address Miriam Hale, this office."

The WEEKLY had many facets. Each week one page was devoted to poetry. It featured an interminable poem in installments called "Nature in a Nutshell," and another which instructed the ladies in the meaning of the latest slang. "Fusil oil" meant whiskey; "spondulix" money; "he's on his back" bankrupt. But the main purpose of the newspaper week in and week out was to boost Victoria C. Woodhull as the ideal President of the United States—on some ticket or other. The WEEKLY wanted to know:

> Are statesmen vain enough to think
>   That they would have been free
> If woman had not lent her hand
>   And fought for liberty?

It might not make much sense, so the gentlemen thought, but they were amused and they read the WEEKLY, while an increasing army of women became suffrage-minded.

Each issue contained a few notes, presumably from readers giving their candid opinion of Victoria. It seemed they all adored her. As one typical letter-writer put it:

"As I was looking at Sister Victoria's picture I involuntarily exclaimed, 'Who can look into that sad, thoughtful, tender but firm, face and not see love, truth, purity and justice enstamped upon every lineament of the countenance?' "

As the WEEKLY continued to gain in circulation the original price of five cents soon was raised to ten, and the advertising rates were high—$1 to $2.50 a line, according to location. Daily newspapers, angered by the loss of revenue to a rival, started to attack the WEEKLY, and the HERALD stopped printing Victoria's column. The politicians, seeing women stirring, became worried. But the readers of the WEEKLY had faith. One letter-writer sent in a six years' subscription in advance. That was real faith.

"Her social theories are most revolting and find but few indorsers," one reporter, who had no faith, said of Victoria, "for their adoption would sap the foundations of domestic life, and bring man down to the status of the brute creation." Another thought the Free Love Queens used lipstick, but few people believed they were as depraved as that.

Finding that she not only enjoyed but reveled in the limelight, The Woodhull cast about for a better Cause. There was a surge of sympathy throughout the nation for women's equality; she herself had occasionally spoken in its favor. The bandwagon was there, waiting, and editor Victoria leaped on it, heels first, and as it happened, into the driver's seat.

. 5 .

Victoria's bid for fame on a more national scale came in January, 1871, when she went to Washington with a Memorial—a petition demanding enfranchisement of women under provisions of the Fourteenth Amendment. Senator Harris of Louisiana obligingly presented it to the Senate, Representative Julian of Indiana to the lower House, and the document then was referred for consideration to the Judiciary Committee.

The Judiciary Committee on the morning of January 11 met to hear the beautiful New York publisher and financier read her Memorial. It so happened that at that time the National Women's Suffrage Association was scheduled to open its third annual convention in Washington. The ladies were dismayed for, with the entrance of what many considered an adventuress, opportunist, and outsider into their private field, their convention was in danger of being ignored. Victoria had not consulted any of the suffragists; indeed, she knew not one of them. Susan B. Anthony, lifelong Suffragette who at first described The Woodhull as "a lady quite déclassée in any society which called itself polite," led a delegation to Senator Samuel C. Pomeroy and asked his advice on how to handle the situation. They informed him that The Woodhull openly admitted she was a Free Lover, that she was bewitching but notorious, and that she supposedly had a fortune.

"Men could never work in a political party if they stopped to investigate each member's antecedents and associates," the politically wise Senator from Kansas told the delegation. (Within a short time Pomeroy was to have his own antecedents investigated and find himself barred from the Senate for bribery.) "If you are going into a fight, you must accept every help that offers."

One of the leading suffragists, Mrs. Isabella Beecher Hooker, half-sister of the famed preaching man, The Reverend Henry Ward Beecher, announced she would snub the newcomer because of her social and sexual opinions and general background. "It would ill become these women, especially a Beecher, to talk of antecedents or to cast any smirch upon Mrs. Woodhull," a gentleman said, stepping forward. "For I am reliably informed that Henry Ward Beecher preaches to at least twenty of his mistresses every Sunday." Mrs. Hooker, who had heard the story before, and who furthermore believed it, was silenced. When Victoria was informed of the conversation she was interested to learn of the reported lapses of The Reverend. She catalogued the curious incident in her memory, and later, when the time was apropos, she used it.

Miss Anthony, Elizabeth Cady Stanton, Mrs. Hooker, Pauline Davis, Laura Curtis Bullard, and other suffrage bigwigs decided Senator Pomeroy's advice was sound. Accordingly, they postponed the opening of their convention to the afternoon and attended the Judiciary Committee hearing. None of the leaders knew, or had ever seen, the oft-publicized Woodhull. To their amazement they discovered that she was not at all the Scarlet Woman type. Instead they found her young and pretty with cropped brown curls, fashionably and quietly dressed. "She was a beautiful woman, refined in appearance and plainly dressed, with a clear, musical voice," Miss Anthony wrote, discarding at once her "déclassé" theory. And Mrs. Hooker, once she was acquainted with suffragism's newest convert, became an ardent, almost slavish admirer. Actually Mrs. Hooker had little use for brother Henry Ward Beecher, for, as

Miss Anthony recorded, "the swimming bath of tears into which he loved to plunge his audience offended her taste."

Victoria was at first flustered as she started to read her petition, for confronting her were such noted Congressional figures as Matthew Hale Carpenter of Wisconsin, General Benjamin F. Butler of Massachusetts, Judge William Loughridge of Iowa, and George W. Julian of Indiana. These four men on the Committee listened to her sympathetically, however. Heartened by the repeated applause of the professional Suffragettes in the room (this "motley assembly" leaned against bookcases "in attitudes which very much resembled the customs of mankind," a newspaper disapprovingly commented), and by the alert attention of the reporters, she soon became spirited as she expounded her views on woman's rights.

Victoria's performance was a great success. "Her contemporaries in the woman's rights or suffrage movement have hitherto ignored her, have frowned upon her as an interloper, and have denounced her as unworthy of the association and confidence of pure and chaste advocates of the great cause," THE NEW YORK TIMES said the next day. But now, the newspaper said, "the cry of the suffragans was anthems to Woodhull."

· 6 ·

That afternoon the suffragist convention opened and Victoria attended, with her sister Tennessee at her side. "Then came the two New York sensations—both in dark dresses, with blue neckties, short, curly hair, and nobby alpine hats, the very picture of the advanced ideas they are advocating," reported the Washington DAILY PATRIOT. The two shared the platform with all the suffragist greats, and in the presence of Senators Nye of Nevada, Warner of Utah, and Wilson of Massachusetts. Victoria, hitherto scorned as being insincere and perhaps even wicked in her private life, was now a guest of honor, heroine of the day. Again she read her petition and was greeted with rolls of applause. Most of the Suffragettes congratulated themselves on their new disciple. Vicky announced that she and Tennessee personally would pay a visit to President Grant to convince him with their charm and logical arguments that women's suffrage could not be denied.

"They had been so much pleased and elated with their capture of the Judiciary Committee, that they imagined they could persuade the chief magistrate to attend the meeting tonight," THE NEW YORK TIMES said. "Of course, they failed."

The next day Victoria—"the little woman with a far-off look," so a visitor described her—again attended the convention, but, far from being bold, sat "sphynx-like" through the proceedings. This convinced more and more of the Suffragettes that The Woodhull was a lady, just like themselves. "General Grant might learn a lesson in silence from the pale, sad face of this unflinching woman," the Philadelphia PRESS stated. "No chance to send an arrow through the opening seams of her mail. She reminds one of the forces in nature behind the storm, or of a small splinter of the indestructible; and if her veins were opened they would be found to contain ice water."

Victoria's veins did not appear to contain ice water, however, when she made her only appearance on the platform. She warmly announced that, as the convention needed money, it was her privilege to subscribe $10,000. The waves of applause were more deafening than ever. "The money doubtless will be forthcoming tomorrow," the hopeful among her audience were saying, for cash was desperately needed. Alas, this money never arrived.

Though the newspapers redoubled their cries that all Suffragettes were now *per se* Free Lovers, the ladies themselves were jubilant. They prepared to storm the galleries of the House and Senate, in the hope of finding the two chambers voting on the petition.

At that point the Committee of the Judiciary, which had been quite willing to listen to the suffragists, but was equally determined to withhold the Memorial from consideration by Senators and Representatives, made its report:

"Resolved: That the prayer of the petitioner be not granted, that the Memorial be laid on the table, and that the Committee of the Judiciary be discharged from further consideration of the subject."

After such a setback any ordinary woman's career might have ended there and then. But Victoria C. Woodhull was not the type to be easily discouraged, any more than the suffragist movement itself could be killed by an unfavorable decision. Victoria was to live down many a professional defeat and even to turn some of them into personal triumphs. She had talent, ambition, enormous vitality, and the singular capacity to fight seemingly hopeless battles from which she might emerge at times, slightly battered, but always intact.

. **7** .

Most of the rank-and-file suffragists were delighted with the acquisition of Victoria, plus her newspaper, but a few professed to be shocked. It was whispered that Victoria's greatest Memorial was the bastard child of old wall-eyed General Benjamin F. Butler, Civil War firebrand known through the South as "Beast Butler." The leaders of the conservative Suffragettes, Julia Ward Howe and Mrs. Mary Livermore, would have nothing to do with The Woodhull, but the bosses of the radical, and stronger, wing supported her stanchly. Susan B. Anthony, who so delighted in being known as "the old war-torn soldier," was called to account by two suffrage groups "for the right hand of, fellowship extended to Mrs. Woodhull—Free Lover." The newcomer's "charm of youth and all that sort of thing, you know," explained Miss Anthony, "will woo men to woman's suffrage."

Elizabeth Cady Stanton, another prominent suffrage warrior, answered the criticism with a left-handed recommendation for Victoria:

"In regard to the gossip about Mrs. Woodhull, I have one answer to give all my gentlemen friends: When the men who make laws for us in Washington can stand forth and declare themselves pure and unspotted from all the sins mentioned in the Decalogue, then we will demand that every woman who makes a constitutional argument on our platform shall be as chaste as Diana. But, if Victoria Woodhull must be crucified, let men drive the spikes and plait the crown of thorns."

As the rumors multiplied about the new disciple's peculiar social ideas and her alleged frequent practice of Free Love in the "Psyche Club," organized for the purpose in New York on Twenty-third Street, Mrs. Stanton retorted that it was a "great impertinence in any of us to pry into her private affairs." Mrs. Stanton, who would have made an alliance with the devil, provided the suffrage cause were furthered, added: "This woman stands before us today as an able speaker and writer. Her face, manners and conversation, all indicate the triumph of the moral, intellectual and spiritual."

Undismayed by the rebuff of the Judiciary Committee and heartened by the support of Mrs. Stanton, Victoria returned to New York and immediately capitalized on the women's rights movement. WOODHULL & CLAFLIN'S WEEKLY (which soon discarded its masthead motto, "Onward and Upward!" and substituted "Progress! Free Thought! Untrammeled Lives! Breaking the Way for Future Generations!") now was full of the subject, and Victoria went on lecture tours in search of converts —and money. Always she would read her Memorial, including the paragraph which for some reason startled her listeners and caused them to gasp: "Woman is a producer, taxpayer, criminal witness, may be loyal, or commit and be punished for treason. She produces her full share of all material wealth, besides the responsibilities and dangers of maternity."

It was scandalous, many people thought, that Victoria had the nerve to mention in public such an intimate function as childbirth.

The first of what were to be hundreds upon hundreds of lectures given by The Woodhull was delivered at the Cooper Institute before a packed house. "Only Criminals, Idiots and the Insane may be deprived of the Ballot—There are No Free Women!" read a poster hanging above the stage. Victoria told those assembled that the prejudice against woman's suffrage was rapidly passing, and that her sex would fight to the bitter end for the pursuit of happiness. "The pursuit of happiness, in bed," sniffed a newspaper the next day.

Victoria, and others in the hall, had by now discovered that she was an orator, a born spellbinder. It was a field in which she had not experimented in all her thirty-two years, and she was an instant success. An historian of the period, Don Seitz, wrote half a century later, "Three women were worth while on the platform: Anna Dickenson, Mary Livermore and Victoria Woodhull—the last the finest speaker." Seitz believed Victoria

was the equal of any of the country's famed male orators—
Webster, Beecher, Clay, Douglas, Douglass, Lincoln.

In another lecture, this time before the Labor Reform
League, Victoria read a lengthy paper on "The Relations of
Capital to Labor," demanding an income tax on the rich. This
seemed quite ridiculous, and her message was ill-received. The
people preferred to hear her talk on a subject which had sexy
connotations. So Victoria discarded labor problems and
turned to suffrage, which for some reason was at the time associated with the awful word, s-e-x. Her speech, "The Great Political Issue of Constitutional Equality," had the respected Mercantile Library Association of New York as its sponsor. She
toured in February, 1871, to Washington, Philadelphia, Syracuse, and back to Brooklyn, giving this oration, and she was
well received. She made many friends for the cause of women's
rights, but, as some suffragists resentfully noted, she made a lot
of money too, which she kept and spent.

Victoria soon found that people liked to be shocked and
would gather in great numbers, and pay cash, for the thrill.
"There is something about her that will not only attract, but
hold an audience," one of her listeners noted at this time. "She
is a radical of the radicals, and boldly, nay, defiantly launches
forth her most ultra and advanced doctrines of Free Love, and,
as we think, often shocks her hearers by preaching extremes of
social and sexual freedom."

Her speaking improved as she became more practiced in the
platform art, and particularly when she was baited.

"She appears best when she is broken up in her discourse by
hisses, or other uncomplimentary interruptions," the same ob-
server commented. "They seem to evoke all the latent powers of
her whole nature, and leaving her desk and manuscript, she
pours forth a perfect torrent of fiery eloquence, freely using
(and effectively too) invective, sarcasm, or ridicule, as the oc-

casion demands, and she is never at a loss for a ready and apt retort."

The Woodhull herself denied she was out to win glory, or money, or to build up a personal following, as the envious claimed. Far from it, she explained. She just felt impelled to act. "Wherever I find a social carbuncle," she vowed, "I shall plunge my surgical knife of reform into it—up to the hilt."

In a world full, then as now, of social carbuncles, Victoria would be kept permanently busy. Since she could not be in all places at all times, the editing of her WEEKLY and the management of her banking house often had to be left to others. Colonel Blood devoted some of his energy to the brokerage firm. However, there is no record to show that he distinguished himself in the world of high finance, and under his half-hearted guidance the business finally deteriorated to the point where it existed only in name. When he was not selling stocks and bonds Blood wrote for the WEEKLY, aided and one might say abetted by Stephen Pearl Andrews and other more obscure figures who did their share of the editorial labors.

One of Vicky's most loyal supporters now was Mrs. Isabella Beecher Hooker, who addressed her with such warm expressions as "My Darling Queen," and tried to bring her sister Catherine to her way of thinking. "My sister Catherine says she is convinced now that I am right and that Mrs Woodhull is a pure woman, holding a wrong social theory, and ought to be treated with kindness if we wish to win her to the truth," Mrs. Hooker wrote in a personal letter. "Catherine asked me to write her a letter of introduction, so that when she went to New York she could make her acquaintance and try to convince her that she is in error to her views on marriage. I gave her the letter and she is in New York now. When she sees her she will be just as much in love with her as the rest of us."

Mrs. Hooker was over-optimistic. Several days later she revealed the sad aftermath:

"Sister Catherine returned last night. She saw Victoria and attacked her on the marriage question, got such a black eye as filled her with horror and amazement. . . ."

From that time on Catherine Beecher habitually referred to Vicky and Tennessee as "The two Prostitutes," a phrase her brother, Henry Ward Beecher, was to take over. And Beecher, orating high in his Plymouth Church pulpit, cited the Claflin sisters as horrible examples of vice, ranking in sinfulness alongside those who indulged in card-playing, dancing, theatregoing, and dining out on the Sabbath Day.

No reply was made, at this time, to the Reverend's attacks. But Henry Ward Beecher was to be answered, pointedly though briefly a few weeks later, and, the following year, in scandalous charges which shook the nation.

. 8 .

On May 11 and 12, 1871, the Suffragette anniversary was celebrated in New York's Apollo Hall. There were strenuous objections by some of the lady crusaders about the propriety of sitting on the same platform with an avowed Free Lover. Astute Mrs. Stanton found a way to give Victoria "sufficient respectability." She sandwiched The Woodhull between herself and old Lucretia Mott, who had been fighting for women's rights before Victoria was born.

The seating arrangement quieted the complainers, but soon new growls arose. The convention was eclipsed by the attention given Victoria, and the ardent suffragists feared the Cause would suffer. Newspapers jeered at the women, calling their meeting the "Woodhull Convention." This came about mainly because Victoria's speech, "The New Rebellion," captured the imagination of the audience, including the working reporters.

"If the very next Congress refuses women all the legitimate results of citizenship, we shall proceed to call another convention expressly to frame a new constitution and erect a new government," declared Victoria. Then she added threateningly, and certainly seditiously: "We mean treason! We mean secession, and on a thousand times greater scale than was that of the South! We are plotting revolution! We will overthrow this bogus republic and plant a government of righteousness in its stead!"

These words were taken in their stride by members of government circles, there being no House Committee on Un-American Activities a century ago, but all agreed that, whether or not the cause of Suffragism was furthered, The Woodhull had had herself a day. There were vague rumors—believed to have been inspired by husband Colonel Blood—that such a stateswoman should stand for the Presidency of the United States with the backing of the delegates. Horace Greeley, who was not radical enough to sponsor women's rights (though he permitted Karl Marx to expound communistic doctrines in his TRIBUNE) wrote that Victoria's was "a spirit to respect, perhaps to fear, certainly not to be laughed at," for "She has the courage of her opinions!"

Capitalizing on her oratorical success, Victoria had the speech printed and the sales topped one hundred thousand.

· 9 ·

Victoria relished publicity. This was probably hereditary, for all the others in her family exhibited the same trait, including mother Roxy. Roxy had left the Woodhull home in a pout and had gone to live at the Washington House. She had probably experienced fits of irrationality before, and she was to have them again, for no discernible reason. Perhaps this mildly unbalanced woman was merely trying to hold her own in a circle of highly self-assertive relatives; or perhaps she just liked a good family row. The true cause for her flights into fancy we shall never know. In any event this time, four days after her daughter's triumph at the convention, evidently yearning for a little public attention herself, she applied in Essex Market Police Court for a warrant. She wanted Victoria's husband, Colonel James H. Blood, alias J. H. Harvey, arrested for threatening to take her life, for ruining one of her daughters while endeavoring to despoil another, and for urging both of them to deny support to their beloved mama.

"I'll tell you what that man Blood is," she shouted to the judge. "He is one of those who have no bottom in their pockets. You can keep stuffing in all the money in New York—they never get full. If my daughters would just send this man away as I always told them, they might be millionairesses . . ."

Roxy insisted that Blood had wrested from her daughters the affection due "their poor old mother," and her opinion of the entire entourage—including Victoria and Tennessee—was low indeed. "I say here and I call Heaven to witness that there is the worst gang of Free Lovers in that house in Thirty-eighth Street that ever lived," she informed the judge.

But this was merely the prelude to a rousing contest among the Claflin clan, who had their own notions of life *en famille*. Mrs. Polly Sparr, a sister who was enjoying Victoria's hospitality at the time, verified Roxy's charges. Polly explained the situation as it appeared to her. The next day THE NEW YORK TIMES —true then as now to its motto, "All the News that's Fit to Print"—sorrowfully remarked, "The evidence adduced was such as to be unfit for publication."

The unprintable evidence was this:

Polly Sparr was asked, "What relation other than that of mother and daughter exists between your mother and Tennie?"

"Something I can't explain, something mysterious and unnatural," replied Polly. "There is a different feeling between Tennie and my mother than between any other mother and child I know."

Colonel Blood then took the stand and denied all of Roxy's charges. He said that though his mother-in-law was "troublesome" he had always behaved toward her as the perfect gentleman that he was.

Under questioning by Roxy's counsel, Blood revealed that he had married Victoria first in 1866, had obtained a divorce from her two years later, and that they soon had remarried.

"Was Mrs. Woodhull divorced when you [first] married her?" asked Roxy's lawyer.

"I do not know," replied Blood.

The lawyer wanted to know how long he had been separated from Victoria.

"We were never separated," said Colonel Blood. "We continued to live together and were afterwards remarried."

The attorney conferred in whispers with mother Roxy and soon returned to the witness, who admitted that Victoria's first husband, Dr. Canning Woodhull, was also living at the Thirty-eighth Street home.

"Do you and Mrs. Woodhull and Dr. Woodhull occupy the same room?" demanded the counsel.

Colonel Blood refused to answer.

The next day Vicky appeared as a witness in defense of her husband. She described her mother as fickle in temperament. Sometimes Roxy would sit on Blood's lap and "say he was the best son-in-law she had," while at other times she "would abuse him like a thief," Victoria said. She dismissed all threats to her mother as utter nonsense, for Colonel Blood was a gentleman. "The most I ever heard him say was—when she would come up to the door and abuse him frightfully, as if she were possessed by a fiend—'If you don't let that door alone, I'll go out and push you from it.'" According to The Woodhull, the reason for Roxy's enmity toward Colonel Blood was quite transparent:

"She wants to get Tennie back to going around the country telling fortunes, and Sparr and his wife were always telling mother that as long as Blood was around she could not get the girl back."

This was the first time that Victoria went on record to reveal her mother's strange *Wanderlust*, a subject on which she usually did not care to elaborate.

After that, it was daughter Tennessee's turn to testify. She said that Colonel Blood treated Roxy much too kindly, considering the vituperation he was exposed to. She blamed the trouble on Polly Sparr, whose husband Benjamin, she declared, had been writing blackmail letters under Roxy's name, though her mother could neither read nor write. And then Tennessee candidly disclosed a little more of the mysterious background of the Claflin tribe:

"Since I was eleven years old I used to tell fortunes with her, and she wants me to go back with her to that business. But Vicky and Colonel Blood got me away from that life, and they are the best friends I have ever had. Since I was fourteen years old I have kept thirty to thirty-five deadheads. Some people in Cincinnati interfered to save me from my good old mother. I am a Clairvoyant, I am a Spiritualist. I have power and I know my power. Commodore Vanderbilt knows my power. I have humbugged people, a great many rich people—Vanderbilt included—I know. But if I did it, it was to make money to keep these deadheads. I have left the degradation of a life where I was almost lost, and I will not return to it, and because I will not, she has instigated the attack on my character."

The assembled reporters were understandably flabbergasted, particularly about the reference to her thirty-five deadheads. Also, as they saw it, it was Colonel Blood's character, not Tennessee's, that was being attacked.

Tennessee told the judge she would either take her mother home or deposit $200 a month with the court for her upkeep. And then, during the wrangle between opposing counsels, she suddenly dashed from the witness chair and tried to clasp her arms around mama Roxy. Sister Polly, who had undoubtedly anticipated this maneuver, was quick to push Tennessee away and yank Roxy to *her* bosom. The judge, bewildered by the incomprehensible conduct of this unusual family, dismissed the suit.

A few days later, just as inexplicably as she had left the home, Roxy returned, happy and contented.

· 10 ·

The INDEPENDENT, a semi-religious weekly owned by Henry C. Bowen, the sometime friend of Henry Ward Beecher, professed to be dismayed at the facts which had come to light concerning the private life of Mrs. Woodhull and family, though the magazine said they had been "no secret before." The INDEPENDENT thought "all gossip is needless" when it came to Victoria's indecencies, and, as for the WOODHULL & CLAFLIN'S WEEKLY, "its coarse treatment of all the sacred things of human life is enough to condemn anyone whose name is associated with it."

The WEEKLY promptly and proudly, if somewhat abstrusely, explained Victoria's stand:

"She believes in and advocates in the highest, purest sense as the only cure for immorality, the deep damnation by which men corrupt and disfigure God's most holy institution of Sexual Relations."

The journal indignantly pointed out that Daniel Webster and William Pitt had been bon-vivants, yet at the same time another great statesman, Victoria C. Woodhull, was being scorned for being just that. "If Mrs. Woodhull has valuable ideas . . . what has her past history to do with them?"

There were appended the warning words, words to be amplified later:

"At this very moment awful and herculean efforts are being made to suppress the most terrific scandal in a neighboring city which has ever astounded and convulsed any community. Clergy, congregation and community will be alike hurled into more than all the consternation which the great explosion in Paris carried to that unfortunate city, if this effort at suppression fail."

The reporters who asked the WEEKLY editors for the name of the accused were told privately to go over to the neighboring city of Brooklyn and ask the Reverend Henry Ward Beecher to comment on the editorial. But even the brashest newspaperman dared not approach the divine with such a question.

Then, as reporters began to prowl about Thirty-eighth Street to verify the acknowledged fact that The Woodhull was living with two husbands, Victoria decided on a bold step. She sent a "card" (an open letter) to the TIMES and to the WORLD. The newspapers quickly forgot their animosity toward her, in the interest of circulation, and printed the letter.

"The fact is a fact," wrote Victoria. "Dr. Woodhull being sick, ailing and incapable of self-support, I felt it my duty to myself and to human nature that he be cared for, although his incapacity was in no way attributable to me."

She conceded that any comment made on her private life was fair play because she had put herself before the public voluntarily and was not ashamed of her conduct, but, she warned:

"I do not intend to be the scapegoat of sacrifice, to be offered up as a victim to society by those who cover the foulness and the feculence of their thoughts with hypocritical mouthing of fair professions, and by diverting public attention from their own iniquity and pointing their finger at me."

She added, mentioning no names:

"My judges preach against Free Love openly, practise it secretly."

Then, again mentioning no names though the identity of the accused was plain to the well-informed, she went on:

"I know of one man, a public teacher of eminence, who lives in concubinage with the wife of another public teacher of almost equal eminence. All three concur in denouncing offenses against morality."

There was the threatening afterthought:

"I shall make it my business to analyze some of these lives, and will take my chances in the matter of libel suits."

. **11** .

In Brooklyn the enemies of Henry Ward Beecher chortled "The jig is up!" but The Reverend made no answer to the anonymous assault. Again the reporters dared not approach him, but it was noticed that his attacks on The Woodhull softened. There was only the unsigned letter soon printed in the TIMES. An indignant "Wife and Mother" wrote:

"I was both surprised and pained to read . . . from a woman who not only lives a life of infamy, but has the unblushing effrontery to uphold and justify her conduct in the sacred name of 'charity.' She must, indeed, be lost to every sense of virtue and decency. Above all, what saith the Redeemer of mankind? 'Whosoever divorceth his wife and marrieth another committeth adultery.' "

Victoria had her answer ready, in another "card" to the TIMES. In an involved sentence she explained:

"If I be a 'notorious woman,' a person with 'soiled hands' and so forth (I need not sully your columns with the filth and impurity of which I have been the target). If I be all this, and thereby am rendered unfit to present and advocate the woman's cause, how is it those—my opponents—who are themselves reprobate, and of impure life and conversations?"

She complained that when her WEEKLY crusaded in the interests of justice "a howl resounds through the Street. 'Those women! Those adventuresses! Blackmail!' "

"Is it fair to treat a woman worse than a man, and then revile her because she is a woman?" Victoria wanted to know.

. 12 .

There were a number of other unfortunate incidents at this time. An actress who styled herself "Princess Editha Lolita Montez" (née Editha Salomon, but she sported many another alias, for example: Ann O'Delia Diss Debar, Baroness Rosenthal and Countess Landsfelt, Vera P. Ava, Mrs. Paul Noel Messant, Mrs. McGood, Mme. Swami, Vina Anandra, Laura Horos, etc.) and who would admit any minute in the day that she was the spawn of the famed Lola Montez and the King of Bavaria, no less, sued Victoria. The "Princess" asserted she had turned over a valuable diamond ring to Woodhull & Claflin, Brokers, for deposit in the company's safe, and now could not get it back.

Victoria testified in court she knew the person in question, that the "Princess" had come to her office, not to deposit any jeweled ring but to beg for help: She needed a New York audience that would listen to her bastardy claims. "I gave her five dollars to pay her board bill and to keep her, as she said, from a house of prostitution," declared Victoria.

The court, diagnosing the case as one brought by an actress wanting publicity, dismissed the complaint and turned over the "Princess" to the correction authorities.

Soon afterward the newspapers punnily headlined: SWIN-
DELL SWINDELLED! and again Victoria, this time with Tennessee, found herself in court. Anne L. Swindell, a schoolteacher,
told her story on the stand. She had taken her life savings from
the bank, come to New York and, because she had read in the
WEEKLY that the "Lady Brokers" guaranteed bona-fide working women against stock losses, provided they patronized the
firm of Woodhull & Claflin, had given her money to the company, with the understanding that no speculation be involved.

"I told her it was a risky business," Victoria testified, "and
advised her if she had any money, to keep it—advice I would
give any woman, unless she understood the business."

"Did you not tell her that if she lost her money in gold speculation you would repay her?" Victoria was asked.

"I did not. I told her I would guard her money as carefully
as I would my own. She understood the matter as well as I did,
and spoke of the fluctuation of gold."

The suit was dismissed, and every broker in New York City,
haunted by the possibility of a precedent having been established whereby he would have to repay customers for gambling
losses, sighed in relief.

On top of this, reports began to circulate in print about the
peculiar background of Victoria, Tennessee, and family, with
special emphasis on the activities of their father, the supposedly rich retired Ohio lawyer. It was whispered he had been
compelled to leave Homer, Ohio, under suspicion of arson and
had taken his daughters with him in a traveling medicine and
fortunetelling show. It was said little Tennessee had sold an
Elixir of Life, with her girlish portrait on the bottle and that
Victoria had practiced clairvoyance on the rustics, while a
brother, Hebern, had posed as a cancer doctor.

These reports the Claflin family haughtily denied.

There were rumors, too, that the family had established a

cancer emporium in an Illinois town and in an ill-inspired attempt to cure cancer by the application of mustard plasters had caused the death of at least one patient. Forced to leave town, so the unverified reports had it, the sisters had gone on to Cincinnati where they had attracted the attention of the sports in the Whiskey Ring, run by friends of President Grant. Also, so the gossip continued, Victoria had traveled through the West with Colonel Blood before obtaining a divorce from Dr. Woodhull. There was a story to the effect that Tennessee, who posed as a single woman, actually was married to one John Bartels, whom she had never divorced, and that Blood had another wife living somewhere in Brooklyn.

The family thought it best not to dignify this new crop of speculations with a denial. In self-protection, the Claflins drew together under the onslaught, and in the absence of any evidence to the contrary one must conclude that they found at least temporary peace in a sphere otherwise so alien to them all—privacy.

. 13 .

In 1871 Henry Ward Beecher, a virile stocky man with a bulgy neck and chest, was, at age fifty-eight, the most popular preaching man in the land. It is difficult today to imagine the veneration commanded by this Man of God. As an orator and lecturer, he drew thousands, mostly women, and books of his sermons were prominently displayed in the better parlors by the faithful. His Plymouth Church in Brooklyn was patterned exactly after Boston's famous Tremont Temple. There was the same high altar in a huge barn of a room with galleries on three sides. When this was filled, folding chairs were put down to clog the aisles, presenting Beecher with the inspiring sight of an unbroken sea of people to harangue. The audience clapped and cheered their idol, as if in a theatre, and they attended the holy tabernacle in the same spirit with which they visited Barnum's Museum. (When Beecher asked Park Benjamin, the editor, why he never came to hear him preach the answer was, "I'd like to, but I make it a rule never to go to places of amusement on the Sabbath Day.")

Henry C. Bowen, a sixty-four-year-old Manhattan merchant, who owned the Brooklyn UNION, a well-known daily newspaper, as well as the INDEPENDENT, had hired Beecher to write articles for his magazine. Bowen was a thin, nervous, sunken-eyed man, who had become rich selling dry goods before he turned to religion and the Plymouth Church, and he paid his star writer large sums. Then the two had parted. Beecher went to edit and write the same homely essays for the CHRISTIAN UNION, a rival to the INDEPENDENT, and to bestow his final accolade on The Above by writing and publishing his first volume of *The Life of Christ*.

Bowen hired an up-and-coming handsome young lecturer, Theodore Tilton, to edit the INDEPENDENT, putting him under contract, but the CHRISTIAN UNION with Beecher's by-line cut into the circulation of the magazine. Bowen determined to get Beecher one way or another. And then, as Samuel Wilkeson, an irreverent journalist said, something happened to Beecher which "knocked the *Life of Jesus* higher than a kite." Wilkeson was right, for what was to come over a period of years prevented Beecher from finishing his great work, forcing his publishers into bankruptcy.

Just exactly what brought the scandal into the open was

never made perfectly clear. According to the Reverend Beecher, one day he received a message from Tilton's wife, Elizabeth, a small, dark, talky and pretty woman. Lib, as she was called, was in terrible distress and wanted his guidance— his spiritual guidance. Beecher said he dutifully called upon her, in broad daylight, to find that the Tiltons had been fighting and that Lib was staying with her mother.

Tilton was an old friend and protégé of Beecher. His side of the story, told later, was radically different. He said the distress caused in the Tilton household was due to Beecher's excessive, unclerical attentions to the attractive Lib, and that his wife had, on December 30, 1870, signed a confession of her sexual sins with the sturdy Brooklyn idol, a most incriminating document. Tilton at first had remained silent about the existence of this confession, preferring to play his hole card later.

In the meantime, Tilton had been shifted from the INDE-PENDENT to become editor of Bowen's newspaper, the Brooklyn UNION, at $5,000 a year under a five-year contract and with a bonus for his on-the-side articles in the INDEPENDENT. But he was not a success on the newspaper and Bowen fired him. Tilton thereupon reconciled himself with Beecher, whom heretofore he had characterized to his friends as a monstrous seducer, and Lib obligingly signed a new document, revoking her former confession. Tilton then proceeded to settle the score with his old friend, his new enemy, Henry C. Bowen.

An article was put in type presumably for publication in the *Golden Age,* a magazine having financial difficulties launched by Tilton, and the proposed article was shown to Bowen. In it the good man was accused of all sorts of scandalous doings, particularly of gossiping about Tilton's close friend, Henry Ward Beecher. It seemed, the article said, Bowen had been circulating false and vile rumors, and raising his eyebrows because the Reverend was sleeping with Tilton's wife Lib.

Alarmed, Bowen hastened to renew his friendship with Beecher and Tilton. The three of them met and signed what later was called the Tripartite Agreement, in which Bowen was absolved of slander and Beecher of seduction. Bowen now decided it would be a wise business move to invest $7,000 in Tilton's *Golden Age.*

So it appeared the troubles of the trio had ended, but this was far from the truth.

Victoria the crusader (for she assured people it was only in this role that she was interested in the sordid Brooklyn matter) had gotten a whiff in the wind of the Beecher scandal—first from an admirer who was present when she read her Memorial in Washington, and later from Elizabeth Cady Stanton, who had the news straight from the mare's mouth, from Lib herself. On May 22, 1871, Vicky summoned Theodore Tilton to her editorial office, laid before him the proof of an article mentioning the hidden misdemeanors of Beecher and Lib, and told him it would be published in the next issue of WOODHULL & CLAFLIN'S WEEKLY. She had called Tilton just in case he, the father of Lib's children, should care to affirm or deny the story. She was willing to lend him space in the WEEKLY to do so, and she thought the article would be a splendid circulation-builder.

The article was not published—at that time. Tilton in a statement made a year or so later said Victoria had informed him of a "wicked and injurious story" which she intended to publish and thus bring more good into the world. Tilton added that by "many personal services and kindly attentions," the nature of which he did not reveal, he managed to dissuade her.

There were many cynical persons who believed that Tilton's services were indeed of a personal nature, an extremely personal nature. It has been said, too, that Victoria "requisitioned" Tilton. Whatever the truth, as the two wrangled over publication of the story, they eyed each other and found each other to their liking. Soon they were out rowing on the Harlem River and driving in a phaeton to Coney Island to bathe—in the nude, it was whispered.

Tilton, thirty-five years old and strikingly handsome, was a six-footer, rawboned, with a slight stoop and a domed brow, and he held an extraordinary fascination for women. He always was clean-shaven, immaculately dressed, and his hair, between red and chestnut, was worn long in what was known as the Grecian style, flopping down to his shoulders. The two made a striking couple and they were together constantly. Tilton began to defend Victoria publicly. "Though preaching extremes of social and sexual freedom, she herself never, never would put them in practice, under *any* circumstances," he assured a friend who feared he was in bad company.

"She has strange traits occasionally, indicating overexcitement of mind," he explained again, in answer to an insulting letter written to Victoria and turned over to him for a reply, "but uses the term Free Love in a sense wholly different from that in which it is understood by the world. But I give my testimony to the fact that she is one of the most upright, truthful, religious and unsullied souls I ever met."

In the columns of his own weekly, the *Golden Age*, Tilton tossed bouquets to The Woodhull. "If the woman's movement has a Joan of Arc, it is this gentle but fiery genius," he proclaimed.

And then he was so carried away, either by caresses, as some said, or by threats and recriminations, as others thought, that he published a biography of Victoria in a *Golden Age* tract. Ordinarily a tract in this magazine was devoted to the denunciation of sinful lives. This biography, running twenty thousand words and taking up the entire issue, was written by Tilton from material graciously supplied by Victoria herself.

· **14** ·

The *Golden Age's* Life of Victoria C. Woodhull was one of the most singular biographies ever written about any man or woman, dead or alive. It was avidly devoured by hundreds of thousands, and many a reader incredulously shook his head and wondered how such a life could be true. Many facts heretofore unknown about Victoria's nebulous background now came to light, usually to a favorable light; for throughout the pages it was stressed that The Woodhull was a martyr, in not one but hundreds of instances, and from the age of babyhood on.

Victoria later commented on her own biography—a rare privilege then as now: "His articles sparkled in every line like rare old wine, which was to be accounted for only [because] he was newly and madly in love, for nothing else would have inspired him to write so grandly."

The biography bore as its motto the Scriptural injunction: "He that uttereth a slander is a fool," Proverbs X, 18. Then the story got under way. Victoria was born in Homer, Ohio, on September 23, 1838, and she was so precocious, in an ectoplasmic sort of way, that spiritual visions flitted before her while she was still in the cradle. The first phantom appeared when she was three, and so startled her that "her little body lay as if dead for three hours." Later, fortunately, she became so accustomed to such appearances from the dim beyond that she thought nothing of them. However, as Tilton explained, drawing deep in the well for some of his sparkling-rare-old-wine lines, there was one rather unusual example of a ghostly exercise:

"In her tenth year, one day while sitting by the side of a cradle rocking a sick babe to sleep, she says that two angels came, and gently pushing her away, began to fan the child with their white hands, until its face grew fresh and rosy. Her mother suddenly entered the chamber, and beheld in amazement the little nurse lying in a trance on the floor, her face turned upward toward the ceiling, and the pining babe apparently in the bloom of health."

During Victoria's childhood "she was worked like a slave—was whipped like a convict" for "her father was impartial in his cruelty to all his children," while her mother, "with a fickleness of spirit that renders her one of the most erratic of mortals, sometimes abetted him in his scourgings." The ancient Hindus had a saying, "One should not strike a woman, even with a flower," but papa Buck Claflin was no ancient Hindu. He often beat Victoria with "a handsaw or a stick of firewood." He would come home late at night and, feeling somewhat restive, would rouse the Claflin children from their warm beds and club them until breakfast time. "I have no remembrance of a father's kiss," Victoria said sadly, according to biographer Tilton.

The Brooklyn EAGLE acidly remarked that Victoria might not remember a paternal kiss but "the fates afterward seemed to have allowed huge osculatory compensation." Other newspapers thought a handsaw or a stick of firewood was rather a large and unwieldy object for beating a child, and they wondered how father Buck and mother Roxy enjoyed reading about themselves (although Roxy was supposed to be illiterate and thus may have been spared the ordeal), particularly since they were living at the time under the same roof with Victoria. The newspapers also speculated on the reaction of the assorted Claflin sisters staying with The Woodhull, when they read the following Tiltonian lines:

"The whole brood are of the same feather, except Victoria

and Tennie . . . for years there has been one common sentiment sweetly pervading the breasts of a majority toward a mi-
nority of the offspring—namely, a determination that Victoria
and Tennie should earn all the money for the support of the
numerous remainder of the Claflin tribe—wives, husbands,
children, servants, all. Being daughters of the horseleech, they
cry 'give!' "

All in all, Tilton concluded, "They are what my friend Mr.
Greeley calls 'a bad crowd.' "

Having disposed of Victoria's and Tennessee's sisters and
parents, Tilton returned to The Woodhull as a young girl. He
revealed that her education consisted of less than three years of
schooling, but that her admiring playmates called her "The Little Queen," not so much because she was named Victoria after
the English ruler but because of her regal demeanor. "She was
a child of genius, toil and grief," a "little steam engine," Tilton
said, because as a tiny tot "she made fires, washed and ironed,
she baked bread, she cut wood, she spaded a vegetable garden,
she went on errands, she tended everything. 'Victoria! Victoria!' was the call in the morning before the cock was crowing."

The EAGLE thought that to comment on this paragraph
"would be to shower hot sands on a garden bed of flowers."

Jumping ahead a few years, Tilton then described how Victoria penned her speeches. It was extremely simple: "angelic
helpers" and "unseen" hands assisted her, and "most often in a
totally unconscious state the words that fall from her lips are
garnered by the swift pen of her husband, and published almost
verbatim as he gets and gives them."

This husband was Colonel Blood, and not Victoria's first
husband, Tilton explained, and his was a harsh view when he
considered spouse Number One, Dr. Canning Woodhull. Victoria's marriage at a somewhat early age (she was fourteen) to
Dr. Woodhull, "a gay rake," was particularly awful, Tilton dis-

closed, because "Her captor, once possessed of his treasure, ceased to value it." Woodhull, who was exactly twice Victoria's age, was shown to be a bad egg: "On the third day after taking his child wife to his lodgings, he broke her heart by remaining away all night at a house of ill repute. Then for the first time she learned, to her dismay, that he was habitually unchaste and given to fits of intoxication."

Tilton described Vicky's feeling on the discovery: "She was stung to the quick."

Things went from bad to worse, according to Tilton, for Dr. Woodhull would leave Victoria at home alone while he was "ordering baskets of champagne, and drinking himself drunk in the company of harlots." Sometimes Victoria would, "half clad and shivering, track him to his dens," but at other, lazier periods she "would watch at the window, waiting for his footsteps, until she heard them languidly shuffling along the pavement with the staggering reel of a drunken man."

"In fifteen months after her marriage," Tilton continued, pulling out the stops, "while living in a little low frame house in Chicago, in the dead of winter, with icicles clinging to her bedpost, and attended only by her half drunken husband, she brought forth in almost mortal agony her first born child . . . On her recovery, and after a visit to her father's home, she returned to her own, to be horror-struck at discovering that her bed had been occupied the night before by her husband in company with a wanton of the streets, and that the room was littered with the remains of their drunken feast. To add to her misery she discovered that her child (Byron, named after the poet and Lord), begotten in drunkenness, and born in squalor, was half idiot; predestined to be a hopeless imbecile for life."

Despite this ugly scene, Tilton wrote, Victoria still showed patience and forbearance. She took her husband and son with her to San Francisco. There Anna Cogswell, the actress, let her play the small part of the country cousin in *New York by Gaslight*. In six weeks' time she was earning $52 a week and was on her way to becoming a great stage star, but one night when she was acting in *The Corsican Brothers* a spirit voice commanded: "Victoria, come home!" She then had a vision of Tennessee, so distinct that she noticed her sister was wearing a striped French calico frock. "The apparition was not to be denied," commented Tilton.

The first commandment of the stage, that The Show Must Go On, meant nothing to Victoria, for "without waiting to change her dress [she] ran to her hotel" and within a matter of hours she had taken a steamer for the Atlantic seaboard.

Arriving in New York, Victoria hurried straight on to Columbus, Ohio, for it was there the spirit voice had informed her that Tennessee would be. The reunited Claflin clan started a tour with a medicine show, with the two sisters giving clairvoyance performances. The spiritual circuit in the Midwest was a gold mine, according to Tilton, for Victoria allegedly had a yearly income of "nearly" one hundred thousand dollars. She had to work hard to earn her money, and this she did by "some apparently miraculous cures." Tilton listed a few of her feats: Curing the lame and deaf, detecting bank robbers with the aid of a tattling spirit, unveiling business secrets, solving physiological problems, and the correct prophesying of future events.

Victoria soon had amassed that nest egg of $700,000 but, for reasons left unexplained by Tilton, hard times hit the Claflin family and none of them had any money. And, as Theodore astutely noted, Victoria's relations with husband Woodhull worsened. "Once during her carriage of her unborn babe, she was kicked by its father in a fit of drunkenness," the biographer related. This inflicted not only "a bruise to her body" but "a greater bruise to her spirit."

Eventually there was an incident that made Victoria at last

conclude that her marriage was doomed to failure. Tilton described in what newspapers called "too disgusting language" the birth of Victoria's second child, Zulu Maud:

"This event occurred at No. 53 Bond Street, New York, April 23, 1861. She and her husband were at the time the only occupants of the house—her trial coming upon her while no nurse, or servant, or other human helper was under the roof. The babe entered the world at four o'clock in the morning, handled by the feverish and unsteady hands of its intoxicated father, who, only half in possession of his professional skill, cut the umbilical cord too near the flesh and tied it so loose that the string came off—laid the babe in its mother's arms—in an hour afterwards left them asleep and alone—and then staggered out of the house. Nor did he remember to return.

"Meanwhile, the mother, on waking, was startled to find her head on the side next to her babe's body in a pool of blood—that her hair was soaked and clotted in a little red stream oozing drop by drop from the bowels of the child. In her motherly agony, reaching a broken chair rung which happened to be lying near, she pounded against the wall to summon help from the next house. At intervals of several hours she continued this pounding, no one answering until at length one of the neighbors, a resolute woman, who was attracted by the noise, but was unable to get in the front door, removed the grating of the basement and made her way upstairs to the rescue of the mother. On the third day after, the mother, on sitting propped in her bed and looking out the window—caught sight of her husband staggering up the steps across the way, mistaking it for his own!"

This was the last straw. "Why should I any longer live with this man?" Victoria asked herself. So, after eleven years of marriage, she applied for a divorce in Chicago.

The realistic passages pertaining to the birth of Victoria's daughter were found by the readers of the *Golden Age* to be utterly horrifying. Yet there were other passages, intended to be taken just as seriously, which left them chuckling. There was the time when Victoria met a public speaker, a Greek, a man whom the history books said had been dead for 2,190 years. He was Demosthenes. When Victoria was a little girl, Demosthenes often had appeared before her, simply clad in his Greek tunic, and had chatted amiably and given her lots of solid advice. But he had stopped visiting her. Victoria never expected to see him again, and then, as Tilton described the scene:

"At length, after patiently waiting on this spirit guide for twenty years, one day in 1868, during a temporary sojourn in Pittsburgh, and while she was sitting at a marble table, he suddenly appeared to her, and wrote on the table in English letters the name 'Demosthenes.' At first the writing was indistinct, but grew to such a lustre that the brightness filled the room. The apparition, familiar as it had been before, now affrighted her to trembling. The stately and commanding spirit told her to journey to New York, where she would find at No. 17 Great Jones Street, a house in readiness for her, equipped in all things to her use and taste.

"She unhesitatingly obeyed, although she never before had heard of Great Jones Street, nor until that revelatory moment had entertained any intention of taking such a residence. On entering the house, it fulfilled in reality the picture which she saw of it in her vision—the self-same hall, stairways, rooms, and furniture. Entering with some bewilderment into the library, she reached out her hand by chance, and without knowing what she did, took up a book which, on idly looking at its title, was (to her blood-chilling astonishment) to be 'The Orations of Demosthenes.' From that time onward, the Greek statesman had been even more palpably than in her earlier years her prophetic monitor, mapping out the life which she must follow, as a chart for the ship sailing the sea.

"She believed him to be her familiar spirit—the author of her public policy, and the inspirer of her published words. Without intruding my own opinion as to the authenticity of this inspiration, I have often thought that if Demosthenes could arise and speak English, he could hardly excel the fierce light and heat of some of the sentences which I have heard from this singular woman in her glowing hours."

Newspapers whooped at the idea of old Demosthenes appearing before Vicky, and they wondered why, if he could write his name in English, he could not speak the language. Even some of Victoria's most loyal followers were hard put to believe in the reunion of The Woodhull and Demosthenes.

The rest of Tilton's biography told of Victoria's divorce from Woodhull, her marriage to Colonel Blood, her sincere interest in suffrage and Free Love, and of the base, slanderous attacks constantly made upon her. "A more unsullied woman does not walk the earth," Tilton firmly declared. As proof, he pointed out that "Twice, she unshakenly believes, she has seen a vision of Jesus Christ, honored thus doubly over St. Paul, who saw his Master but once, and then was overcome by the sight." Tilton said that every time he heard this pure and innocent soul maligned he was reminded of Tennyson's line on King Arthur:

"Is thy white blamelessness accounted blame?"

. 15 .

Newspapers roared at the spectacle of Tilton "dazzled and blinded by the moral effulgence of Mrs. Woodhull." The EAGLE called her "the polyandrous nymph of Broad Street" and spoke disapprovingly of the "votive biography," and of Tilton languishing "in the adulterous arms of his mistress." The all-inclusive description used by many newspapers for the sisters was "those abandoned women."

"We hear of abandoned women, but not a word of abandoned men, and yet there are ten times the number of abandoned men than there are of women," the WEEKLY replied on June 31. "Eight millions of dollars are paid by men in the city of New York to support this infamous business by which they gratify their damnable lusts. Men reeking with the foul abomination of fancy houses and street walkers, just from the moral degradation of promiscuousness and polluted beds, bought with money and the price of souls, are countenanced and fellowshipped by virtuous men and chaste women."

The Brooklyn SUNDAY PRESS printed two billets-doux, reputedly sent by Tilton to Victoria. Rival newspapers accepted the authenticity of these notes, as the editor of the PRESS, James M. McDermott, was said by pun addicts to be the "bosom friend" of Tennessee, or Victoria, or both. The first note read:

June 15. [1871]
Fifth Avenue Hotel
My dear Victoria: Put this under your pillow, dream of

the writer, gather the spirits about you, and so, good night.

Theodore Tilton

In the second and undated note Theodore evidently had come to know The Woodhull intimately enough to change the salutation from *Dear* to *Dearest* and to sign off with his first name:

The *Golden Age*
My Dearest Victoria: I made haste, while yet able to sit up, for I am giddy with ******* this morning.

Theodore

The seven asterisks, explained the PRESS, stood for a vulgar expression that could not be printed in a family newspaper in deference to propriety. It had something to do with sex.

POMEROY'S DEMOCRAT later had its own version as to why the biography had been written by Tilton. It declared Theodore had "lived up to the professions of his new faith, until at last the Woodhull and Claflin tribe had him where the ambrosial locks adorning his head were so short that he was either obliged to pay the musician or write a little book to prove that Victoria was one altogether lovely, and Free Love was the best dish ever partaken by him."

HARPER'S WEEKLY jocularly remarked: "If apples are wormy this year and grapes mildewed, and ducks' eggs addle, and bladed corn be lodged, it may be ascribed to the unhallowed influence of Mr. Tilton's Life of V. W.," while *Frank Leslie's Budget of Fun* solemnly proposed the perfect combination to run for the White House: "Theodore Woodhull for President and Victoria Tilton for vice."

. 16 .

Looking for broader worlds to overwhelm, Victoria now turned to Marxism. She announced she always had been a devout believer in the Fourier movement, but after much study of the subject had turned into a sincere disciple of the newest and most radical *ism*, Communism. Victoria and Tennessee both joined Section Twelve of the International, one of two such organizations in New York. And, once the sisters had obtained a foothold in this new field, they soon dominated the group, and then brought the other one, Section Nine, under their grip.

Controlled by the sisters, the two sections issued a document calling for the exclusion of aliens from the cause—the aliens who were the backbone of the movement—and for concentrating on the furtherance of women's rights and Free Love. The members of the two New York groups, a majority of whom were foreigners, dutifully went along, though their perplexity was great, but the other chapters in the United States and elsewhere did not.

Prompted by Karl Marx himself, the International expelled the two New York sections, but this only redoubled Victoria's zeal. She called upon all Marxist factions the world over to unite with Sections Twelve and Nine in New York and form a new Communist Party of their own, and to supplant the tyrant Karl Marx, who was no Marxist at all, with Victoria C. Woodhull.

As long as Victoria stuck to the cause, she was energetic. She marched at the head of the International Workers' Party pa-

54 • *Vicky* •

rade of fifty thousand who protested the deaths of Flourens and Dombrowski in the Paris Commune, while in the newly formed Union League Club shudders shook the chairs. But, eventually, Vicky lost interest. *Frank Leslie's Magazine* published a sketch of the parade, commemorating the Paris Commune, with Tennessee in the fore, holding aloft the banner, "Complete Political and Social Equality for Both Sexes." But where was Victoria C. Woodhull? Nowhere in the picture. The newspapers, too, gave little space to Victoria's communistic activities. They just did not seem to know a good story. So The Woodhull turned in her party card and quit.

For Victoria, this was an abortive, and final, interest in Communism. Indeed, it is sad to relate, and puzzling it was to red-hot Communists, that from then on Victoria seemed to dislike the creed. The interest of the sisters in Communism accomplished little, but enough for future historians of the movement to term them, half a century later, as "probably the most seductive pair of reformers the country has ever known."

Victoria became a tiny footnote in Soviet history, however, for the WEEKLY was the first newspaper in the United States to print the Communist Manifesto. Today in the Marx-Lenin Institute in Moscow, which scarcely can be said to specialize in Americana, there can be found the complete file of WOODHULL & CLAFLIN'S WEEKLY. And the Soviet reference volumes have at least paid her a negative compliment: There is no denunciation of Victoria C. Woodhull as being the first American Trotskyite.

· 17 ·

Two outbursts by members of the Claflin clan now upset the comparative serenity of Victoria and Tennessee. One was caused by their sister, "Dr." Polly Sparr, the other by mother Roxy.

Theodore Tilton had remarked, accurately it would seem by the record, that most of the members of the family were horse-leeches who lived off Victoria and Tennessee and who then were prone "to curse the hand that feeds them." Tilton wrote in his biography:

"What language shall describe them? Such another family circle of cats and kits, with soft fur and sharp claws, purring at one moment and fighting the next, never before filled one house with their clamors since Babel began. They love and hate—they do good and evil—they bless and smite each other. They are a sisterhood of furies, tempered with love's melancholy."

"Dr." Sparr (her academic title was self-assumed, as she had no medical training or degree and was, in her own words, "an electric magnetic doctor") started the furore off. Her husband, Dr. (legitimately so) Benjamin Sparr, was found dead in a New York hotel. Queried by reporters, Polly declared he had been murdered. Murdered by whom? By her sisters Victoria and Tennessee. The motive? Robbery. Dr. Sparr had left their happy home with $5,000 in his pocket. and he had returned, on his bier, without it.

The accusation, made by a sister who at the time was living with Victoria and Tennessee, was not taken seriously, even by newspapers avid to "get" the sisters. It soon was established that Dr. Sparr, who never had been known to carry more than five dollars at a time, had died, nude and raving drunk, from apoplexy. The incident was scarcely hushed up when mother Roxy, who, to indulge in understatement, was a violently emotional character, went on another rampage.

The quiet Murray Hill neighborhood was in an uproar one June morning when husband Colonel Blood rushed from the door of 15 East Thirty-eighth Street in a most undignified and unmilitary fashion, with Roxy in hot pursuit. "You vile Free Lover!" shouted mama Roxy as she pursued the fleeing Blood.

As always, the reporters were quick to arrive. They found the fiery Roxy only too willing to talk. "Oh, my girls are virtuous —I've given them a Christian mother's example," she confided. It was "this hell-hound Blood" she did not fancy. Roxy tried to explain the fascination Blood held for women: "Blood has something about him that infaturates and he infaturates my daughters."

The reporters were somewhat puzzled by Roxy's English, but before they could recover Tennessee shooed her mother away. The good lady, she said, could neither read nor write and, for that matter, not think any too clearly. Tennessee invited the newspapermen inside. Edging close to them as she talked, she then revealed a little more, just a little more, of her misty past:

"I'm nearly twenty-six years old and yet they treat me as if I had no rights above those of a child of five. I have been the ruin of my relations—by giving them blood until they became the merest leeches. For years they have lived this contemptible life, and now enervated and useless like so many bloated corpses, they utter the screams of the infirm when I attempt to clear myself of the dead weight. We will show you up in the newspapers, we will ruin you. This has been the cry at every attempt of mine towards independence."

As the reporters scribbled away industriously, Tennessee continued:

"I told such wonderful things as a child that my father made from fifty dollars to a hundred a day at hotels simply by letting people see the strange clairvoyant child. As I grew older and the deadheads accumulated around me, I was forced to humbug. I didn't want to but I was obliged to make money. Mother was constantly in fear that I would marry and stop the income. I never had any happiness until I came to live with my darling sister Vicky. With Colonel Blood I made fourteen thousand dollars in six months. In all that time I bought myself only two calico dresses."

At this juncture, Victoria took over. "We don't want any scandal," she said. "I believe Tennie ought to use the gift God has given her, but not in the mercenary way she was forced to use it. She has no right to prostitute her powers."

The reporters left and the interviews were faithfully reported in the newspapers. A day later, it was announced that Roxy had made up with her daughters and was sitting on Blood's lap. It had been merely a "misunderstanding."

· 18 ·

Encouraged by the attention and the ensuing publicity, Tennessee decided to branch out, break up the sister act for a change and make some news on her own. In August the German-American Progressive Society met in Irving Hall and nominated Tennessee to run for Congress from the 8th District.

She was endorsed because of her "practical wisdom and extensive knowledge shown by her different works on the subject of political reform."

Tennessee accepted the honor, speaking to her would-be constituents in halting German, Roxy's native language. She said first she intended to get a majority of votes and win, pointing out (wrongly) that though women could not ballot, they were not forbidden to be candidates. She would make a test case of the action, and carry it up to the Supreme Court, if necessary. This statement greatly excited the several hundred in the hall. They escorted Tennessee to her residence, serenaded her until late hours, and that was the last ever heard of Tennessee Claflin the Congressional candidate.

Tennessee now made up her mind to produce some works on political reform, inasmuch as the German-American Progressive Society had credited her with the feat. The subject had always interested her, she said. With the aid—total aid, some believed—of Stephen Pearl Andrews, Colonel Blood, and Dr. Joseph Treat, a radical litterateur, she proceeded to turn out a mass of pamphlets. They were collected and published in book form under the title *Constitutional Equality of the Sexes*. There were the envious who said no one knew more about sex than Tennessee Claflin, but why bring in the Constitution? Nonetheless, the book sold well.

"It has been freely circulated through the press that we are simply notoriety seekers," Tennessee stated in her book. In an effort to explain away the accusations she added:

"Do people usually invoke upon themselves continuous persecution, merely to obtain notoriety? Do they consciously invoke the terrible power of the press to crush them, to brand them before the world by every vile and detestable epithet known to language? Do they seek the hoots and jeers of the common multitudes, and the sneers, and upturned noses of the select few wherever they go—merely to become simply notorious?"

"Nay, my friends!" said Tennessee, quickly answering the question herself. "It requires stern convictions of duty, unflinching allegiance to purposes, undying devotion to principles, and an unswerving faith to enable any one, and especially frail women, to endure unto the end under all these trials."

Tennessee made it clear that she and Victoria were not brassy creatures, insensible to censure:

"If the public knew what it has cost us in sleepless nights, in heartaches and laceration of soul, to be able to perform our duties, under the heavy hand that has at times been laid upon us, you would wonder, not that we have maintained ourselves, but that we could ever presume to think of living at all!"

Intrigued by the spectacle of Tennessee the author, the reporters gathered again at the Thirty-eighth Street residence, in search of Tennessee the broken reed, the lacerated soul. They found, not to their surprise, a gracious and pretty hostess who was pouring champagne.

"When engaged in conversation upon any topic which interests her, she is all animation, talking not only with her tongue, but with her eyes, face, hands, and *all over*," reported one of the visitors, and the italics are his. "One would think her whole physical structure was inlaid with a thousand sensitive spiral springs," he added thoughtfully.

The newspapermen also noticed Tennessee's "careless freedom" and the fact that, because she "has mingled largely and freely with men of the world, she will say and do the most *outré* things, but with an air of the most childlike and unsophisticated innocence." Some people thought this "innocence" was calculated, but the newspapermen liked the celebrated Tennessee, though not alone for her "careless freedom," but also for the champagne which was so freely served at the

Claflins'. They also liked what today would be known as her sex appeal. "Victoria's sphere is the editorial room, but Tennie's that of the outside business *man*," wrote one newspaperman, but he hastily added, "to get subscribers and secure paying advertisements," of course.

As she filled the champagne glasses, Tennessee stated her theory of social equality of the sexes. If a woman who violates the laws of social purity is ostracized by society, her male partner in guilt should suffer the same penalty. If, Tennessee said, prompted by Blood and Andrews hovering beside her, the libertine and seducer is well received into and petted by society, his female victim must be equally well received. If Hester Prynne—"Hester Prynne is the name, isn't it?" she asked Colonel Blood—yes, if Hester Prynne be compelled to wear the scarlet letter in the market place, then her reverend seducer should stand beside her, wearing the same insignia of shame.

Asked if she had anyone in mind when she mentioned a "reverend seducer," Tennessee winked and replied, "Draw your own conclusions."

. 19 .

While Tennessee was thus exerting herself in her own behalf, sister Victoria made news too, first in an ethereal way, then in a more down-to-earth fashion. The National Association of Spiritualists met in Troy, New York, and elected her, most famed of the profession, President. And in Vineland, New Jersey, a convention of Communists, Pantarchists, Spiritualists and assorted radicals convened and nominated her for the Presidency of the United States.

At once Victoria Leagues were organized (their backers were not known but it was believed the WEEKLY editors were in the picture somewhere), also proposing The Woodhull for the Chief Executive's job. Victoria, as Theodore Tilton had recorded in his biography, never would "write at all except for those spirit-promptings which she dare not disobey." The promptings evidently were hovering about her, for she immediately dispatched a letter to the Victoria Leagues. She did not accept the honor, but she graciously admitted that, inasmuch as another Victoria ruled another great people, "it might grace the amity" between the two countries "if a twin sisterhood of Victoria were to preside over the two nations."

The Woodhull at first seemed to think her chances of becoming President were good, for:

"It is true, also, that in its mere etymology the name signifies *Victory!* . . . and, as the great Napoleon believed the star of his destiny, you will at least excuse me, and charge it to the credulity of woman, if I believe also in fatality of triumphs as somehow inhering in my name."

At that time doubts were raised as to whether Victoria was the actual author of the speeches, editorials, and pamphlets attributed to her name. Her book, *Origins, Tendencies and Principles of Government,* sold well at the high price of three dollars a copy. She had published "A Lecture on Constitutional Equality," "Speech on the Principles of Finance," and another tract, "And The Truth Shall Make You Free," all of them moneymakers. Many believed it more likely that Colonel Blood or Stephen Pearl Andrews or Dr. Joseph Treat, or any of the scriveners on the WEEKLY staff, were acting as ghost writers. These rumors were now refuted once and for all, by Victoria herself. It was officially announced that the letter to the Victoria Leagues was her own, as were all The Woodhull's literary products, though, true, they were penned by Colonel Blood. The words "fell from her unconscious lips," as Tilton reported, and as they fell, Colonel Blood copied them down. This particular letter was described as a prime example of "a composition which she had dictated while so outwardly oblivious to the dictation that when she ended and awoke, she had no memory at all of what she had done."

. 20 .

Unhappily, there was a minimum of popular demand that Victoria run for the Presidency. Like a true politician who has his ear glued to the ground, Victoria made it known she did not think the time ripe to announce her candidacy for such a high office. That could come later.

So The Woodhull went on a lecture tour. At Cleveland she spoke before an audience of three thousand on suffrage. At Plymouth, Massachusetts, she advanced the then novel proposition that parents should reveal the secrets of sex to their children. The stork should not be blamed. This was regarded by many as more horrifying than Free Love. "If our houses of prostitution were searched and their inmates questioned," declared Victoria, "none would be found whose mother had the good sense to teach them the objects and functions of their sexual systems." No authority was given for her dictum.

When she was scheduled to lecture in Hartford, Connecticut, some of its citizens were indignant. "Can any Christian woman," asked "A Lady of Hartford" in a letter to the town's COURANT, "sanction in any way the efforts of such a woman?" The Hartford Lady predicted no decent person would dare attend the lecture of a female who maintained that a wife was guilty of prostitution if she fulfilled her conjugal duties after love had flown out of the window.

"Fair Play" spoke up for Victoria in a letter to the newspaper a few days later. Victoria was "too much of a lady" to talk on such subjects, at least in Hartford. Victoria intended to speak only on suffrage problems. The next day "A Citizen of Hartford" demanded that Governor Hawley should ban the meeting, because The Woodhull's intercourse and language with men was well known, though admittedly of a nature hard to prove by eyewitnesses.

Governor Hawley did nothing of the kind, but he felt himself duty-bound to write a signed editorial in the COURANT. He damned Victoria's WEEKLY as a "disreputable journal" not fit to be introduced "into respectable households where there are virtuous girls."

Due to the happy interchange of publicity, seven hundred persons were attracted to the Hartford Opera House. They came to be thrilled, perhaps shocked. They were disappointed. Victoria delivered a quiet plea for suffrage which apparently offended no one. That disgusting thing, s-e-x, was not mentioned once, and the Connecticut Yankees felt that they had been "sold."

· 21 ·

Victoria announced her lecture tour would be climaxed by an oration in New York City's Steinway Hall on "The Principles of Social Freedom, Involving the Question of Free Love, Marriage, Divorce and Prostitution." With an all-inclusive title such as that, a full house of listeners was assured.

But that was not enough for Victoria C. Woodhull. She sat down and wrote a letter to Henry Ward Beecher, a letter which truly deserved to be called an inspiration:

Nov. 19, 1871

Dear Sir:

For reasons in which you are deeply interested as well as myself and the cause of truth, I desire to have an interview with you, without fail, at some hour tomorrow. Two of your sisters [Harriet Beecher Stowe and Catherine Beecher] have gone out of their way to assail my character and purposes, both by means of the public press and by numerous private letters written to various persons with whom they seek to injure me and thus to defeat the political ends at which I aim.

You doubtless know that it is in my power to strike back, and in ways more disastrous than anything that can come to me; but I do not desire to do this. I simply desire justice from those from whom I have a right to expect it; and a reasonable course on your part will assist me to it. I speak guardedly, but I think you will understand me.

I repeat that I must have an interview tomorrow, since I am to speak tomorrow evening at Steinway Hall and what I shall or shall not say will depend largely on the result of the interview.

Yours very truly,

Victoria C. Woodhull

P.S. Please return answer by bearer.

The import of this letter was only too clear to Beecher. Frightened, he consented to the interview. No witnesses were present. Beecher never disclosed what happened, but, according to Victoria, the famed Man of God arose from a sofa in agitation when he found out what she wanted him to do—to introduce her at the Steinway Hall lecture. He went on his bended knees before her, and taking her face in his hands—an acrobatic feat in itself—begged off between sobs.

"I should sink through the floor," he supposedly confessed. "I am a moral coward on this subject and I know it, and I am not fit to stand by you, who go there to speak what you know to be the truth. I should stand there a living lie."

These were Beecher's words as reported by Victoria. Offhand, such abjectness on his part is almost unbelievable, but the Reverend never flatly denied this one-sided description of the interview.

After Vicky had gone, Beecher reread the letter, realized more fully its implications and rushed to an old friend, Frank Moulton, who obligingly asked Victoria to his home for the second meeting of the day. Tilton also attended the parley, and as he was afraid The Woodhull might make dangerous remarks in public unless she were appeased, he pleaded with the Brooklyn pastor to introduce her. He suggested that Beecher say he disagreed with Victoria's views but believed in her right to present them. Victoria said that, considering the circumstances, this type of weak-kneed introduction would be acceptable to her.

"I cannot, cannot face this thing!" moaned Beecher. Tilton and Victoria alone are the authorities for this alleged admission.

All in the room realized that Vicky might illustrate her Free Love theories by mentioning the Lib-Beecher affair, and, as she turned to leave, their fears were justified, for she declared threateningly:

"Mr. Beecher, if I am compelled to go upon that platform alone I shall begin by telling the audience why I am alone and why you are not with me."

Frantic, the Reverend Beecher turned to Tilton and secured his promise to introduce The Woodhull in his stead. It was believed that Victoria, mollified, would not mention the affair. This, as it happened, was true; but surely all concerned knew that the disclosure of the scandal had merely been postponed.

. **22** .

High winds and a rainstorm roared through the city on the night of November 20, yet at seven o'clock, an hour before lecture time, Steinway Hall was jammed with three thousand people. The Standing Room Only sign was posted, then taken down, and late-comers were turned away.

Victoria and Tennessee were somberly dressed in full black, but their costumes were brightened by a red rose pinned at the throat. They received in their dressing room a battery of reporters who, to their amazement, were served tea. However, the tedium of such an ordeal was relieved somewhat when Tennessee, with a seemingly unconscious gesture, retied her shoelace and in doing so happened to show a shapely expanse of leg. The newspapermen dutifully recorded this significant fact the next day in their stories.

Tennessee soon left the dressing room to occupy a box at the right of the stage. In the box at the left was seated Utica, another Claflin sister. She had been drinking whiskey all day long —a habit she had developed early in life—and that night for some obscure reason she was angry at Victoria. Utica, along with her other sisters and her parents, alternately adored and hated Victoria and Tennessee.

Those massed in the audience applauded as Theodore Tilton escorted The Woodhull onstage. Theodore seated her, bowed low in tribute, turned to quiet the cheers, and said:

"Ladies and Gentlemen—happening to have an unoccupied night, which is an unusual thing for me in the lecture season, I came to this meeting actuated by curiosity to know what my friend would have to say in regard to the great question which has occupied her for so many years of her life. I was met at the door by a member of the committee who informed me that several gentlemen had been applied to—particularly within the circuit of these two or three neighboring cities—to know whether they would occupy the platform and preside on this occasion. Every one had declined . . ."

There were hisses and boos from the audience, for the news had leaked out that the Reverend Henry Ward Beecher of Brooklyn had feared to make the introductory speech.

"Every one had declined," Tilton continued, stilling the rising jeers, "one after the other, for various reasons, the chief among them being—first, objections to the lady's character. I know it, and believe in it, and vouch for it.

"As to her views, she will give them to you herself in a few minutes, and you may judge for yourself. It may be that she is a fanatic; it may be that I am a fool, but before high heaven I would rather be both fanatic and fool in one than to be such a coward as would deny a woman the right of speech."

And amidst the cheers Tilton took Victoria by the hand and led her to the lectern.

Entirely composed, The Woodhull started to read her speech from manuscript. Judging by the response of the audience, about half of the people favored her views, while the other half violently opposed them, for when she declared that a loveless union should be dissolved because it violated the laws of nature and of God, and that all current laws of marriage were despotic toward womankind, the hall rocked with competing hisses and cheers.

"If any gentleman or lady in the audience who is hissing will come to the platform here . . ." Victoria started to say. To her astonishment, she was cut short by sister Utica. Utica stood up in her box, swayed, and asked querulously: "How would you like to come into this world without knowing who your father or mother was?"

Again applause vied with boos. Victoria had an answer. Leveling her finger in the general direction of the audience, although she might well have been pointing at Utica, she replied:

"There are thousands of noble men and women in the world today who never knew who their fathers were."

This somehow quieted Utica, and she sat down. Tilton, up on the stage, stirred uneasily, but relaxed when Victoria returned to the script in front of her. A few minutes later, however, Utica in a wobbly way pulled herself to her feet. Victoria, who was touting Free Love, did not desire to be interrupted. "I have a better right to speak," she said, "as one having authority in this matter, since it has been my province to study it in all its various lights and shades."

Utica continued to reel back and forth, and it was evident she intended not only to ask a question or two, but to make a speech of her own.

An officer entered the box and laid a commanding hand on the young lady. "Shame!" screamed half the audience. "Throw her out!" cried the other half. The policeman backed away.

Victoria stepped back to Tilton's chair behind the lectern, pulled the reluctant man to his feet, escorted him to the front of the platform and, tugging at his coat sleeve, asked him to say a few words to quiet the audience. It was feared a free-for-all was in the making. Tilton was, for the moment, nonplused. Victoria went to the front of the stage and called out to Tennessee, "Can't you get Utie to leave?" Tennessee thought it best to sit quiet.

As the tumult gradually subsided, Tilton regained his wits. He told the audience that perhaps the lady in the box should be heard from, for he believed in free speech for everyone, but only after the speaker of the evening, Victoria C. Woodhull, had had her say. Again there were mingled boos and cheers, and when the commotion had died down Victoria returned to her subject, asserting Free Love was the only true religion of the future.

"Are you a Free Lover?" demanded a voice from the audience.

"Yes, I *am* a Free Lover!" screamed the exasperated lecturer, and, to Tilton's horror, she threw her manuscript to the floor, advanced to the footlights and began to speak extemporaneously. "It was not the printed speech that did the damage," Tilton afterward said, "it was the interjected remarks in response to the audience—for she said violent things."

And to an audience gone wild with conflicting emotions Victoria shouted:

"I have an inalienable, constitutional, and natural right to love whom I may, to love as long or as short a period as I can, to change that love every day I please!"

This was strong meat. The next day the newspapers were to append three, and sometimes more exclamation points to this frank statement. Victoria's listeners gasped at her audacity, while Tilton, who realized she was publicly committing hara-kiri and perhaps damaging his own reputation as he had introduced her, wrung his hands.

"And with that right neither you nor the law you can frame have any right to interfere," Victoria cried. "And I have the further right to demand a free and unrestricted exercise of that right, and it is your duty not only to accord it, but as a community to see that I am protected in it. I trust that I am fully understood, for I mean just that and nothing else."

Without giving her listeners time to digest these words, Victoria continued, her eyes flashing, her voice rising:

"I deem it a false and perverse modesty that shuts off discussion, and consequently knowledge, upon these subjects. Free Love . . . is the law by which men and women of all grades and kinds are attracted to or repelled from each other, and does not describe the results accomplished by either. These results depend upon the condition and development of the individual subjects.

"Promiscuity in sexuality is simply the anarchical stage of development wherein the passions rule supreme. When spirituality comes in and rescues the real man or woman from the domain of the purely material, promiscuity is simply impossible.

"The love that I cannot command is not mine. Let me not disturb myself about it, nor attempt to filch it from its rightful owner. Shall I forcibly capture the truant and transfix it with the barb of my selfish affection and pin it to the wall of my chamber? Rather let me leave my doors and windows open, intent only on living so nobly that the best cannot fail to be drawn to me by an irresistible attraction."

Not all her words made sense to the audience, but everyone in Steinway Hall agreed they had had their money's worth—they had heard a daring speech. The papers thought so too, and news of it was sent over the wires to the country's waiting presses. From the Middle West Isaac S. Kalloch, renowned as the man with the Golden Voice, the preacher turned editor and politician, wrote tersely in his SPIRIT OF KANSAS:

"Mrs. Woodhull says she claims the right to choose the father of her children. For our part, we are not disposed to deny her the right, but we would like for her to tell us how she is going to convince the child as to which of the fathers is his."

Victoria's name again was on every lip. She was in demand to present her views in lectures throughout the nation, but another result of her notoriety was less fortunate. The immediate social ostracism that struck the whole family was more than a mere nuisance. Several angels of the WEEKLY withdrew their financial support, and the entire Claflin tribe was evicted from its Thirty-eighth Street home. The landlord argued he was a moral individual, a churchgoer to boot, and so could not tolerate such tenants, even though there was money in it for him. For the time being the family could find no place to live except a cheap boarding house. No money was available until Victoria would start on her lecture tour. The handsome landau and horses were sold, and—loathsome indignity!—the Claflins were forced to ride in the new cable cars on the Ninth Avenue elevated.

. 23 .

When by-election day came in the fall of 1871, Victoria and Tennessee marched to the voting booths and were refused ballots. This surprised no one, including the assembled reporters. A few months earlier, on registration day, the sisters had remonstrated so vociferously at the booth at 682 Sixth Avenue that they had been arrested. That had been their first arrest, and quite welcome to people devoted to getting themselves into print. This time, however, though the publicity was gratifying, their luck did not hold, for no official volunteered to take them into custody. As the reporters jotted down their notes, the inspectors of the Democratic Party, which meant Tammany Hall, patiently explained that it was against the law of the United States to permit women to vote. The Republican inspectors, who had nothing to lose, inasmuch as it was unlikely that even their own votes would be counted by Tammany Hall, said they welcomed Victoria's and Tennessee's and, for that matter, any woman's ballot. Victoria wrote a letter to the TIMES, declaring, "The inspectors, under law, are guilty of felony for preventing a legal voter from voting."

The publicity was good enough to bring demands from a few more towns for The Woodhull to entertain them on the lecture platform. All desired to hear the extemporaneous speech she had made in Steinway Hall. So Victoria decided to educate the great but unenlightened Middle West. She sent Tennessee ahead to book the dates and hire the halls. The newspapers darkly muttered that Tennessee was accompanied by a male, who did not shrink from taking her to respectable hotels where they would take a room and sleep together, as man and wife; but this was not proven.

Sometimes, when the December weather of the plains prevented Victoria from keeping a lecture date, Tennessee would act as substitute. Audiences found her social views as daring and heady as sister Victoria's, though she lacked her stage presence and charm.

"If the loss of purity is a disgrace to unmarried women, then the same should be held of men," Tennessee would tell her startled Midwestern natives. "If the mother of a child out of wedlock is ostracized, then the father should share the same fate. If a life of female prostitution is wrong, a life of male prostitution is equally wrong. If Contagious Diseases Acts are passed, they should operate equally on both sexes."

Tennessee was a fair speaker and acceptable enough in an emergency, but there was never any great demand for her to give lectures on her own.

Victoria's tour led her first to Washington, then on to Cincinnati, Chicago, Milwaukee, Evansville, Kansas City, and other Midwestern cities. Large crowds came to her lectures, despite the unanimous warnings of newspapers that no decent man or woman should attend, and the money poured in. Soon Victoria and the Claflins were again in luxury.

As 1871 waned and the new year came on, Victoria stopped off at the convention of the National Woman's Suffrage Association in Washington. The newspapermen noted she was stylishly dressed in a quiet double-breasted blue broadcloth coat which displayed a rich chinchilla collar. They were disappointed, however, by her conduct. She made no effort to dominate the convention or, so at least the reporters thought, to put forward a single radical view. According to the newspapermen, The Woodhull was retiring, "proper and alluring," and, they wrote with disgust, she "acted the perfect lady."

A later generation would have found her views radical enough. Victoria proposed in a speech before the delegates that the countries of the world loosely unite and adopt one and the same constitution, but the significance of this suggestion—which was to become apparent three-quarters of a century later when the basis for the United Nations was laid in San Francisco—escaped the reporters.

Much Ado About Blackmail

NEW YORK: 1872

. 1 .

When The Woodhull returned from her lecture tour she found
that the hostility of New York landlords, who are notorious for
their short memory when the tenant has a long pocketbook, had
abated. She was able to rent a private house at 118 East
Twenty-third Street, in a stylish district near the "Psyche
Club," reputedly the den devoted to Free Love orgies. The new
home was spacious enough, but the moment she moved in the
place was crammed, as usual, with her two children, with the
assorted sisters and their husbands and offspring, with Andrews, Dr. Woodhull, Buck Claflin, mother Roxy and others
dining at the family board.

It was at this time that Victoria announced that her daughter
Zulu, now eleven, would be trained for a stage career. She
would coach Zulu herself, as she had been an actress and would
have become a great star had she not turned to another profes-

sion. Victoria claimed Zulu had great potentialities. Alas, nothing more was ever heard of Zulu's stage career.

The lecture tour had been a financial success, but, by the time Victoria returned to Manhattan, rumors spread that the WEEKLY, hard hit by the withdrawal of angels, was resorting to blackmail to pick up needed revenue. It was said prominent citizens had been shown galley proofs of articles which depicted them in a most unfavorable light, and that the stories would be kept out of print providing a "donation" was given to the magazine. The Springfield REPUBLICAN claimed Mrs. Elizabeth B. Phelps, the wealthy backer of a suffrage journal, *Revolution*, had been so approached. Mrs. Phelps would not be quoted. The Hartford POST declared Mrs. Mary Livermore, the prominent suffragette, was a victim. Mrs. Livermore refused to affirm or deny the accusation. The Worcester SPY said Reverend Doctor Bellows had been blackmailed. Reverend Bellows said the charge was false. Two other alleged victims, Lillie Devereux Blake and Laura Curtis Bullard, refused to talk. The newspapers admitted, however, that these "attempts at extortion" had been made in Victoria's absence.

The rumors gained credence when it was recalled that, a few weeks before, a letter containing various veiled threats had been printed in the WEEKLY, a letter which had frightened many a New Yorker who had strayed from hearth and wife. Numerous people felt it was extortionary; others, more lenient, pointed out it was a sure-fire circulation-builder. The communication signed by one "Mary Bowles" read, in part:

"At twenty years of age, by a train of circumstances, an uncongenial marriage, an abandonment, inexperience, desperation, total want of comprehension and sympathy from my own family—by my own folly, if you will—I found myself the inmate of a house of ill-repute in this city. I discovered in myself a shrewd business capacity, and after a few years I found my-

self the successful mistress of the house of the kind I had been
an inmate before.

"From the time that I opened my house I have kept a record
of men who have visited it. I procured a large ledger, and sub-
sequently a second, and entered in a business way the names
and residences and some of the incidents of each visit of all the
visitors at my establishment.

"My business has been successful but I am tired of it. I am
arranging to break it up and go to Europe. If you, in the prosecution of your blessed mission as a social reformer, have any
need to see more behind the scenes and to understand the real
state of New York society better, I will give you access to my
two big books, or would leave them with you in my absence.
You will find in them [anyone from] doctors of divinity to
counter-jumpers . . ."

This letter was addressed "with love and admiration" to
Vicky, but sister Tennessee answered it while Victoria was
away:

"I curse and denounce a virtue which is forced on women as
slaves, by men who are making themselves confessedly steeped
in the same vice. I have to associate with male prostitutes in my
business, everywhere, and if I then condemn and avoid women
of equally bad character, am I not glaringly false and traitorous
to the dignity and equality of my sex?

"In respect to the books you speak of, I do not know what
use can be made of them, for my sister and myself have scrupu-
lously adopted the policy of avoiding personalities when possible. But the time may come when that policy will have to be
abandoned, for our enemies do not scruple to resort to them in
the most scandalous manner."

When this correspondence appeared the agonized bellows of
errant New Yorkers could be heard, demands were made that
the authorities stop the threatened exposé, and anonymous

notes poured into the WEEKLY office, decrying such a move. The tumult was so great that Victoria felt obliged to step forward and explain the situation. She did admit the Claflin clan needed money: there was the expense of keeping such a large troupe under one roof, and the high printing costs of the WEEKLY. This prompted some people to remember that only a year or so before the sisters had bragged about the $700,000 windfall they had made on the 'change. Had they spent this fortune? Or had they ever made any money at all as Lady Brokers? And if they had, why was it they had suddenly abandoned such a "profitable" business?

Victoria announced that even though money was needed, the sisters never, never would resort to blackmail. It just was not in them. And, finally, the rumpus had been raised over nothing, for the letter had been composed and answered by editor Tennessee herself, as a hoax. The good folk who were whorehouse visitors need not be alarmed, for the Mary Bowles yarn had been concocted as a circulation-getter.

Disclosure of the forgery brought no criticism from the press of that age. The rival editors enviously wished they had thought up the stunt themselves, and the WEEKLY was complimented for its journalistic coup.

. 2 .

Most suffragists had accepted Victoria into their ranks because their leaders had so insisted. Now there were demands that the "blackmailer" be expelled. The *Woman's Journal*, a conservative spokesman for suffrage, called on the organization to get "rid of the Free Love incubus which has done incalculable harm to the cause." It warned that "Women, like men, are known by the company they keep." Harriet Beecher Stowe, famed author of *Uncle Tom's Cabin* (though she herself said "God wrote it," and this was widely believed), attacked Victoria's "vile immorality" in the CHRISTIAN UNION. Mrs. Stowe, who was to become broad-minded enough to enjoy friendship with George Sand and George Eliot, was believed to have been inspired by her brother, the Reverend Henry Ward Beecher, editor of the CHRISTIAN UNION.

Undaunted by the accusations of extortion, the WEEKLY in its April 6 issue defended attempts at "what is called blackmailing." If a helpless woman is extorting from a certain type of man, a man who is a "cunning animal," the WEEKLY declared, woman must "meet cunning with cunning, fraud with fraud." To illustrate its point the newspaper printed a letter from "One Who Knows," telling of the encounter of an innocent young lass with a wealthy deacon of a church, "an ignorant fellow, fond of that bawdy talk which is pure obscenity, without any relief of wit or humor." Due to imperative, but undescribed, reasons the little lady needed money. The logical thing to do, she reasoned, was to get it in a house of prostitution.

The anonymous letter writer then explained how, in certain cases, blackmail is justified:

"Never having been to such a place before she requested me to go with her. As I believe that all places should be known to the wise, I did not hesitate to accompany her. She was there introduced to Shank, who after treating us to wine, retired with my companion. This rich and pious deacon gave to this necessitous girl, to her terrible disappointment, but half the price usual in the house. She complained to me, and but for my remonstrance he would not have given the balance, which he afterwards did."

The inference was that "the balance" Deacon Shank gave afterward was considerably more than what was owed, and that was blackmail; it was not made clear how the Madame of the house would permit a customer to pay half the regular price.

"One Who Knows" of course was a woman, and the fact that she was closely associated with the WEEKLY was brought out at the end of the letter, in an ominous invitation to the readers of the journal:

"Indeed, I say to my sex, 'Have you been deceived, maltreated, abandoned, or to comprise it all in one word—beat—write out your experiences, state the plain truth, give names and incidents with all possible particularity. Send these statements to WOODHULL & CLAFLIN'S WEEKLY that they may be published and broadcast over the land. . . .' "

.3.

In February, 1872, Victoria, who had bathed in columns of newspaper publicity when defying the sanctity of marriage, or boosting Free Love, or defending herself against charges of blackmail, found that when she attacked the sanctity of monopoly and accumulated wealth—perhaps a hangover from her Communist days—she was, comparatively speaking, ignored. This disappointing discovery came during her lecture at the New York Academy of Music on "The Impending Revolution."

The hall was packed an hour before lecture time, the street

outside was impassable because of the carriages, and scalpers were hawking tickets at $10 apiece. But when Victoria stepped to the rostrum, dressed in a black silk dress and jacket, with high-heeled boots, her hands sparkling with what looked like diamond rings, the avid audience found that they were to hear no talk on Free Love or Sex. The Woodhull instead was campaigning against the revered rich.

"An Astor may sit in his sumptuous apartments and watch the property bequeathed to him rise in value from one to fifty millions," she cried, "and everybody bows low before his power. But if a tenant of his, whose employer had discharged him because he did not vote the Republican ticket, fails to pay his month's rent to Mr. [William Backhouse] Astor, the law sets him and his family into the street."

As another example Victoria mentioned the owner of the city's biggest department store, which paid out the most money to newspapers for advertising:

"Mr. [A. T.] Stewart by business tact and the various practices known to trade, succeeds in twenty years in obtaining from the customers, whom he entraps into purchasing from him, fifty million dollars . . . and builds costly public beneficiaries, and straightaway the world makes him a philanthropist. But a poor man who should come along with a bolt of cloth which he had smuggled into the country and which consequently he could sell at a lower price than Mr. Stewart, who paid the tariff and is thereby authorized by law to add that sum to the price, would be cast into prison."

As was the custom in those days, the TIMES did not print a line about an attack on an advertiser, but two days later it condemned The Woodhull's "periodic exhibitions of bitter language" and commented sourly, if irrelevantly, on the fact that she had been married not once but twice, and maybe more—who knew? The TIMES declared, probably to the bewilderment of its readers who knew nothing of her speech, for the paper had suppressed it:

"She is capable of mischief in inflaming the unthinking hostility of the poor to the rich, and in fostering in the minds of the working man who applauded her during her recent lecture, the conviction that capitalists have no rights which working men are bound to respect."

The TIMES was upset not only because the biggest advertiser in town had been insulted, but because Victoria's WEEKLY was defending the striking coal miners, exposing "grabs" by politicians and delving into the practices of insurance companies and shady city bond deals. The WEEKLY, whatever its faults, was at the time, thirty-four years before Theodore Roosevelt used the word, a real "muckraker."

. 4 .

One of Victoria's vulnerable spots—the fact that her first husband was living in peaceful conjunction with spouse Number Two—was removed early in 1872. Dr. Canning Woodhull was taken off his morphine diet by a physician. The withdrawal symptoms were too much for him and he died.

"I intend to take revenge on the family," sister Utica confided between hiccups to a newspaperman, and soon after that the Coroner was informed the Doctor had died under suspicious circumstances. Victoria and Tennessee immediately insisted that a post-mortem be held. The examination showed Dr. Woodhull had died from pneumonia.

The WEEKLY frankly explained the relationship that had existed between the two husbands side by side in the same home:

"No clearer nor better testimonial of the deep regard, aye, love, than the deceased had for our present husband could be had than the care bestowed upon him during several violent attacks of illness . . . These two people were not rivals. They were brothers, and in spite of all attempts to make them enemies, they remained friends to the last."

. 5 .

Whenever things quieted down in her life Victoria became unhappy. She had to keep moving, and her nervous energy gave her no rest. She moved in many directions, sometimes backward, but more often forward, and the only thing she could not do was to stand still. When she found that the question of accumulated wealth and reform would never yield the spectacular results commensurate with her ambition, she abandoned it and began to engage more actively in the straight political field.

In the spring of 1872 WOODHULL & CLAFLIN's WEEKLY announced that "the undersigned citizens," acting under the auspices of the National Woman's Suffrage Association, was calling a convention at Steinway Hall in New York on May 9 and 10 to form a new political party and to nominate a candidate to run for President of the United States. The undersigned included all the big guns of the suffrage brigade—Elizabeth Cady Stanton, Susan B. Anthony, Isabella Beecher Hooker,

Matilda Gage, editor of the feminist journal *National Citizen*, and others. Without exception, it was the first that any of the signatories had heard about the matter.

"Mrs. Woodhull has the advantage of us because she has the newspaper, and she persistently means to run our craft to her port," declared Miss Anthony on hearing the news during a lecture tour far away in the West. "If she were influenced by *women* spirits, either in body or out of it, in the direction she steers, I might consent to be a mere sail-hoister for her, but, as it is, she is wholly owned and dominated by *men* spirits." Miss Anthony demanded that her name be removed from the list of sponsors and took a fast train for New York.

After Mrs. Stanton had called the suffrage meeting to order on the night of May 9, Victoria C. Woodhull arose, adjusted her costly chinchilla wrap and asked for the floor. She said that a newly formed "People's Party," devoted to political and industrial reform, would convene jointly with the Suffragettes. She envisioned a great future for the fusion of two such powerful bodies.

Mrs. Stanton, president of the Suffragettes, appeared willing, as did Mrs. Hooker, but Miss Anthony barred the twin convention and demanded that the "People's Party" adherents be evicted. The ladies split. Mrs. Stanton resigned her presidency and, with Mrs. Hooker, joined forces with Victoria. Miss Anthony was elected the new head of the organization, or what was left of it. As she was about to adjourn for the evening, "To my amazement," as she told her biographer years later, "Mrs. Woodhull came gliding in from the side of the platform and moved that 'This convention adjourn to meet tomorrow morning at Apollo Hall.' "

The motion was quickly seconded from the floor, but Miss Anthony refused to put it. None daunted, Victoria put the motion again, and it was adopted in a sea of yeas. Miss Anthony cried the whole procedure was out of order, as a majority of the members present did not belong to the Association. Victoria started to present her side of the case, but the wily Miss Anthony stopped, for the moment, the secession by ordering the janitor to turn out the gaslights. Victoria talked in the dark for a while, and then gave up. But she was to have the last word, for, as the future biographer of Miss Anthony was to write half a century later, "Victoria Woodhull was better able to take care of herself than the women were to take care of the National Woman's Suffrage Association."

The next morning but a scattered few attended the proceedings in Steinway Hall, while in rival Apollo Hall there were five hundred "delegates." It was a curious olla-podrida. Many were faithful WEEKLY readers, some were Spiritualists, Communists, Free Lovers, some even suffragists, but all were radicals of one sort or another, and whatever their merits or demerits, they all wanted to improve the status quo.

At the morning session, presided over by the respected Judge J. D. Reymart of New York City, a left-wing platform was adopted and the permanent name, "Equal Rights Party," was chosen. (It did have permanence; as recently as 1947 a women's "Equal Rights Party" met in Washington.) Victoria C. Woodhull was asked to address the evening meeting.

"From this convention will go forth a tide of revolution that shall sweep over the whole world," Victoria shouted that night, a trifle optimistically, as events have shown. She demanded that "the inalienable rights belonging to individuals shall be jealously guarded against encroachment," and threatened that in America "a revolution shall sweep with resistless force, if not fury, over the whole country, to purge it of political trickery, despotic assumption, and all industrial injustices," unless the Equal Rights Party came into political power.

At this juncture Judge Carter, a prominent lawyer from Cincinnati, stepped to the platform and nominated Victoria C. Woodhull to be the new party's candidate for President of the United States. There were great cheers, and no dissensions.

"I thank you from the bottom of my soul for the honor you have conferred upon me tonight," said Victoria, stifling down some sobs. She seemed quite surprised she had been tendered the nomination. "I have stood by you so long, sometimes meriting your applause, and sometimes encountering your rebuffs, but I have been always faithful to my principles . . .", and then she cut it short and said, yes, she would accept the honor.

There were some jovial souls in the audience who favored the nomination of Colonel Blood as Vice-President, so Victoria would not be lonely in the White House, but these requests seemed to stem from the press gallery. Spotted Tail, the Indian Chief, also was suggested, but the majority appeared to favor Frederick Douglass, the great Negro Reformer, and he was unanimously named as running mate. Years later, when Douglass got around to writing his autobiography, he thought it best to omit the fact that once he had been nominated for the Vice-Presidency of the United States in such peculiar company.

Acting in the manner of a truly great political party, the Equal Rights organization held a "ratification convention" at Cooper Institute, and there Victoria formally accepted the nomination. The hall was filled with the faithful and the curious, and all joined in to sing, to the tune of "Coming Through the Rye," the baby party's ringing campaign song:

Yes! Victoria we've selected
For our chosen head.
With Fred Douglass on the ticket
We will raise the dead.
Then around them let us rally
Without fear or dread

And next March, we'll put the Grundys
In their little bed.

• 6 •

The spectacle of a lady—if she *was* a lady, so mused the editors—running for President of the United States was unprecedented in the history of the country, and the idea was greeted raucously by the press.

From far-off California came jeers. The GOLDEN CITY printed the toast made at a banquet, a toast thought most daring: "To the rights of women—if she cannot be captain of a ship may she always command a smack!" The ALTA CALIFORNIA in San Francisco sniffily quoted the words of the Duke of Argyle on suffrage: "A woman has no right to appear upon a platform except when she is going to be hung—then it is unavoidable."

New York newspapers pointed out that The Woodhull was ineligible for the Presidency for, among other reasons, she lacked the constitutional minimum age. And the powerful *Harper's Weekly* entered the fray, calling upon its great cartoonist, Thomas Nast, to caricature her. Vicky was depicted as a vulturous-looking female Satan who is championing Free Love. In the background is a woman, with babies clutching her, saying, "I'd rather travel the hardest path of Matrimony than follow your footsteps." As to Victoria's assertion that she gradually was abandoning the gospel of Free Love to concentrate on the more important subject of political reform, the magazine re-

called the defiant words she had flung at her audience in Steinway Hall:

"To those who denounce me for this I reply, 'Yes, I am a
Free Lover! I have an inalienable, constitutional, and natural
right to love whom I may, to love as long or as short a period as
I can, to change that love every day if I please!' "

Victoria denied ever making such remarks, though they had
appeared in a hundred newspapers. She said that she had been
misquoted, adding that, anyway, her Free Love enthusiasm was
a thing of the past now that she had entered the political lists.

That was not good enough for *Harper's Weekly*. It made
its point, as was customary at the time, by quoting from the
Scriptures:

"If this mischievous talk does not emanate from Satan,
whence does it come? Certainly it can not have Divine approval, else what comes of the injunction uttered by the Sa-
viour, 'What therefore, God hath joined together, let not men
put asunder'?"

THE NEW YORK TIMES chimed in with its stern appraisal, on
March 31. "When either member of the firm of Woodhull-
Claflin appears in public as a lecturer, it is well understood that
her motive is to gain notoriety." The newspaper explained why
Wall Street men (who incidentally advertised each week in the
sisters' journal) would have nothing to do with Tennessee, then
business manager of the WEEKLY:

"When a woman attempts to combine flirtation with business
and tries to gain business favors in exchange for familiarities
too freely offered to be attractive, the ordinary man of business
is annoyed and disgusted, and naturally declines to submit to
another interview of the kind."

The TIMES was particularly "annoyed and disgusted" because Tennessee, who two days before had made her New York
debut as a public speaker at the Academy of Music on "The

Ethics of Sexual Equality," a subject designed to draw an audience, had made an embarrassing disclosure: The TIMES paid its male typesetters forty-five cents per one thousand ems as compared to forty cents for women workers. She condemned such discrimination.

"Praise or abuse is probably alike welcome to these diffident women," the TIMES said in its editorial. "Of the two, perhaps, violent abuse—better suits their purpose than mild or brief approval. The more prominently the rather ungracious fact of their existence is kept before the public the better their trade is advertised, and the more keenly their vanity pleased."

This appeared to be a shrewd diagnosis. In any event, it was added grist to the publicity mill, and so the reporters once again began to gather to interview the sisters. The New York correspondent of the Chicago TIMES found the Presidential candidate, Victoria, alone in her Broad Street offices. Newspapermen always delighted in interviewing Victoria, for, as one of them fondly recalled years later, "She is apt to call things by their right names, and is guiltless of prudery or sham modesty, but speaks out boldly what she thinks." This, of course, always made for a good story. In this instance, however, the journalist from Chicago had to be content with mere financial details.

"In sheer adventure, I concluded to call on the most notorious adventuress of our country, Victoria C. Woodhull," he informed his readers. "My first impressions of her were agreeable. There was a bright, intelligent face, lit up by two soft, dark-blue or changeable eyes. She smiled sweetly, and greeted me in tones tender and plaintive as a flute. She was stylishly attired, and at that moment was partaking of a dish of luscious berries, a generous quantity of which had been sent in to the 'sisters' by some anonymous millionaire (probably old Vanderbilt). She remarked, in her animated way, that she would receive a million votes.

" 'You look incredulous,' she went on to observe, 'and I do not wonder, for it takes money to conduct a great campaign, and of that we shall have abundant supplies. Look here!' she exclaimed as she drew forth what I at first mistook for a U.S. bond. 'Here,' she continued, 'here is a bond we are issuing, and upon which we shall raise $200,000, or twice, or thrice that sum if needed.' Then, with a fascinating smile and a pensive and tender glance from her mellow eyes, she softly and confidingly whispered: 'The next time you call you shall have one of these bonds. They draw seven per cent interest.' "

. 7 .

Tennessee had dabbled in Pacifism and Communism, when suddenly a militaristic streak cropped up in her nature. Jim Fisk, Jr., the playboy and Erie railroad stock manipulator, who was shot to death by Edward S. Stokes after seducing Stokes's sweetheart Josie Mansfield, had been Colonel of the 9th Regiment of the National Guard. Tennessee, who always said a woman could fill any man's shoes, now applied for the job. She reminded TIMES readers in a letter that "Joan d'Arc also was a woman," and "while I do not make pretensions to the same military genius she possessed, I may state it always has been my desire to become actively connected with the service."

The newspapers viewed this sally into the masculine military world quite jocosely, referring to Tennessee as "Miss Napoleon." The TIMES visualized the troops of the 9th Regiment acting as bodyguard for Victoria when she was elected President, and "Col. Claflin mounted on a gorgeous side-saddle, leading her regiment down Broadway to be inspected by Col. Blood and blessed by the Pantarch [Andrews]."

When the 9th Regiment declined her proposition, Tennessee, bitten by the militaristic bug, turned to the 85th Regiment, composed of Negro soldiers who were in great need of uniforms. She promised to outfit the six hundred members in rainbow suits, and to dress herself in a wonderful costume—not neat but gaudy—something half male, half female in style. She promptly was elected the regiment's Colonel, and so now there were, with Colonel Blood, two of such rank in the Woodhull ménage.

The TIMES feared Tennessee's white face would stand out among the Negro troops and suggested that she don burnt cork and go black-faced, but two days later the newspaper discarded its attempt at satire and declared that women "even blush to acknowledge her" as of their sex, and that the presence of two such sisters in one family "would surpass belief, did not the fact stare one in the face." Tennessee never was commissioned Colonel, inasmuch as the 85th Regiment demanded its promised uniforms before the induction ceremony, and that was the last heard of Tennessee's foray into militarism.

. **8** .

Now the consensus among astute political observers was that Ulysses S. Grant, and not Victoria C. Woodhull, would be the next President, but there were some who actually feared her candidacy. The Grand Opera House rented its facilities to the Equal Rights Party for a mass meeting, and then suddenly canceled the arrangement. And the Twenty-third Street landlord of The Woodhull evicted the family "for their immoral doctrines." The entourage was able to find accommodations at the Gilsey House—but not for long.

The time came when Vicky suffered what she felt was the unkindest cut of all. A few months before she had been nominated for the Presidency, Theodore Tilton could always be relied upon to rush to her aid. "What if foul-mouthed scandal, with its many tongues seeks to defile her?" his *Golden Age* had asked. "Shall we ignore a champion like this?"

The answer, at that time, was nay, and Theodore let it go at that. Later, the editor, her "intimate friend," as he was discreetly described, seemed to lose interest in The Woodhull. The two seldom were seen sipping champagne in the fashionable cafés, and no longer did they take buggy rides into the country or eat at the exclusive Woodmansteen Inn. And then, suddenly, Theodore really deserted the "champion." He announced he would support Horace Greeley, and not Victoria C. Woodhull, as next President of the United States. Greeley had secured the Democratic nomination, and also that of the left-wing Republicans who could not stomach their party man, Grant.

Those close to The Woodhull were surprised at the vehemence of her reaction to this "act of perfidy." One would think, it was remarked wonderingly, that Tilton's backflip actually had robbed her of the election. And so it was at this time that Victoria was moved to explain, in so many words, the exact nature of her friendship with the irresistible Theodore. Months after this interview, which was published in the Chicago TIMES, Victoria repudiated her words, for tactical reasons, saying she had been outrageously misquoted, but during the intervening period she repeatedly affirmed its genuineness.

"I ought to know Mr. Tilton," Victoria allegedly said when questioned by the TIMES reporter, "for he was my devoted lover for more than half a year, and I admit that during that time he was my accepted lover."

The newspaperman gasped at her frankness. Ladies, and sometimes even gentlemen, never acknowledged such things. He took a firm grasp on his pencil and recorded the words: "Of course we were lovers—devoted, true, faithful lovers."

The reporter asked if he might quote her. "Certainly," said The Woodhull, and went on:

"A woman who could not love Theodore Tilton, especially in reciprocation of a generous, impulsive, overwhelming affection such as he is capable of bestowing, must be indeed dead to all the sweeter impulses of our nature. *I* could not resist his inspiring fascination."

"Do I understand, my dear Madam," asked the TIMES man, possibly thinking fleetingly of Victoria's husband, Colonel Blood, "that the fascination was mutual and irresistible?"

"You will think so," answered Victoria, "when I tell you that so enamored and infatuated with each other we were that for *three months* we were hardly out of each other's sight and that during that time he rarely left my house *day and night*. He slept every night in my arms . . ."

"Theodore," The Woodhull continued briskly, "was then estranged from his wife, and undergoing all the agonies of the tortures inflicted upon him by the treachery of his 'friend,' Mr. Beecher."

As the newspaperman was to remember years later, during the entire journey by horse cab to the telegraph office, the thought kept drumming through his head that three months of days *and* nights was a long, long, a very long time.

. 9 .

In the opinion of Theodore Tilton, Victoria was no lady—she had kissed, and told. The handsome but disillusioned Theodore sadly related the aftermath of his affair with The Woodhull in a long poem, "Sir Marmaduke's Musings," which for some unfathomable reason has found its way into various anthologies. One of the verses read:

> I clasped a woman's breast
> As if her heart I knew,
> Or fancied would be true.
> Who proved—alas, she too!
> False like the rest.

Victoria was asked by a newspaperman to comment on the poem. She replied she never read trashy literature.

. 10 .

The bonds, those beautiful gilt-edged seven per cent bonds the Equal Rights Party intended to sell by the bale, went begging. The depression was on and Victoria found the expense of feeding and housing the numerous members of the Claflin family

was draining her purse dry. Advertising in the WEEKLY slacked
off during the hard times, and soon there was no money to put
out the journal. With the issue of June 22, 1872, the WEEKLY
temporarily suspended publication. Soon after, the proprietor
of Gilsey House, who had been out of town when the celebrated
Woodhull crew had moved into his fashionable hotel, asked
Victoria to get out and take her people with her. He said his
distinguished Southern clientele was threatening to leave en
masse, as they did not fancy living in the same hotel with a
woman who had a Negro as a Vice-Presidential running mate.

The Woodhull pointed out they could not be evicted unless
charges of misconduct were presented and proved, but to the
landlord that was a trifling objection, and one afternoon she
found their baggage piled on the sidewalk and the way into the
hotel barred. Victoria, Blood, Tennessee, and daughter Zulu
tramped the streets but could find no refuge for the night. They
climbed over the transom of their WEEKLY offices at 48 Broad
Street, and there they camped for a week. The management
raised their office rent fivefold, demanding payment in advance. Eventually, new and cheap quarters were found a few
doors down the way, at 44 Broad Street.

Desperate, Victoria wrote a letter to the Reverend Henry
Ward Beecher, whom she believed to be responsible for her
ordeal:

". . . Now I want your assistance. I have been shut out of
hotel after hotel . . . and am hunted down by a set of males
and females, who are determined that I shall not be permitted
to live even, if they can prevent it. I have submitted to this persecution just so long as I can endure. My business, my projects,
in fact everything for which I live, suffers from it, and it must
cease. Will you lend me your aid in this?"

The preacher did not reply to this "whining letter," as he
called it.

Through friends, Vicky was able to find a more congenial home for herself and the rest of the Claflins at 237 Fourth Avenue, but her troubles were not over. In August she was brought into court for nonpayment of debts. She testified that the very clothes she wore were borrowed, and that she had no money or property whatsoever.

Apparently Victoria, along with the whole Claflin family, was faced with ruin. This, as it turned out, was far from the truth; their fortunes were merely at low ebb. According to The Woodhull, the master mind behind the scenes was the sinister Henry Ward Beecher who was bent on driving her into bankruptcy. She decided to fight back.

Victoria had warned the preacher, though she had not named him, that "I do not intend to be made the scapegoat of sacrifice to be offered up as a victim to society by those who cover over the foulness of their lives . . . by diverting public attention from their own iniquity by pointing the finger at me." Now she set out to borrow money from any and every quarter to resuscitate the WEEKLY. The task was slow and difficult, but, once it was carried through, she was determined to tell all.

· 11 ·

Early in September, 1872, the New York TELEGRAPH printed an obscure item that prophesied a prominent clergyman was about to get his come-uppance. No name was used. A few days later when Victoria went to the National Spiritualists' Associa-

tion convention in Boston, the stronghold of conservatism, there
was a name mentioned, and it was that of The Reverend Henry
Ward Beecher.

Victoria had announced that with her entrance into the political arena her interest in spiritualism had become secondary,
but that she felt it her duty to make her final report as President of the organization. Perhaps, as she fingered her dry notes
on the platform she thought back to her former eminence, and
then of the man who she believed was the cause of her mis-
fortunes, the man who within a few days was to be feted and
glorified for completing twenty-five years as shepherd of the
Plymouth Church flock. Whatever her speculations were, she
suddenly threw aside her notes and: "Seized by one of those
overwhelming gusts of inspiration, which sometimes come
upon me, from I know not where, I was taken out of myself,"
Victoria later explained. She then told in detail all she knew of
the cohabitation that had taken place between the Brooklyn
Reverend and pretty Lib Tilton.

The Woodhull was careful to point out that Lib was not the
only member of the Beecher harem:

"He preaches every Sunday to dozens of his mistresses, who
are members of his church, sitting in their pews, robed in silks
and satins and high respectability!"

Victoria asserted virtuously she was making the matter
known publicly for the sole reason that all hypocrisies must be
uncovered. She said that as she herself believed in complete
social and sexual freedom, and practiced it, she realized
Beecher had the right to his own lecherous convictions.

A listener in the audience, Mrs. E. A. Meriweather, reported
on the event in the Memphis APPEAL:

"A sort of electric shock swept over the assembly, striking it
to a dead stillness, as if awaiting a thunder clap. Mrs. Woodhull

tossed back her hair, in high tragic style, and poured out a torrent of flame. It made our flesh creep and our blood run cold."

Mrs. Meriweather then described The Woodhull as she made her sensational charges:

"Her features are delicate and clear-cut, the nose slightly aquiline. Her skin, smooth and pale, except when under the excitement of speaking, then two crimson spots burn on her cheeks, and in her eyes is a lurid light. When speaking she has all the action and fervor of a tragic actress. Her face, the saddest I ever saw, tells of the wrecked hopes and a cruel battle with life."

In her speech, which Mrs. Meriweather described as "fiercely denunciatory, fiery and scandalous," Victoria declared that the facts of the Beecher-Lib-Tilton scandal had been withheld from the public for five long years. She again justified the "sexual freedom" enjoyed by herself, which she thought was Beecher's right too, and at the end of the oration defiantly cried: "If there is a single immaculate being in the hall, he should rise to his feet and cast on me the stones!"

A seedy character clutching a carpetbag and umbrella solemnly rose in the rear of the auditorium. He cleared his throat and started to talk but, overwhelmed first by rising titters and then by jeers, the "immaculate being" cowered back in his chair. The meeting was adjourned.

Public mention of the scandal, it would seem offhand, made for a good newspaper story, and yet there was but one journal in the country (the Memphis APPEAL, which as a Southern paper had a sectional dislike for Beecher the terrible Abolitionist) that named the Brooklyn divine in connection with Victoria's speech. Bringing the all-powerful Henry Ward Beecher into disrepute was to be compared with tipping the Pope: it was not done.

The Boston JOURNAL cautiously remarked that Victoria swore profusely in her talk about a "prominent New York clergyman." "They tell me that I used some naughty words," replied Victoria. "All that I know is, that if I swore, I did not swear profanely. Some said, with tears streaming down their eyes, that I swore divinely."

The facts of the Beecher-Tilton scandal were an open secret in newspaper offices, yet no editor dared print a line about it, so great was the prestige of the preacher and the fanatical faith of his myriad admirers. The entire press, however, was willing to print the story if it could be picked up from another source. That way, the publication of the exposé could be descried and at the same time its spicy facts bared. Victoria decided she would be that source. She returned to New York and redoubled her efforts to relaunch the WEEKLY. In this she was at last successful, and it was believed old Vanderbilt had guaranteed the printing bill. It was in the revived issue of November 2, 1872, that Victoria printed the story that shook the country.

· 12 ·

The Woodhull explained to her WEEKLY readers that she had been hounded by Beecher and his cohorts for months, that she had been forced to discontinue her journal and stock market activities and had been driven from home to home. "After carefully considering all these things, can anyone wonder that we have been compelled to turn on our accusers?" she asked. "Can anyone wonder, after our treatment at the Gilsey House, if we

take the roofs off the hotels and expose the damned lechery that
exists there so closely concealed?"

But it was people, not hotels, who were to draw the fire. "We
have five hundred biographies of various persons, in all circles
of life, many of which persons are the present oracles of society, the facts of which biographies are similar to those presented in this article," wrote Victoria in a sentence that sent a
chill down the back of many a sporty New Yorker.

Two were the "biographies" used in the November 2 issue of
the WEEKLY. The first, covering eleven and one-half solid
double-measure columns of small type, was headlined:

THE BEECHER-TILTON SCANDAL CASE
The Detailed Statement
of the Whole Matter
by Mrs. Woodhull

Victoria justified "the ventilation of one of the most stupen-
dous scandals which has ever occurred in any community" by
saying that, unless she did so, she would be guilty of collusion.
"Was I not, in withholding the facts and conniving at a putrid
mess of seething falsehood and hypocrisy," she asked her
readers, "in some sense a partaker of these crimes?" There
were, of course, some quibblers who wondered why Victoria
had withheld the facts for years.

Beecher was dared to defend himself and to sue (he never
did), for, Victoria explained, "We are prepared to take all the
responsibilities of libel suits and imprisonments." She said that
as far as the Reverend was concerned personally, "I am impelled by no hostility whatever to Mr. Beecher, nor by any personal pique toward him or any other person," but, deep down
in the columns she forgot her lack of prejudice and found that

"I am prone to denounce him as a poltroon, a coward and a sneak."

Victoria hoped "that this article shall burst like a bombshell into the ranks of the moralistic social camp," and one can safely say that her hopes were justified, because the exposé *was* a bombshell. No scandal in the United States ever approached the Beecher affair in national and international interest; no other trial (which was to come later) ever was consumed with such greediness by such millions of newspaper, magazine, and book readers. No other scandal ever remained in the minds of the people for so long.

Victoria's "Detailed Statement of the Whole Matter" made it clear that she did not frown in the least upon the divine's lapse of morals. What she objected to was his hypocrisy in conducting clandestinely his many love affairs, and his attacks upon those, such as herself, who practiced the same freedom out in the open:

"I condemn him because I know, and have had every opportunity to know, that he entertains, on conviction, substantially the same views which I entertain on the social question, that, under the influence of these convictions, he has lived for many years . . . That he has permitted himself nevertheless to be overawed by public opinion, to profess to believe otherwise than he does believe, to have helped to maintain that very social slavery under which he was chafing. The fault with which I therefore charge him is not infidelity to the old ideas, but unfaithfulness to the new."

Victoria said the story was told to her by Mrs. Elizabeth Cady Stanton, who got it first-hand from Tilton and second-hand from poor Lib. But her primary source for the story was Tilton himself, and even Beecher had implied to her that he was guilty. Lib had admitted that she had been so carried away by her husband's grief over the discovery of her disgraceful conduct that she had been shocked into a miscarriage. This unborn child, Victoria declared in her article, was, according to Tilton, of doubtful parentage. (The respected New York SUN flatly stated later that Beecher through Lib's own mother brought about the abortion of his "love babe," a fact, the SUN added, "which is so widely known that it is strange that the newspapers have kept silent about it.")

Knowing it made interesting reading, Victoria spoke compassionately of Beecher with his "demanding physical nature," and of his "immense physical potency" and even "physical amativeness," and of the terrible restrictions upon a clergyman's life, imposed by that public opinion ignorant about physiological laws, and of Beecher's need for the "embraces" of women:

"Passional starvation, enforced on such a nature, so richly endowed, is a horrid cruelty. Every great man of Mr. Beecher's type has had in the past, and will ever have, the need for and the right to, the loving manifestations of many women."

Hammering away at the stern call of "duty" which had driven her to reveal the scandal, Victoria again and again placed the Woodhull seal of approval on certain actions of Beecher:

"It is the paradox of my position that, believing in the right of privacy and in the perfect right of Mr. Beecher socially, morally and divinely to have sought the embraces of Mrs. Tilton, or of any other woman or women whom he loved and who loved him, I still invade the most secret and sacred affairs of his life, and expose him to the opprobrium and vilification of the public. What I do is for a great purpose. The social world is in the very agony of its new birth. Somebody must be hurled forward into the gap. I have the power, I think, to compel Mr.

Beecher to go forward and to do the duty for humanity from which he shrinks."

Though she sympathized with Beecher, in this left-handed way, Victoria had but scorn for her old lover, Theodore Tilton. His life, she said, was worse than Beecher's, by far. The fact that his feelings had been wounded when he discovered his wife's infidelity was caused by "bogus sentimentality, pumped into his imagination, because our sickly phariseeism had humbugged him all his life into the belief that *he ought to feel and act* in this harlequin way on such an occasion." Hers were the italics.

Victoria said that Theodore "was not exactly a vestal virgin himself," and here she appeared to be speaking authoritatively. She thought his childish whining and stage-acting, put on only because Lib had slept with "her Reverend lover," was a disgrace. She did not weep, either, over Lib's plight. "Mrs. Tilton had in turn grown increasingly unhappy when she found that Mr. Beecher had turned some part of his exuberant affections upon some other object," said Victoria.

Then, considering the three as a whole, Victoria wrote:

"I hold that Mr. Tilton himself, that Mrs. Beecher herself, have no more right to inquire, or to know or to spy over, with a view to knowing, what transpired between Mr. Beecher and Mrs. Tilton than they have to know what I ate for breakfast or where I shall spend my next evening."

It is probable that, unprecedentedly frank as this article was, and even though its toned-down version went humming over the wires to newspapers through the country, Victoria and her associates would never have been called to the bar had it not been for "Biography Number Two" in that same issue of the WEEKLY. Beecher sued neither then nor later, but an insignificant broker named Luther C. Challis did, and as events were to show, the fat was on the fire not only for Victoria C. Woodhull but for Henry Ward Beecher.

The second exposé was headlined:

THE PHILOSOPHY OF
MODERN HYPOCRISY
Mr. L. C. Challis
The Illustration

The story of Challis' misdeeds, presumably written by Tennessee, was merely an account of what supposedly had happened during the French Ball at the Academy of Music, as observed by Victoria and Tennessee, who had attended "incog.," probably to gather material for social study. The French Ball attracted, so one newspaper said, "Three thousand of the best men and four thousand of the worst women."

"My sister and myself went closely dominoed," Tennessee said, and then:

"After a while I saw Mr. Challis and a gentleman with him whom I will call Smith, though his real name is one of the oldest and best in the annals of New York society. We made ourselves known to them, and they joined us, accompanied by two young girls not more than fifteen or sixteen years of age. These girls had come on fresh from school in Baltimore, and in the best society of New York had fallen in with these middle-aged roués, and had in their innocence been led by them in the ways that lead to ruin.

"Wine was called for, and while the men drank but little, these young girls were plied with it, until I remonstrated and begged them not to drink any more. My effort to influence them was met with an insulting request from the men to let them alone. You may be sure I followed these girls up, and got the history of their connection with these men. They were seduced by them."

There followed the leering but carefully phrased description of the alleged seductions, and the statement that Challis, no gentleman he, had boasted publicly of his amatory success.

· 13 ·

The WEEKLY, pre-dated Saturday, November 2, went on sale at noon the preceding Monday, October 28, and at once a smash first-run sellout of 100,000 copies was assured. Before additional press runs could be made, copies were sold first at fifty cents, then at $2.50, and, according to a journalist, "one extraordinary lover of literature is reported to have invested forty dollars in a copy. Owners of the paper then leased it to other readers for a dollar a day."

A newspaperman assigned to cover the story rushed to the WEEKLY offices and found that "the army of newsboys and news-dealers wishing to leave orders actually blocked Broad Street for hundreds of feet," and police were called out to clear the crush. "Hundreds of dollars per hour were flowing into their coffers," the reporter noticed. According to another newspaper, "The sales reached 150,000 copies [the first day] and promise 2,000,000," even though the American News Company had refused to place the paper on its stands.

Once the lid had been blown off the kettle, other newspapers felt at liberty to help fuel the fire. "No event since the assassination of Abraham Lincoln attracted so much notice from the press," wrote a reporter. Nevertheless, few reputable citizens would comment on the story. One of them, Parker Pillsbury the distinguished philanthropist, did. He declared that, if the WEEKLY revelations were true, "No matter though Mrs. Woodhull were an imp of hell, she should have a monument of polished Parian marble as high as Trinity steeple, and every father and mother of daughters should be proud to contribute a stone."

One newspaperman wrote that "[the sisters'] appearance among the infuriated bulls and bears of Broad Street always produced a sensation," but that none ever had equaled what followed publication of the story. This reporter saw Victoria and Tennessee in their office and found: "The conspirators were jubilant—the exposé had gone off like buttered hot cakes."

The general feeling at first was that there was a conspiracy of some sort. A typical reaction was contained in a pamphlet, "Ye Tilt-on Beecher, or Ye Muddle of Ye Mutual Friends," a hurry-up job issued to capitalize on the scandal. As the anonymous author [Charles J. Stedman] of the booklet saw it:

> This rat of a Scandal, then, dirty and dead,
> With folly for body and crime for a head,
> Fell into the hands of two raven-ous Sisters,
> (Most women are Blessings, but these two were Blisters)
> Who seized on ye Scandal-ous rat by ye tail,
> And hawked it around to ye papers for sale.

. . .

> 'Twas *weekly*, but still it was strong enough quite
> To bear a dead rat through the darkness of night;
> So they handed ye rat to their own special crow,
> Who bore it aloft, while all ye people below
> Looked up at ye carrion crow with a stare,
> And held each his nose while it flew through the air.

All through the day of publication the newspapermen clamored for interviews. That evening the reporters from the New York HERALD and the Chicago TIMES were admitted to Victoria's Fourth Avenue home. An expensive grand piano in the apartment first received attention, and then the prying eyes quickly, and appreciatively, noted that:

"We were ushered into a spacious parlor, at the further end of which long flowing lace curtains, gently drawn apart, half-disguised and half-disclosed a magnificent mahogany bedstead —the chief article of furniture in Tennie's perfumed bedroom."

If the presence of the bed in the perfumed bedroom was exciting to the reporters—although ordinarily a bed would be the piece of furniture one would expect in such a place—their interview with Vicky was even more titivating.

The Woodhull informed the visitors that she had "peculiar and extraordinary proofs" of the accuracy of the WEEKLY's articles. She said she knew Beecher well, and as for Tilton, her one-time "devoted lover," she had known him *most* intimately. The TIMES man from Chicago gave the interview as follows:

Correspondent: Pardon me, but I presume that it was under such circumstances and during such intimacy that Mr. Tilton unlocked the secrets and griefs of his breast to you?

Mrs. Woodhull: Yes sir, we were naturally mutually confiding. And it was during this time he so eloquently wrote of me, in the little brochure of a biography from his pen.

Cor.—You speak of Mr. Tilton's sorrow over his friend Beecher's treachery. You refer, I presume, to the alleged seduction of Mrs. Tilton by Henry Ward Beecher?

Mrs. W.—Yes sir, as we have stated in the WEEKLY, giving the true relations existing at one time between Beecher and

Mrs. Tilton. You observed we did not blame either. To do so would be inconsistent.

Cor.—So I understand that Mr. Tilton gave you an insight into his trouble directly from his own lips?

Mrs. W.—As sure as God rules the spheres he did. He confided in me and won my entire sympathy, and I tried to solace him by pointing out to him that *our* teachings in the WEEKLY and our lectures were natural and not abnormal, as shown in his own family and that of Henry Ward Beecher.

Cor.—Did I understand you to say, Mrs. Woodhull, that you were personally acquainted with Mr. Beecher?

Mrs. W.—Oh, yes sir, I know Mr. Beecher very well.

Cor.—Permit me to ask if Mr. Beecher ever exhibited toward you his especial friendship in any unmistakable manner. I have a particular reason for making this inquiry.

Mrs. W.—Indeed he has. His private carriage could have been seen waiting before our door every afternoon for many months, to take us riding in Central Park. You would, perhaps, call that *some* indication or evidence of personal friendship.

Cor.—Yes, Madam, I would most unquestionably consider it a very practical proof of regard, if in my own case. I presume all this occurred months ago?

Mrs. W.—Yes, months ago, before Mr. Beecher discovered that the Argus eyes of the world had detected him practicing one system and preaching another. Compelled to choose, he preferred to be open in his preaching, and, I presume, to *cloak* his practices. It *pays* better, you see.

Cor.—I will not ask you, Mrs. Woodhull, if your intimacy with Mr. Beecher extended beyond the carriage rides.

Mrs. W.—I leave you to your own inferences. But I must not be understood as suggesting that Mr. Beecher and Mr. Tilton ever occupied precisely similar *personal* relations towards myself. I never loved Mr. Beecher. By the way, here is a letter I have just received from an eminent lawyer in Brooklyn. He affirms that it has become a kind of playful gossip among the outsiders who merely *look* on the play, as to *which one* of Mr. Beecher's score of female lovers in his flock (dames and virgins) is, at the time, basking in his smile."

At the conclusion of the interview the TIMES reporter had the feeling that "Mrs. Woodhull's calm and sympathetic eyes, her tender and motherly voice, and her chaste manner indicated to me that she is, whatever else may be said, a *truthful woman.*" The italics belong to the Correspondent.

· 14 ·

The first few days after the exposé the Reverend Beecher refused to be quoted for publication. And, when the following Sabbath found his Plymouth pews packed as never before, he did not mention the odious subject. As newspapers through the country began to devote more and more space to the scandal— always careful to point out the vile story was that of WOODHULL & CLAFLIN'S WEEKLY, not theirs—he is credited with saying: "In passing along the way any one is liable to have a bucket of slop thrown upon him. It is disagreeable, but does not particularly harm."

Beecher was overoptimistic. The aftermath of the WEEKLY article was a trial followed breathlessly by the nation and the world. At the same time, however, there were trials, trials in the literal sense, for Victoria and company. For, when curiosity about the reputed divine-seducer continued to mount and a horde of out-of-town newspapermen started digging deep into the story, the Beecher forces decided to take the offensive. Several copies of the WEEKLY were ordered to be sent to the office of the INDEPENDENT, the magazine owned by Beecher's friend, Bowen. It was requested that these copies be sent through the United States mails.

· 15 ·

Comstock—the name which has become an epithet.

Comstock was the first professional reformer who made a comfortable living in the United States, and his counterparts are alive and prospering today. Comstock was the head of "The Committee for the Suppression of Vice," which was backed by the Young Men's Christian Association. He condemned pornographic literature, and especially the dime novels, those "traps for the young," as he called them, which were then so popular. Comstock had lobbied a law through Congress prohibiting the circulation of obscene publications through the mail, and the wording of the statute was so loose as to include anything a determined individual might think obscene. "A cheap and dirty hypocrite," the magazine JUDGE called him, and, after thinking it over, added, "a sneak *and* a hypocrite."

As soon as the copies of the WEEKLY had arrived at the offices of the INDEPENDENT, Anthony Comstock secured a warrant from the United States District Attorney for the arrest of Victoria and associates, and for the seizure of all the offending

issues of the journal, on the charge of sending obscene literature through the mails. In the meantime, Luther C. Challis the
broker secured a warrant in the 2d District Police Court for the
arrest of Victoria C. Woodhull et al on the charge of libel.

Deputy United States Marshals Colfax and Bernhard won
the race for their arrest. The officers found Victoria and Tennessee at 12:15 P.M. in their carriage on Broad Street. In the
carriage they found three thousand copies of the WEEKLY
which were promptly confiscated, and the sisters were taken for
arraignment in the Federal Building before United States Commissioner Osborn, with a large crowd tagging at their heels.

The prisoners were perfectly composed as they appeared in
court, their only criticism being that the Marshals (who were
ugly men, a little old) had treated them with "endearing famil-
iarity" by insisting on sitting in their laps on the way to the
Federal Building. It was plain that Tennessee enjoyed the commotion thoroughly. A reporter of the New York DISPATCH described the scene:

"They were dressed in plain dark suits of alpaca, and wore
hats of the most jaunty style. Tennie was flushed like a rose,
and her blue eyes sparkled nervously. As she glanced round the
room, a smile of contempt seemed to gather about her ruby
lips. She has splendid teeth, and takes care to show them. In
fact, Tennie is a pretty-looking woman, round faced, with well-
cut features, and a bright, animated expression."

General Noah Davis, the United States District Attorney,
asked that each of the sisters be held in $10,000 bail. He ex-
plained why the prosecution wanted such an excessive sum:

"Not only have the defendants, by circulating an obscene
publication through the mails, committed an offense against the
law, but they have been guilty of a most abominable and unjust
charge against one of the purest and best citizens of this State,
or in the United States, and they have, as far as possible, ag-

gravated the offense by an atrocious, malicious, gross and untrue libel upon the character of the gentleman whom the whole country reveres, and whose character it is well worth while the Government of the United States to vindicate."

The name of this great character never was mentioned in court.

Judge J. D. Reymart, counsel for the sisters, pointed out that the defendants were charged with sending obscene literature through the mails, not with libel. He said this was not the time or place for the Government to defend the character of the unnamed and absent personage.

"An example is needed and we propose to make one of these women!" thundered Commissioner Osborn. Whereupon he set prohibitive bail, $8,000 for each of the defendants.

In the meantime, Challis with a handful of warrants had caused the arrest of Colonel Blood, Stephen Pearl Andrews, William A. Smith, publisher of the WEEKLY, William D. Nyse, a stereotyper, and D. C. Miles, husband of a Claflin sister, who was employed by the WEEKLY. All five were arraigned in Jefferson Market and charged with libel.

"See here, where is George Francis Train?" jocularly asked a New York newspaper. "This is the first fight that he hasn't taken a hand in, and hasn't fired a single pistol shot at the air or made a single speech. Come to the front, George, and wake snakes. Speak for Ireland, for Woodhull, the devil, or anybody."

These words were addressed to a prominent and rich eccentric who, before the words had appeared in type, already had come to the front. "The language of your paper has been splendid," Train told the sisters as he appeared in Commissioner Osborn's courtroom. "The truths you are defending are eternal. I should be happy to go your bail. I am satisfied the cowardly

Christian community will destroy you, if possible, to cover up the rotten state of society."

Train offered to put up the $16,000 bail in cash, if necessary, but on advice of counsel Victoria and Tennessee declined the offer. Their attorney told them that, once they were at liberty, they would be rearrested on Challis' libel warrants and then thrown into the Jefferson Market prison, known as one of the worst jails in the country. They decided to remain overnight Saturday and Sunday (being due to appear before Commissioner Osborn on Monday) in the Ludlow Street Jail, where the food was better and quarters were cleaner.

The sisters were taken to the Ludlow Street calaboose at 3:30 P.M., followed by a large crowd which roared, "Where's Theodore?" Mr. Tilton did not make an appearance. They were escorted to cell No. 11 by Deputy Warden William H. Gardner, who presented them with a copy of Pope's poems, which, he pointed out, contained a stanza couched in more indecent terms than anything ever printed in the WEEKLY. Warden Gardner even insisted on reading aloud the censurable words, and did so with gusto. Victoria and Tennessee began to receive visitors. George Francis Train, attired in his $500 sealskin overcoat, the inevitable flower in buttonhole, was the first to arrive. He took a piece of charcoal and dramatically scrawled on the whitewashed wall a couplet denouncing the base attack upon two of the most spotless reputations in the land.

The clustering reporters could not wedge their way into the tiny eight-by-four-foot cell, what with Victoria and Tennessee in it and with Train attempting to stalk about. They conferred with the sisters through the bars. They saw that the cell contained two cots, one of which was occupied by Tennessee sitting there "half dressed." Victoria refused to say anything except that their quarters were "not wholly unpleasant." Tennessee gave the reporters a long talk, the substance being that they were martyrs to the holy cause of Free Love.

Meanwhile, police armed with warrants signed by Mayor Hall—who was on trial at the time, charged with fraud—raided the Broad Street offices, confiscated all copies of the WEEKLY, pied and scattered the type, rifled trunks and private letter files, broke the furniture and seized the company's books.

The next day the HERALD characterized Tennessee and her sister, who was at one time the newspaper's columnist: "These women cannot even be classed with unfortunates. It is a greater depth of infamy to which they glory to belong." The TIMES editorially believed that "The female name never has been more disgraced and degraded than by these women." The SUNDAY MERCURY was equally outraged, but over comparative trifles: it said Tennessee used swear words, smoked segars, and liked to wear men's pants.

· 16 ·

When the case of Victoria and Tennessee was called in the United States Circuit Court on Monday, November 4, the crowd that filled the room saw that the pretty defendants had dropped Judge Reymart as counsel and had hired the expensive criminal law firm of Howe & Hummel—the notorious legal guardians of professional thieves and killers, counterfeiters and confidence men, forgers and bucket-shop operators, and darlings of the theatrical world. Abe Hummel (Victoria's mother was born a Hummel, but of no relation) usually did the spadework for cases and then remained in the background. William F. Howe, a flamboyant character, was the tear-jerker before the jury.

Dressed in plaid pantaloons, purple vest and a blue satin scarf, upon which was pinned a diamond the size of a bird's egg, Howe shouted that "this case is instigated by the malice and revenge of certain persons in high station, who dare not come forward and face public opposition." If the WEEKLY was obscene, he loftily pointed out to the court, then "future generations may be denied the beauty and consolations to be found in Shakespeare, Byron and the Scripture itself." Howe added that the case simply was a flagrant example of malicious persecution, and he called upon the newspapers to support the defendants and thus preserve freedom of the press, which was being threatened. "Mr. Howe looked in his glory," remarked the New York DISPATCH. "His face seemed as fresh as a peach, and the glitter of diamonds was like the gleaming rays of the sun."

Commissioner Osborn pondered and reluctantly found that, inasmuch as bench warrants had been issued by the Circuit Court and the grand jury had brought indictments against the sisters, the case was out of his jurisdiction. Victoria and Tennessee were taken before the bar and discharged, and as they stood glumly by, they immediately were arrested on the grand jury indictments and taken back to Ludlow Street Jail. They were to be held there in their cell for one whole month.

Challis took reporters aside, told them he was willing to spend $100,000 to secure convictions, and explained how he had become involved with Tennessee. He knew her but vaguely, and it was plainly a case of blackmail, he said. Tennessee half a year before had written and demanded $200 from him. When he refused to give what she described as "a loan" she had forwarded him a proof of the article published alongside the Beecher story in the WEEKLY. No, he said in answer to a reporter's question, unfortunately he had not kept the printer's proof. Was the Reverend Beecher behind him in this suit? No, Challis replied firmly.

Tennessee summoned the newspapermen to cell 11 and gave them her side of the story. Challis, she said, had been on "intimate terms" with her. The reporters might consider this expression to mean anything they liked. She had written a routine letter to Challis, asking him if he would like to contribute a small sum to defray expenses for the Steinway Hall lecture. She said Jim Fisk, Henry Clews, and other brokers had often chipped in on such occasions. Also, said Tennessee, she had some loving letters from Challis in her possession, and, when the time was ripe, she intended to release them for publication. The letters would make interesting reading.

· 17 ·

On Friday, November 8, "the sensational comedy of Free Love," as the HERALD called it, opened before another packed courtroom, in Jefferson Market Court. Howe, garbed in a Scotch plaid vest, a huge diamond breastpin, with a hawser-like watch chain stretched across his belly, saw to it that Zulu, Victoria's daughter, was sitting demurely by her side. Little Zulu seemed quite melancholy.

Challis testified that he scarcely knew Tennessee, that he had met her but once, at the French Ball the previous winter. Ordinarily he never would have attended such a dance, but he had felt in the mood for slumming. He and a male companion, each in full evening dress, had met Vicky and Tennessee at the party, both unescorted and masked. He said they also had met two fairly young girls at the ball, but had drunk only one small bottle of wine with them during the entire evening. Tiring of the spectacle, the two gentlemen had gone home early.

"This *poisoned Challis*," as Howe labeled him, denied under cross-examination he had ever courted Tennessee, or become her sweetheart, or kissed her, or given her silken underthings.

Victoria took the stand and said Challis had visited them in Ludlow Street Jail and offered a bribe if they would deny the scandal. Of course, she added in a horrified tone, she and her sister were appalled at such a suggestion. Vicky said Challis often had visited Tennessee in their Fourth Avenue home, but when she started to explain exactly what sort of an individual he was, the District Attorney asked the court to interfere. Her remarks "boded indecency," he said.

Laura Cuppy Smith, the well-known suffragist, testified that The Woodhull was a lady, a woman, a mother. She said she had met Challis in Victoria's Murray Hill residence in February, that he had kissed Tennessee most familiarly and told her she "looked charming." When Mrs. Roxy Claflin had entered the room he had said, "Good evening, Mother."

Decision on the matter was reserved, and the defendants were taken back to cell 11.

· 18 ·

George Francis Train was making a nuisance of himself with the authorities because, as a rich man well able to provide high bail, he offered to put up the money, in cash if necessary, to free the sisters. Train has been described as the most eccentric and picturesque character New York has ever known. At the time he was forty-three, supposedly worth a million dollars. He owned a showplace at Newport, was the friend of Louis Napoleon, the Empress Eugénie, and the Queen of Spain, yet professed to be a Communist. He was a man of many interests. He had built and operated a fleet of world-girdling ships, had helped lay the Union Pacific railroad, built the first streetcar lines in Europe, was one of the organizers of the Crédit Mobilier in 1864, had been active in bringing on the Marseilles Commune in France, was an ardent Fenian, and his trip around the world, accomplished in the unbelievable time of eighty days, had inspired Jules Verne to novelizing.

Train was a believer and follower of many doctrines, but not Free Love, and yet he rushed to the defense of Victoria and Tennessee because he felt they were being unjustly persecuted. "This may be libel, but it is not obscenity," he said after reading the Beecher and Challis articles in the WEEKLY. Defying Comstock to arrest him, he issued a magazine called the TRAIN LIGUE, in which he reprinted much of the WEEKLY's story on Beecher verbatim. The authorities refused to make another test case. Train demanded the arrest of the Bible Publishing Company for printing "disgusting slanders on Lot, Abraham, Solo-

mon and David," quoting three columns of verses from the
Bible, pointing out how much more obscene they were than the
offending passages in the WEEKLY's articles.

Pushed, Comstock secured an indictment from the state
court for Train's arrest. His guilt was to publish a second TRAIN
LIGUE, and not the reprint of excerpts from the Beecher story.

George Francis Train was given "the treatment." He was
taken to the Tombs and shut up in Murderers' Row. He was
jailed on a felony charge, but his twenty-three fellow inmates,
who all were under sentence, or awaiting trial for, homicide,
elected him president of "The Murderers' Club." Train was put
into a cell seven by three and one-half feet, which had no running water, ventilation or sanitation facilities, and there he was
forced to remain for five months before the authorities would
permit him to stand trial. For a while, Train delighted in his
martyrdom. He invited a SUN reporter to his cell and outlined
the actions he intended to take in retaliation. He was going to
become dictator of the United States. Then he was going to
establish a bloody Commune. He would hang, first, the murderers. Second, the thieves. Third, the politicians. Fourth, a good
many editors. Fifth, all Congress. George Francis Train seemed
to think the distinction between these five groups was minute.
"Just call me 'Champion of the People,' " he instructed reporters.

The help given Victoria and Tennessee by this Champion of
the People was to prove costly to him. Long after the case of the
sisters had been settled, the eccentric was kept behind bars and
branded as a lunatic. He was dismissed only after he signed
papers agreeing to a ban of declared lunacy. In the eyes of the
law he remained a monomaniac—insane on one or more subjects, but not generally crazy—for the next thirty years, until
his death.

· 19 ·

Though Train's predicament was soon forgotten, popular opinion began to swing in favor of the incarcerated Victoria and Tennessee, and, during their month's stay in cell 11, outside forces worked constantly to bring about their release. A good many newspapers and individuals did not care for their views, but nonetheless felt that the Government was overplaying its hand by keeping the sisters in jail and denying them the constitutional right of trial. They began to be known as "Heroines," not as "depraved Priestesses."

The clamor was started by Victoria herself, who wrote another open letter to the HERALD. Shrewdly phrased to arouse sympathy, the letter was reprinted in other papers through the country. It read, in part:

> Sick in body, sick in mind, sick at heart, I write these lines to ask if, because I am a woman, I am to have no justice, no fair play, no chance through the press to reach public opinion. How can anybody know for what I am accused, arrested, imprisoned, unless the public are allowed to see the alleged libel?
>
> If the paper is suppressed and I charged with crime, in what way can I substantiate the truth, when the judge before whom I only appear as a witness, constitutes himself as plaintiff, prosecuting attorney, judge, jury and witness? When has it ever been known in this land of so-called religious freedom and civil liberty, that pulpit,

press and people tremble before a cowardly public opinion?

Is it not astonishing that all Christian law and civilization seemed to be scared out of their senses at having two poor women locked up in jail? Suppose, Mr. Editor, that some enemies of yours should throw you into a cell for publishing the Challis article, suppress the HERALD, arrest your printers, prosecute your publisher, shut up your business office, close all the avenues of press and lecture hall against your honorable defense? Would not every land ring with the outrage?

> Victoria C. Woodhull
> Cell 11
> Ludlow Street Jail

The leading suffragists were the first to come to Victoria's support. Elizabeth Cady Stanton wrote Susan B. Anthony that, if her testimony would rescue Victoria, and yet at the same time dethrone Henry Ward Beecher, then she was willing to give it. Miss Anthony forgot her differences with Victoria and said she felt the same. "We have had women enough sacrificed to this sentimental, hypocritical prating at purity," Miss Anthony declared, quoting from a letter she had sent Victoria the year before. "This is one of man's most effective engines for our division and subjugation. He creates the public sentiment, builds the gallows, and then makes us hangmen for our own sex. Women have criticized the Mary Wollstonecrafts, the Fanny Wrights, the George Sands, the Fanny Kembles, of all ages; and now men mock us with the fact, and say we are ever cruel to each other. Let us end this ignoble record and henceforth stand by womanhood."

Mrs. Stanton feared a precedent would be established and that women's rights' leaders soon would be thrown in jail, and she began to work hard to secure Victoria's release, and for her right to stand trial. In a private letter written Lucretia Mott, Mrs. Stanton came "to the conclusion that it is a great impertinence in any of us to pry into her private affairs." Mrs. Stanton saw The Woodhull as valuable to the suffrage cause because she "stands before us today as an able speaker and writer."

The Reverend Henry Ward Beecher was hypercautious. He limited his comment on the situation to a single word. A Plymouth Church parishioner spoke of the "Woodhull outrage" and said everyone knew "the whole thing was a fraud from beginning to end."

"Exactly," the preacher replied. This was his first public utterance on the matter, and the last he was to make for some time.

Miss Anthony was prompted to write Beecher's sister, Mrs. Hooker, saying that if God ever struck anyone dead for telling a lie, He should have done so then.

Mrs. Hooker in turn wrote brother Henry, pleading with him to tell the truth, and nothing but the truth. "The one radical mistake you have made is in supposing that you are so much ahead of your time, and in daring to attempt to lead when you have nothing to conceal," she told him.

Henry Ward Beecher had little support in his own family circle. One of his many brothers, Thomas, also a Reverend, wrote Mrs. Hooker:

"I respect, as at present advised, Mrs. Woodhull, while I abhor her philosophy. She only carries out Henry's philosophy, against which I recorded my protest twenty years ago, and parted (lovingly and achingly) from him. In my judgment Henry is following his slippery doctrines of expediency, and in the cry of progress and nobleness of spirit, has sacrificed clear, exact integrity. Of the two, Woodhull is my hero, and Henry my coward."

Brother Thomas' advice to Mrs. Hooker was: "You cannot help Henry. You must be true to Woodhull . . ."

Eventually these letters found their way into print, and to Henry Ward Beecher's consternation, were not disowned by the writers. This was explained away by the friends of the Brooklyn pastor. All the offspring of Lyman Beecher always had been known as a crazy lot—except Henry Ward—they said.

The press chimed in on Victoria's side. It was pointed out that the most risqué words in the Challis article were "token" and "virginity," neither of which was obscene. The powerful Brooklyn EAGLE, which so often had opposed The Woodhull, condemned the "irresponsible action of the more zealous than sensible Comstock," and flatly declared further:

"We can discover no intention on the part of authorities to try these women at all. The seeming disposition indefinitely to incarcerate them is discernible. If the lies and libels they print were true, then most certainly they ought to have been printed. Being untrue, it is a folly to persecute women who deserve prosecution. . . ."

The Hartford TIMES believed if the Beecher article had appeared in THE NEW YORK TIMES the authorities would never have brought an indictment. The Troy DAILY PRESS thought Comstock had "struck a dastard's blow at liberty and law in the United States." The New York SUNDAY MERCURY also had no use for Comstock. It agreed that the phrase, "this illiterate puppy," as used by the sisters, was apt and just, and concluded:

"It does not seem right that the whole machinery of the Federal Government, with its courts and marshals, should be placed at the back of a man who has, somehow or other, chosen it for his private business to deprive this woman of her liberty."

And the Chicago TIMES pointed the finger at Beecher and

sneered at "the cowardice of those who have *communed* with her . . ." Beecher, the newspaper believed, was a modern Arbaces—insatiate luxury masked in the idol of a god.

Of course, not all newspapers championed the sisters. To the Philadelphia STAR, for instance, the horrendous reputation of Victoria and Tennessee was such that nothing they said could be believed. "I should render myself liable to persecution by Mr. Comstock if I were to describe the 'free life' of these women as it is notorious in downtown conversation, probable by unimpeachable evidence, if that were called for," the New York correspondent of the STAR declared.

· 20 ·

Victoria the Presidential candidate learned of the election returns while languishing in cell 11, Ludlow Street Jail. She had lost. The results were:

Ulysses S. Grant, Republican:	3,597,123 votes.
Horace Greeley, Democrat, Ind. Rep.:	2,834,125 votes.
Charles O'Connor, Taproot Democrat:	29,489 votes.
James Black, Prohibitionist:	5,608 votes.
Victoria C. Woodhull:	0 votes.

Corruption, not the voters, had re-elected Grant as President, The Woodhull told reporters. "If Jesus Christ had been running against this man, he'd have been defeated." As others figured it, if the Lord had run on the Equal Rights Party ticket he would have lost, too, for it was not allowed on the ballot.

· 21 ·

Reluctantly, the authorities gave in, but not much. On December 5, after thirty-one days in Ludlow Street Jail, Victoria and Tennessee were given their freedom after Dr. Augustus D. Ruggles and James Kiernan, both from Beecher's bailiwick in Brooklyn, had put up $8,000 bail each.

The sisters, however, were immediately rearrested, this time on three different counts in three different courts.

They were ordered to appear on charges of slander and of sending obscene matter through the mails by a state court. Ruggles and Kiernan again supplied bail. They were rearrested by an officer from the Jefferson Market Police Court on a criminal suit filed by Challis. Ruggles and Edward MacKinley put up bail. They were tapped on the shoulder by a deputy from the Sheriff's Office, and asked to produce bail on the action brought by Challis in Supreme Court for damages of libel. The patient Ruggles and MacKinley paid again.

· 22 ·

It was not to be expected that Henry Ward Beecher would lift a finger to alleviate the triple-troubles besetting the sisters, but there were those who were puzzled at the steadfast, sphinx-like attitude of Theodore Tilton, who refused to aid Victoria in any way. After all, it was reasoned, Theodore should bear a grudge against Beecher, for it was the pastor who presumably had slept with his wife, and not Victoria. Both Beecher and Tilton declined to give interviews, but the latter did permit a personal friend from the Chicago TIMES to visit his modest two-story house at 174 Livingston Street in Brooklyn. He was not allowed to quote Tilton, but was given permission to meet and describe Lib.

The newspaperman found Tilton, "the handsome hero of the greatest scandal of our time," lounging in dressing gown and slippers before a fireplace. The reporters looked over an "exquisite portrait on canvas" of Mrs. Tilton, and found the subject "a wealth of silken brown hair, soft and soulful eyes of richest hazel, a mouth carved by the gods, and lips full, warm and suggesting robustness of modest passion."

When he met the original face to face he found her equally fascinating. "Mrs. Tilton is of medium height, perfectly, voluptuously developed, not very vivacious," he wrote. "She is in the prime of life, enjoys good health and her manners are most winning."

Then he philosophized, taking Beecher's guilt for granted: "The world has learned to bear no malice toward Mark Anthony for his fall before Cleopatra. Some time it may be equally generous with Beecher's fall before lovely Mrs. Tilton."

POMEROY'S DEMOCRAT was equally generous toward Lib, but it did not fancy husband Theodore.

"It is quite clear in evidence at the present writing," declared the newspaper, "that several years after Theodore Tilton became the husband of his present wife, he adopted the Moses Hull and Victoria Woodhull view of life and plunged boldly into the free-love swimming pond, with a result somewhat heavier than expected. Mrs. Tilton refused to follow him into the mire and slime of this social nastiness, not willing to become a common prostitute and to emulate the example of those free-love men and women who, having no money to pay for dissipation, obtain it on the cheap plan of religion."

· 23 ·

Victoria was again at liberty. Far from being broken by this harassing experience, she seemed to have drawn strength from it, determined as ever to continue her various crusades. After all, her fight against the orthodox, the conventional, against Respectability itself, had only begun.

Contributions poured in from sympathetic outsiders and so the WEEKLY was able to resume publication with the December 28 issue, which touted a speech Victoria was to make in Boston's Music Hall on the subject of "Moral Cowardice and Moral Hypocrisy, or Four Weeks in Ludlow Street Jail."

Governor Claflin of Massachusetts (who hastily pointed out that he was not even a distant relation of the Free Love sisters) thought otherwise. He stated, rather harshly:

"We have enough bad women in Boston now, without permitting this one to come here and further demoralize us. Why, she might repeat the vile stories about Mr. Beecher, or even attack some of us in Boston. No, sir! This cannot be permitted. This prostitute shall not disgrace this hall or insult this city by speaking in it. She is no better than a panel thief or a common street walker, and I will see that she don't open her vile mouth in the city which so recently was honored by Mr. Beecher's presence."

"Governor Claflin," moaned Tennessee, "he has thrown down a grand old name."

Prompted by the Governor's words, the Mayor of Boston stepped in and banned Victoria's appearance on any of the city's many lecture platforms. There were, however, numerous people, even among the town's rock-bound conservative set, who questioned this denial of a constitutional right. Among the liberal elements the uproar was considerable. The Reverend Octavius Brooks Frothingham rebuked the bluenose-Grundys in a sermon from his pulpit and was faced with boos from the churchly audience. "Hiss if you will," declared Reverend Frothingham. "I have nothing to detract."

Despite the protests, Victoria could find no sounding board in Boston. While in the city she conferred with an admirer, D. W. Miles, well-known as a publisher. Through him The Woodhull's name has been linked with a figure no less famous than Goethe. A year before, at the publisher's request, she had written an introduction to the poet-philosopher's *Elective Affinities*. Victoria by now had an imposing list of literary credits. To her numerous publications issued in 1871, she now added "Carpenter and Cartter Reviewed," "Campaign Documents of the Equal Rights Party," and "Freedom! Equality!! Justice!!!" Tennesee was an author, too. Her book, *Constitutional Equality,* retailed at two dollars and one-half a copy, and she was about to print and distribute her speech, "The Ethics of Sexual Equality."

The spectacle of the sisters turning out a flood of books and pamphlets was greeted with jeers in some quarters. It was believed Colonel Blood was the pen behind the inkstand, and the belief was strengthened when it was disclosed that Victoria's manuscripts were sent to the printers in her husband's hand-writing.

Colonel Blood smoothly explained in a public letter how Victoria composed her literary masterpieces:

"At about eleven or twelve o'clock at night, two or three times a week, and sometimes without nightly intervals, Victoria and I hold parliament with the spirits . . . Victoria goes into a trance, during which her guardian spirit [Demosthenes] takes control of her mind, speaking audibly through her lips, propounding various matters for our subsequent investigation and verification, and announcing principles, detached thoughts, hints of systems and suggestions for affairs . . . I make copious notes of all she says, and publish it without correction or amendment."

The statement presumably cleared Victoria. No attempt was ever made to explain just how gay Tennessee wrote her books.

· 24 ·

Barred from Beantown, Victoria gave her lecture in more hospitable Springfield, Massachusetts. She warned that all the forward-thinking and social-minded people had best guard their civil liberties, and to accomplish that they should go from state to state "and sow the seed of social revolution, which, springing up, shall sweep the despots like chaff before the fan from their thrones built upon the liberties of the people." She also vividly described the horrors of her thirty-one-day incarceration.

The crusty Springfield REPUBLICAN found the talk "singularly pathetic." Those in the audience enjoyed it, and they contributed liberally to collection plates which were passed.

So ended the eventful year of 1872—eventful at least for the sisters Claflin.

The Woodhull Compromise

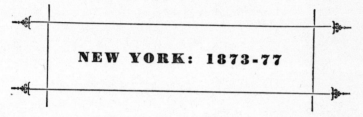

NEW YORK: 1873-77

Victoria announced she would lecture on "The Naked Truth"
at Cooper Institute on January 9, 1873, with special reference
to Mr. Anthony Comstock. Within two days the hall was sold
out.

Comstock's riposte was to lay a trap. Discovering that the
banned WEEKLY was being retailed under the counter, he sent a
letter to the journal, enclosing money to have several copies of
the Beecher issue forwarded—through the United States mails
—to a nonexistent "John Beardsley" in Greenwich, Connecticut.

When the copies arrived he hustled to New York and at once
obtained new warrants against Victoria, Tennessee, and Colonel Blood. On the scheduled day of the lecture Blood was arrested, but he managed to send a warning to the sisters before
he was taken to prison. Tennessee hid in their Fourth Avenue
home and the cook drove away the officers when they attempted

to search the place, while Victoria slipped out the back door and took the ferry to Jersey City.

Before lecture time that night half a dozen United States marshals and squads of police ransacked Cooper Institute and, finding no Victoria, stationed themselves at the entrances to inform people there would be no meeting. Nonetheless, on that bitter, icy night the vast hall (where Lincoln had made his famous Cooper Union speech a quarter of a century before) was packed. The audience waited for a full hour. Then the people grew restless and impatiently began to clap.

Laura Cuppy Smith came on the stage. "The enemies of free speech have another order of arrest for Mrs. Woodhull," she said. "She cannot appear tonight, lest she be again thrust into an American Bastille." Mrs. Smith said Victoria had deputized her to read the speech she had intended to deliver. The throng grumpily accepted the substitute.

At this moment an old, old lady garbed in Quaker gray, wearing a floppy bonnet and shawl, and heavily veiled, limped past the marshals stationed at the main entrance. One of the officers assisted her through the crowd, and when he found she was slightly deaf he helped her work her way down front.

The audience tittered as the doddering old lady wandered aimlessly to the stage, and then something happened which brought the crowd to its feet, cheering wildly. As one onlooker described the occasion:

"With the celerity of a flash of lightning the old Quaker lady dashed from behind the pillar. Old age, coal-scuttle bonnet and gray dress disappeared like magic. Had a thunderbolt fallen upon the audience, they could not have been more surprised and astonished. There stood Victoria C. Woodhull, an overwhelming inspirational fire scintillating from her eyes and beaming from her face.

"The Quaker costume lay coiled at her feet, and, with her

breast heaving in long suppressed nervous emotion, her arms raised aloft in nervous excitement, her hair in wild and graceful confusion, and the head thrown defiantly back like the head of the Apollo Belvedere, she looked like the personification of Liberty in Arms. Her voice rose in clear and piercing tones, like a song of love, blended with the war-cry of battle, and the pent-up forces of her soul rushed forth in an impetuous and irresistible torrent of burning, glowing words, thought and voice being full to repletion with the musical and magnetic energy of the Marseillaise."

Alarmed by the tension of the audience, knowing well what would happen if they tried to serve their warrants, the marshals and police stood dumbly by as Victoria, in an event long re-membered, loosed a tumbling wave of words. She denounced Comstock as the self-appointed agent of Christ, the tool of Beecher and a Pickwick as a prosecuting official. "By some mental obfuscation of such a public functionary," she cried, "there is no telling how soon some women may be arrested for adultery—for kissing their own baby boy." On and on she went, for one hour and a half. Challis was vindictive, a monster backed by Beecher the unspeakable, she shouted. The Challis article had been reprinted by the HERALD and other newspapers, but why were *they* not prosecuted? The newspapers had not given her side of the case. Officers of the law had ruined her business, stolen her private papers, pied the WEEKLY's type, held her incommunicado in prison for a month. Her answer to this savage harassment was this: She would reprint in its en-tirety the suppressed issue of the WEEKLY. Let the authorities do what they would.

And, when finished, she bowed low to three marshals stand-ing in the wings, and extended her wrists submissively to re-ceive handcuffs. The marshals shamefacedly advanced, took her gently by the arm and amid jeers and catcalls from the throng conducted her once more to Ludlow Street Jail. There Victoria was put in a cell with husband Blood.

. 2 .

When the case came up the next day for examination before Commissioner Davenport, Tennessee walked in, smiled sweetly at Comstock and sat down by Victoria and Colonel Blood. She said it was not a case of her surrendering to the law. She had not known she was wanted on a warrant, having been up some days and nights with a sick friend.

William F. Howe, who was wearing a bright orange waistcoat and a fingerful of diamond rings, Abe Hummel, J. Parker Jourdan, and Edward MacKinley were lawyers for the defense. They concentrated on Comstock. Howe wanted to know if Comstock thought the Book of Deuteronomy in the Holy Bible was obscene. Comstock thought not. Prancing over to the jury box Howe revealed that a five-line sentence on which the obscenity charge was based had been lifted straight from Deuteronomy, Chapter 22. Howe asked Comstock if he favored censoring Lord Byron, Shakespeare, and Fielding. Comstock refused to answer. Abe Hummel suggested maybe he wanted Smollett barred. Jourdan wondered if *Hudibras* should be read in this country. Comstock thought Hudibras was a fairly clean author. "Hudibras," Jourdan informed him, was the title of a book written by Samuel Butler in the seventeenth century. MacKinley wanted Comstock to produce some of his own literary efforts; he believed they might prove to be obscene.

Commissioner Davenport reserved decision and released the defendants in $5,000 bail each. Again, the indefatigable Dr. Ruggles obligingly put up the security.

That night Comstock optimistically wrote in his diary: "Their counsels were very anxious to break down my testimony, but utterly failed. Truth was too much for them. They do not take stock very largely in that commodity."

But, according to the SUN, the righteous man had contradicted himself and made a thoroughly bad impression, and other papers felt that, in general, the professional reformer had made a fool of himself.

Victoria, Tennessee, and Blood soon found their court troubles were just starting. On January 22 the District Attorney granted bench warrants for their arrest on a new charge, preferred by Challis, of sending an obscene article about him through the mails. A Sheriff and two deputies took the three to the District Attorney's office and, though it was only mid-afternoon, learned he had gone home. The officers felt "compelled," as the TIMES put it, to lock up the trio overnight in the dank Tombs prison.

In the Court of General Sessions the next day Attorney Howe pleaded for reasonable bail. He pointed out that the defendants were, on a simple misdemeanor, under $60,000 bail in various suits, while Boss Tweed, who was accused of looting the City treasury of millions, was under $51,000. Bail was set at $2,000 for Blood, $1,000 each for the sisters. Victoria and Tennessee were able to secure bail backing, but Blood was not, and so he was taken back to the Tombs.

Commissioner Davenport gave his decision on the third of February, and to the dismay of Anthony Comstock it was evident that on that same day he had read an open letter in the SUN to Victoria from General Benjamin F. Butler. Butler declared that The Woodhull had no need of his legal services, as she had requested, because no lawyer at all was needed by the defense. The action of the government was based upon a misconstruction of the obscene literature statute, which was meant to cover only lithographs, prints, engravings and books of a pornographic nature. Commissioner Davenport was like-minded. He said in his opinion the Challis article was obscene, but that he was convinced the law as drawn was not intended to cover such an article published in a newspaper or magazine. Under ordinary circumstances, he said, he would release the prisoners, but, owing to "the importance as well as the subtlety of the questions involved," he was holding them for the grand jury.

The Commissioner "was never of more than microscopic magnitude, mental and physical," snarled the Brooklyn EAGLE in its disappointment that the sisters were not to be tried on the charge.

. 3 .

Victoria took advantage of this breathing spell and went on a two weeks' lecture tour, giving "The Naked Truth" talk. Everywhere she was greeted, if not with respect, at least with great interest. She was even able to speak in Boston, which a few months before had barred her from presenting her opinions.

This came about after Ezra Hervey Heywood, a militant radical, heard that Tremont Temple had canceled a contract with the New England Labor Reform League, all because The Woodhull was scheduled as a speaker. This vehement pamphleteer founded the New England Free Love League in 1873.

(This year, for Heywood, was the beginning of a new chronology; for from then on he dated his letters Y.L., meaning the Year of Love, instead of using the conventional A.D. style.) He was somewhat eccentric—his children were quaintly named Hermes, Angelo, Vesta, and Psyche—but he was respected in the community, though a defender of advanced views. Heywood saw to it that the Labor Reform League hired several smaller halls for its convention, and that Victoria gave two formal lectures and a number of impromptu talks.

Meantime, the WEEKLY was published in New York at indefinite intervals, and it was defiant in tone. The Beecher-Tilton affair was kept alive in every edition, with comments on the latest developments of the case. Per its promise, the WEEKLY in its May 17 issue reprinted in its entirety the old November 2 number which had been suppressed. Comstock and Beecher noticed it not. There was no suit.

On February 15 the WEEKLY reproduced several advertisements from the New York HERALD, which was notorious for its sponsorship of ads paid for by contraceptive dealers, abortionists, venereal disease quacks, and whorehouse Madams. "If you mean business, here is a game worthy of your steel," the WEEKLY challenged Comstock and his Vice society. "Will you venture to assail it? Or are you only valorous enough to attack women?"

Comstock, who momentarily had lost his keen scent for obscenity, as he was to do throughout his life when a powerful newspaper was concerned, lay low. The WEEKLY called his backers the "Protestant Jesuits," and as for Comstock himself, he was "this pious puppy," but, the journal conceded, "We should no more think of comparing Comstock, alias Beardsley, alias****, with Torquemada than of contrasting a living skunk with a dead lion."

The Brooklyn EAGLE, edited by Tennessee's close friend,

James M. McDermott, professed to be horrified in its jeering item:

A CALL TO COMSTOCK

Does Anthony J. Comstock know that the portrait of Beecher is exhibited on Fulton Street to the naked eye? Is he aware that this picture is gazed on daily by thousands of innocent young girls on their way to school? Is he cognizant of this appalling fact? We call upon him to act at once.

Again Comstock was mute.

Emboldened by the inactivity of the Vice czar, Edward H. G. Clark, editor of the Troy, New York, WHIG, published a special edition of a newspaper called the THUNDERBOLT, giving the True Story of the Beecher Scandal in twenty columns. Clark loathed Beecher, Tilton, Victoria, and Tennessee, and he was against Free Love. But, as he said, "Through these two women, American law has been outraged, the rights of the press assailed, freedom of speech endangered and the functions of the republican government usurped, to cloak the reputation of one or two prominent individuals." His comment on Victoria was:

"She ought to be hanged, and then have a monument erected to her memory at the foot of the gallows."

"She loves notoriety more than any other being on earth, yet she loves her notions of duty more than notoriety," wrote Clark in trying to explain The Woodhull's mixed personality. "At one time she sinks every vestige of shame in the absorbed expression of ideas; and at another she would steal the genius of a friend to aid in her 'putting on airs.' "

The THUNDERBOLT took Beecher's guilt for granted, inasmuch as he had not publicly denied it. "If Beecher himself would only be honest, and not try to garrote the prospects of his race to cover his own frailties, I could hug him in ten minutes," wrote Clark. "But he prefers the 'orthodox' embraces of 'twenty mistresses' and a few million fools."

The THUNDERBOLT was widely sold, but Clark was never indicted. The Chicago TIMES reprinted the long THUNDERBOLT article, adding an unspecified charge of its own, much more serious than adultery. People racked their brains, wondering what that could be. Incest? Homosexuality? Necrophilia? And no one, not even Henry Ward Beecher, sued the Chicago TIMES.

Victoria had gained a certain amount of sympathy in high quarters but, it seemed, lost it in lower places. She herself told the story of stepping aboard a Broadway stagecoach and sitting down beside a well-dressed woman, when she heard the whisper in her ear: "For Heaven's sake, Mrs. Woodhull, don't recognize me—it would ruin my business."

The woman, according to Victoria, was a well-known keeper of a house of prostitution. "I am ostracized by those whom the world calls prostitutes almost as fearfully as I am by those whom I call the real prostitutes," was her dejected comment.

"Yet she loves her notions of duty more than notoriety," editor Clark had written of her. In doing so, he displayed a fine gift for character analysis. It is true she could not tolerate to be ignored. But notoriety alone had not driven her into her reformist career and her fight against respectability. She had a sharp feeling for what was right and wrong in her world, and if she sometimes confused her methods she seldom confused the issue.

. 4 .

Early in June, 1873, Victoria fell ill. Harassed by the thought of lawsuits, so Tennessee dramatically announced to reporters, her sister was dying. Two doctors were summoned. One pronounced her dead, as her breath could not be seen on a looking glass. The other physician thought The Woodhull was alive, and was right.

The reaction of the press, which assumed Victoria was dying or already dead, was mixed. "Her influence over people of intelligence and refinement, women as well as men," the New York GRAPHIC somberly said, "is a phenomenon which has yet to be satisfactorily explained." But the Pittsburgh LEADER thought the illness was a staged trick on the part of the "obscene sisters," an appeal for sympathy. If she died, the newspaper coldly stated, "The world will be rid of one of the most remarkable, albeit terrible and dangerous, women who ever lived in it."

"At the door of death!" mourned POMEROY'S DEMOCRAT in its June 14 issue on receiving telegraphic news that Victoria's demise was imminent. "Mental anxiety, overwork and the unnatural excitement of weeks in prison or at the bar of incompetent courts, have combined against her vitality, and one of the bravest, if not the most discreet, women in the world is prostrate."

The DEMOCRAT, which ordinarily had little love for Victoria, but even less for the Reverend Henry Ward Beecher, continued:

"The hoary-headed hypocrites of Plymouth Church, and the happy husbands who had been cuckolded by Beecher in the name of the Lord, smiled, and in joy made presents to their little ones as they contemplated the burial of the woman who preferred honest devils to sneaking saints.

"Woodhull is dying!

"Bulls, bears, boars and Beechers of Broad Street and Brooklyn:

"Let the woman alone. She is what she is . . .

"She will not yet die."

. **5** .

The DEMOCRAT was right. Vicky had an engagement to keep on the evening of June 25, and her health recovered miraculously. On that night Henry C. Bowen, H. B. Claflin the wealthy businessman (whose repeated avowals that he was not related to the sisters were as vehement as Victoria's and Tennessee's), and several Plymouth Church elders came to Victoria's brownstone house at 6 East Thirty-fourth Street, to find out if she had any documentary proof of Henry Ward Beecher's possible misconduct.

When the grave churchmen were led into the parlor they found Victoria sitting beneath an immense oil painting depicting the Virgin and Child, and backed by an imposing array of consultants—Judge J. D. Reymart, George H. Ellery, a millionaire from Indiana and one of her admirers, J. Parker Jourdan, her personal attorney, and others.

The solemnity of the occasion was temporarily shattered when her sister Utica reeled into the room and started expounding upon the characters of the assembled "sons of bitches." Utie, who had been drinking a little too much whiskey, was forcibly escorted from the parlor. Then the visiting emissaries inquired if Victoria was acquainted with one Mr. Theodore Tilton and a certain Reverend Henry Ward Beecher. They received a frank answer:

"Did I know Theodore Tilton?" cried Vicky in astonishment. "I stayed with him at his house days and nights. And I know Henry Ward Beecher. I have stayed with him at his house days and nights, too, gentlemen, and when I say I stayed with him, I mean no myth."

This expression, "I mean no myth," was relayed to the outside world by the Brooklyn EAGLE, and for years it was nationally known as what later generations would describe as a wisecrack.

The delegation demanded that Victoria produce proof to substantiate her assertion. She said she had in her possession a number of love letters written by Beecher. She paid tribute to Beecher's prowess in bed, a comment which was received in silence by the stony-faced friends of the Brooklyn divine. The elders asked her to show the love letters, for according to the Reverend Beecher, he had written her only twice in his life, once in refusal to preside at her Steinway Hall lecture, and then again in refusal to give money to the Suffrage cause.

"Any one of sense would have known that after several months of intimacy with Mr. Beecher, being with him frequently and alone, our correspondence was not one of mere platonic affection," Victoria told her guests.

She showed Beecher's signature on several notes but she never displayed the context of the alleged billets-doux.

. **6** .

Victoria and Colonel Blood were tried in the United States District Court starting June 23, on the charge of circulating obscene literature. And, after all the fuss raised, the result was anticlimactical.

"In God is my trust," Comstock scrawled in his diary at the time. The defense lawyers placed their trust in Judge Blatchford. His Honor found that the statute as originally drafted applied only to books and pamphlets, and not to newspapers, which the WEEKLY was. Judge Blatchford instructed the jury to return a Not Guilty verdict. It did.

AN INGLORIOUS FAILURE was the headline in the Brooklyn EAGLE, while other papers denounced Comstock. He salved his conscience by having a man named Simpson arrested for selling dirty books. Challis was determined to stick to it, however. He convinced governmental authorities to find new indictments, to bring prosecution under the new act of 1873 which amended the old statute to include such publications as the WEEKLY in the ban against sending pornographic literature through the mails.

. 7 .

The day Victoria and Tennessee were cleared by the jury, Utica, the unruly alcoholic in the family, who had so often caused them trouble, was at it again. Presumably under the influence of prolonged drinking the young lady informed the newspapers that Victoria and husband Blood had assaulted her and kicked her from their home. Now, she complained angrily, there was no one who would buy her whiskey.

In a letter to the SUN Victoria replied to these charges, and the peculiar home life of the Woodhull ménage was once again bared. The letter, dated July 1, read:

Statements of yesterday that Colonel Blood and I committed an assault on Utica Brooker are unqualifiedly false. Mrs. Brooker, in a drunken or insane rage, attacked Mrs. Miles— her sister—with a heavy chair, for which and her subsequent acts Mrs. Miles had her arrested for disorderly conduct. It was, however, at my specific solicitation that Mrs. Miles did not appear against Mrs. Brooker. It was expressly understood that she would not return to the house further to molest us; but no sooner released than she did return, and at once began her insane and disorderly conduct. Her complaint is purely malicious, and by her own avowal was made to effect the public against me.

Woodhull and company often used the columns of the SUN to explain their side of matters. Johnnie Green was Tennessee's

sweetheart, her Number One sweetheart, and he was city editor
of the newspaper.

Utica's frustration, as she freely admitted in the neighborhood saloons, was due to the desertion of a beloved husband
and to the fame of her two sisters, a fame which she could not
attain herself. She drank more and more heavily until a week
later she died. Her death came after an overdose of drugs and
bay rum, which she had taken when no one would buy her
Bourbon whiskey.

Mother Roxy's first impulse was to announce that she intended to sue the druggist for selling a poisonous product, and
the HERALD cautiously mentioned "the strange death of Mrs.
Brooker." Victoria and Tennessee insisted on an autopsy. It
was officially established that Utica had died of Bright's disease.

The WEEKLY candidly explained the reason for Utica's erratic behavior. "She yearned for love, but she cursed those who
would have labored to set her free, and all other women like
her, free," it said. "She was married twice, and while either of
those to whom she was married would have made any ordinary
woman happy, they were restraints that at the time both curbed
and nettled her proud spirit and kept her constantly on fire. All
this led to narcotics and stimulants, and she was cut off at thirty-
one by death." Victoria followed up this strange encomium
with a long lamentation on her sister, "In Memoriam."

. 8 .

Having failed to be elected President of the United States, Victoria's interest in politics waned, while there was an upsurge in favor of the formerly soft-pedaled doctrine of Free Love. She expounded her beliefs in Vineland, New Jersey, and all the major New York newspapers sent reporters there when they heard the subject would be "The Scarecrows of Sexual Freedom." The HERALD afterwards declared The Woodhull "made the most outrageous address ever yet delivered by her," and, thus carefully placing itself on record as being against the speech, proceeded to print her words.

Victoria's main complaint in her lecture was on the awful state of affairs which forced married people to live and sleep together, for though a prostitute could refuse to cohabit, a wife could not. "Sexual intercourse obtained by force" was the only crime, she said, and she asked her audience, "What is it to you whether I live on fish or flesh?" Victoria related the sad tale of an unnamed friend whose husband's "brutal approaches, when first married, made sexual reciprocity impossible for her. He knew but one thing, selfish gratification, and was oblivious to everything else."

Turning dramatically and leveling a finger at Colonel Blood, who stood startled and transfixed on the platform, The Woodhull cried:

"There is my lover, but when I cease to love him, I will leave him, though I trust that will never be."

· 9 ·

Victoria's "Scarecrow" speech was in great demand throughout the country, and so she decided to go on a lecture tour to the West Coast and back. Working, as Parker Pillsbury, the Abolitionist and suffrage leader expressed it, "like a plantation of slaves," she was everywhere a sensation, a notorious sensation, and again the money started to pour into the family's coffers.

Old Roxy Claflin always sat on the platform, lending a pure and maternal touch to the proceedings, as her daughter was preaching radical sexual measures. Only the Claflins shared in the profits and Colonel Blood, who qualified as a Claflin, opened the meetings by selling pamphlets and books written by Victoria and Tennessee, while daughter Zulu usually read a few poems. Incidentally, this was the closest this frustrated girl ever came to performing on the legitimate stage. Once the preliminaries were out of the way, Victoria would step to the lectern, dressed severely in black, with a tea rose at her throat, and the bored audience would prick its ears, sit on the edges of their seats, stare avidly and give their entire attention to every word of the Free Love Queen from the big city.

While lecturing in Chicago, Victoria further elaborated her views of sexual freedom. The Midwest found her, as usual, frank. At one time, as she was expounding her advanced doctrines, a man in the hall sprang to his feet and shouted that in furthering "the glorious work of Suffrage [you have been] prostituting yourself sexually," thereby luring prominent persons to the cause. Amidst a tattoo of boos the man demanded that Victoria "come out and divulge the whole thing—in connection with uncovering individuals from Butler [General Benjamin F. Butler] down."

"A man questioning my virtue!" cried Victoria, and her indignation somewhat startled the audience. She demanded that the complaining person identify himself by name, but the man was silent. And she continued:

"I declare that I never had sexual intercourse with any man of whom I am ashamed to stand side by side before the world with the act. I am not ashamed of any act in my life. At the time, it was the best I knew. Nor am I ashamed of any desire that has been gratified, nor of any passion alluded to."

Then, with overwhelming frankness, Victoria answered her challenger's charge:

"When I came out of prison I came out a beggar. I went to bankers, presidents of railroads, gamblers, prostitutes, and got the money that has sent you the paper you have been reading; and I do not think you are the worse for handling it. I used whatever influence I had to get the money and that's my own business and none of yours. And if I devoted my body to my work and my soul to God, that is my business, and not yours."

Her listeners sat aghast, but she had not finished:

"Are there any of you who would have come forward and put your bodies in the gap? If you will not, don't put me before you as needing to confess anything that in your self-sanctified spirits you may conceive to be prostitution. If I want sexual intercourse with one hundred men, I shall have it!"

There were handclaps, but only scattered handclaps, from the petrified audience. As one Chicago newspaperman reported, the general reaction to the famous Victoria C. Woodhull was—"Whew!"

As Victoria paused to recover her breath, some of those in

the assembly thought the lecture had ended, and wiping their red foreheads with handkerchiefs, groping for hats and umbrellas, they began to stumble to the aisles in a state of shock. But The Woodhull was not through. She commandingly motioned them back to their seats and continued:

"I am charged with seeking notoriety, but who among you would accept any notoriety and pay a tithe of its cost to me? Driven from my former beautiful home, reduced from affluence to want, my business broken up and destroyed, dragged from one jail to another, and in a short time I am again to be arraigned before the courts and stand trial for telling the truth. I have been smeared all over with the most opprobrious epithets, and the vilest names, am stigmatized as a bawd and a blackmailer.

"Now, until you are ready to accept my notoriety, with its conditions—to suffer what I have suffered and am yet to suffer —do not dare to impugn my motives. As to your approval or disapproval, your applause or your curses, they have not a feather's weight with me. I am set apart for a high and sacred duty, and I shall perform it without fear or favor."

The Chicago TRIBUNE editorially found the lecture "was unfit to listen to." When the telegraphic news of Victoria's outburst reached New York, the WORLD declared The Woodhull had confessed publicly to being a whore and strumpet, and was proud of it. Now, for the first time, some of her stanchest followers began to disown her. But Emily B. Ruggles, well-known for her defense of the slaves of whoredom, was ecstatically delighted. She cried:

"I felt that I had clasped hands with one who would bring me nearer into contact with the so-called fallen women than I had ever come before, that she being lifted up would draw all women after her, so, when the editors of the New York WORLD told me that Victoria was a prostitute, I said, 'Well, show me the worst prostitute in New York and she is the one I want to clasp hands with and bring up from such a life.' "

This long-winded, well-intentioned defense of Victoria lost Emily B. Ruggles a friend for life. Victoria never spoke to her again.

After the Chicago explosion, The Woodhull was more careful when she delivered the lecture in smaller towns. There the reception by the press was better. The Saginaw, Michigan, COURIER found her "entrancingly lovely." The Galesburg, Illinois, REPUBLICAN said her advice was a "profitable lesson" for mothers. "She has created more stir, more sensation in our city than any man who ever trod the dust of its streets," commented the Dubuque, Iowa, HERALD.

Strangely, the Midwest, so traditionally conservative, treated her most kindly and with more respect than San Francisco, known as a wide-open, liberal town. Victoria caused no commotion in a metropolis which had a Barbary Coast, in a city used to scandal and brawling. When she gave her daring "Scarecrow" speech in Platt Hall the CHRONICLE found it "a nice little talk." In this "nice little talk" Victoria declared, "It would be better if a woman bore twelve healthy children by twelve different men, than twelve such children . . . by one man."

· **10** ·

Victoria was exhausted when she returned East after the cross-country tour. She sent mother Roxanna and an older sister, Mrs. Margaret Ann Miles, to represent her at the meeting of the

Philadelphia Spiritualists, where the audience was treated to an entertaining, if unscheduled, airing of the Claflin family's internecine strife. A somewhat bewildered reporter from the Philadelphia RECORD described the scene:

Vicky was denounced by a speaker from the floor for disgracing the Spiritualist movement by her "wild platform statements." A Miss Dumar arose and suggested that Victoria alone was responsible for what she said; that she spoke for herself while on lecture tours, and not for any other individual or cause.

Few people visualized that such an inoffensive comment would enrage mama Roxy, but it did.

"Tisn't so! You lie!" shouted the unpredictable Roxy, leaping to her feet. "My daughters are not responsible for what they do or say. They're psychologized by that devil of a Blood! But they're my daughters and I love them, and I'll defend them! But you're a liar!"

The chairman pounded his gavel. The audience screamed, "Throw her out!"

Roxy retreated up the aisle, waving her umbrella in a menacing fashion, while she continued her harangue. The situation was further complicated when her daughter, Mrs. Miles, dashed into the fray, though it was hard to tell whose side she was on. She abused sisters Victoria and Tennessee in terms "more energetic than decent," but she also belabored Colonel Blood, while defending someone whom people vaguely thought was herself, possibly her mother.

"The assemblage broke up in the greatest confusion," remarked the RECORD.

. 11 .

Vicky lectured again in Boston in the fall of 1873, and there she renewed her acquaintance with an alert, handsome, and interesting youth she had met six months earlier. Bennie Tucker, scarcely more than half her age at nineteen, was interested in radical movements. While a student at the Massachusetts Institute of Technology he had attended Victoria's lectures the year before and she had become his idol. Several months later he and some college mates heard her talk again, and their cheers had vied with the predominant boos in the audience. And so, when Colonel Blood came to Boston to prepare Victoria's speaking engagements in New England, young Bennie offered to help out. He approved of woman's suffrage, and he wanted to know Victoria C. Woodhull. Bennie secured halls in Salem, Lynn, and Lawrence, over the opposition of the town bigwigs who resented the idea of having "the New York witch" speak in staid Massachusetts, and thus he earned the favor of husband Blood: The Colonel told Victoria about this bright, youthful admirer, and to Bennie he relayed the information that the Great Lady would be charmed to grant him an audience.

Young Bennie later became known as Benjamin R. Tucker, well-known as a publisher and chief exponent in this country of individual anarchism. Tucker lived until 1939, aged eighty-five, and during his long life he was an interesting, if minor, figure. A newspaperman on the Boston GLOBE, he later launched *Transatlantic*, a first-rate literary journal, and, afterward, *Liberty* magazine. From 1926 on he lived in retirement

in France and Monaco, turning out numberless tracts, ⌐
autobiographical material which no publisher would ⌐
treatises on pacifism and anarchism and what not, for⌐
dedicated to many isms, -ists and reforms. Besides being a
"consistent anarchist," he had been, so he fondly recalled, "an
atheist, a materialist, an evolutionist, a prohibitionist, a free
trader, a champion of the legal eight-hour day, a woman suffragist, an enemy of marriage, and a believer in sexual freedom."
Like George Francis Train, he was a man of many parts.

In 1873, however, Bennie was a man of no parts, and despite
his advanced views, he was a virgin. He is one of the few individuals who has left a written record describing an intimate
friendship with The Woodhull—the sort of friendship for
which she was notorious in the public eye. His story was told in
1928, eleven years before his death, in *The Terrible Siren* by
Emanie Sachs, a biography of Victoria C. Woodhull.

Bennie met Vicky during one of her visits to Boston. He
went up to her suite in the Parker House hopefully looking forward to, as he put it, his "ruin." And, according to Bennie, he
was ruined, all right, though it took some doing. Victoria, after
discreetly taking the precaution of hanging a wrap over the
doorknob to cover the keyhole, had to make all the advances,
kissing him and sitting in his lap until she had excited him
sufficiently enough to bundle him off into bed and down to
business. As young Tucker remembered it, husband Colonel
Blood thoughtfully left the room so as they could be alone.

When Vicky returned to New York, Bennie sent her his first
love letter. She did not answer it; instead Colonel Blood sent
him a friendly note. This mystified Bennie. A year later young
Tucker saw Victoria again, as we shall see, and by this time he
knew her well enough never to be mystified by any of her actions.

. 12 .

The Challis suit for libel against Victoria, Tennessee, and Colonel Blood was set on the calendar for trial January 16, 1874, in the Court of General Sessions. Charles W. Brooke, who had represented the trio in the Government's obscenity case, was the senior counsel of three defense lawyers. He asked for a postponement, explaining The Woodhull was two thousand miles away, lecturing to the godly in Kansas. The case was put over to March 5.

When that time arrived, Victoria had returned home, and an entire day was taken to select a jury. Through the wrangling, it was evident that Judge Sutherland favored the prosecution and loathed the defendants. The spectators cramming the courtroom, however, were friendly to Victoria and company, and particularly sympathetic because her little daughter, Zulu, was present. Zulu sat tensely at her mother's side, holding her hand pathetically, trying hard to be brave, but there were many who feared the girl and her mother would break into tears.

Once the jury was chosen, Judge Sutherland again showed his bias by refusing to set bail. Instead he remanded the prisoners to the Tombs. Zulu cried profusely as she was separated from her mother, and the jurors could not help noticing her grief, but Victoria told her, in a voice that carried all the way to the jury box, not to worry too much while she was incarcerated behind cold bars. Victoria, Tennessee, and Colonel Blood were to remain behind these cold bars during the ten days taken to hear the case.

The next day the trial opened. Attorney William Fullerton, Challis' lawyer and, significantly enough, a crony of Henry Ward Beecher, was permitted by the court to question Victoria on her social beliefs. "In your opinion, should a woman desert her husband and live with another man, if prompted by such a desire?" he demanded to know.

Lawyer Brooke tried to point out that such a question was immaterial to the case, but Judge Sutherland ruled it in. And, while her mother was on the stand, the jurors observed that Zulu occasionally would dab at her eyes, and quietly gulp down a sob or two. "It was a sad, heart-rending sight," a juror later told a reporter.

Victoria waved aside her lawyer's appeal to the court and said she would be happy to answer the question. However, she seemed to have trouble concentrating, for, as the jury noted, and they all were intelligent persons, her mind apparently was riveted on her daughter, who sat next to her mother's empty chair, her body now racked with sobs. There was a moment when it looked as if Victoria herself was close to a little cry, but she perked up when Tennessee leaned over and gave the child a tender auntie's pat on the head.

In answer to the lawyer's question about a wife deserting her husband to live with another man, Vicky replied:

"If her will takes her away from a man, she surely ought to go," answered Victoria briskly, her mind now strictly on the subject matter. "I hold that any man or woman, whether married or unmarried, who consorts for anything but love, is a prostitute."

Judge Sutherland often interrupted the questioning by interpolating neat moral lectures on the utter indecency of such social theories. Lawyers in the courtroom, who were on a busman's holiday to hear an interesting case, believed the jurors resented his bias almost as much as the presence of the defendant's poor, poor little girl who had to listen to such vile goings-on.

Judge Sutherland instructed the jury in his summing-up speech that nothing but a Guilty verdict could be returned, or even considered. The jurymen retired shortly after noon on Friday the thirteenth, deliberated all night, and came in with their decision at 11:05 in the morning. The verdict, reached on the one-hundredth ballot, was Not Guilty.

"We wish to express our unanimous and most hearty concurrence in the sentiments expressed so eloquently by Your Honor," so read the foreman in a prepared statement to the court, and he quaked as he conned the paper, "but decide to yield to the defendants that charitable presumption of innocence where there is a reasonable doubt . . ."

The veins were standing out, red and hot, on His Honor's neck as he stilled the applause in the courtroom, stopped Vicky and Tennessee from shaking hands with the jurors, and growled:

"It is the most outrageous verdict ever recorded. It is shameful and infamous, and I am ashamed of the jury who rendered such a verdict!"

Perhaps Zulu was meant to be an actress, after all. It was undeniable that her tender talent had blossomed even without encouragement. Victoria, in any event, affectionately hugged her little girl as she swept from the courtroom, and, outside—so did attorney Charles W. Brooke.

. **13** .

After her "vindication" Vicky immediately took off on a six months' lecture tour, again traveling to the Middle West, and then, heartened by her reception—for she drew large crowds everywhere—she went on to the West Coast. Few Californians had any recollection of Victoria's visit fifteen years before, when she had aspired to become a great actress under Anna Cogswell, but they had been reading about her impact on the eastern seaboard for years and remembered her previous lecture in San Francisco. For one hundred and fifty consecutive nights Victoria gave her talk, "Tried As By Fire, or, The True and The False Socially." It was another anti-marriage sermon. "The marriage law is the most damnable social evil bill—the most consummate outrage on women that was ever conceived," Victoria told her awed audiences. "Those who are called prostitutes are free women sexually, compared to the slavery of the poor wife."

The message was such a success, particularly among married women who comprised most of the listeners everywhere, that it was incorporated into a forty-four-page pamphlet, which sold well. (Interestingly enough, the Oberlin College Library today catalogues this title as *"F*ried by Fire . . .")

. 14 .

When Victoria returned to New York she found that Beecher had been brought to dock—to a friendly dock. Alarmed by the slathers of publicity, the Plymouth Church elders had appointed a Committee of Investigation to ascertain the truth or falsity of the charges that its beloved pastor had seduced Lib Tilton. Each of the six committeemen was a member of Plymouth Church, and each was personally devoted to its Shepherd.

The dark question of the hour was: Would The Woodhull, instigator of the scandal, testify at this private investigation? It was known that the Plymouth Church deacons would not relish hearing her evidence, that they considered her an unqualified, prejudiced witness—and yet she, as being responsible for the exposure, possibly should be heard from. There were covert rumors in newspapers that some persons, who were interested in a whitewashing verdict, had approached Victoria and her friends and convinced her, in some way, that she should not enter into the "trial" picture in any way. In other words, the implication was that she had been bribed into silence.

Whether or not this was true is not known. The facts are these:

On July 29, 1874, a Brooklyn EAGLE reporter went to interview Victoria. He found her in shabby offices, walking three flights up rickety stairs at 111 Nassau Street, where the WEEKLY had established itself after being evicted from its old headquarters on Broad Street. No newspaperman in New York or any other city had ever known Vicky to be at a loss for

words. To his surprise, the EAGLE man found her strangely in-
articulate. She would not comment on the Beecher Investigation Committee's hearing, nor on anything else.

Two days later, Victoria and Tennessee and James M. Mc-
Dermott, editor of the Brooklyn SUNDAY PRESS (who had become an intimate friend of Tennessee, and whose newspaper
peculiarly enough was now minimizing the importance of the
investigation, though months before its columns had been full
of denunciations of Beecher), appeared before the Committee
and asked if their testimony would be required. The Committee courteously thanked them for their thoughtfulness and informed them that, no, their evidence was not needed.

The trio accepted the decision with great grace. To inquiring
newspapermen they said benignly they did not question the decision, they did not intend to protest it. Vicky herself refused to
say anything one way or another on the subject of The Reverend Henry Ward Beecher.

A badgering reporter confronted Victoria with a clipping
from the November 2, 1872, issue of the WEEKLY, asking her to
comment on it. The clipping read: "I have been charged with
attempts at blackmailing, but I tell you, sir, there is not enough
money in these two cities to purchase my silence in the matter."

Victoria replied she had nothing to say.

She was asked if she had repudiated the interview given
months before to a Chicago TIMES newspaperman, which told
of the many rapturous nights she had spent in bed with the
Brooklyn divine.

Victoria replied she had nothing to say.

. 15 .

Bennie Tucker had come to New York in February on his way
to Europe. He did make the trip, but that was half a year later,
for he stopped off to say good-by to Victoria and decided to
postpone his journey.

According to the indiscreet and somewhat unreliable memories of Bennie, Tennessee was attracted to his splendid person
just as much as Victoria, and maybe more so. He went to the
WEEKLY's offices in Nassau Street, and, according to his story:

"There were two persons in the single room of which the
office consisted—Tennie, seated at a desk, and Zulu, sitting opposite her. Both were in street costume and busily engaged in
doing nothing at all. I stepped up to Tennie's desk and asked
her if Mrs. Woodhull was to be seen. She answered that her
sister was just returning from a Western lecture tour, and was
expected to arrive together with Colonel Blood, that evening. I
told her that I had come from Boston, and that my name was
Tucker.

" 'What! Is this Bennie Tucker?'

"I allowed that she was a good guesser.

" 'Why!' she exclaimed. 'Vicky just thinks the world of you!
She'll be awful glad to see you. But isn't this weather terrible?
Just look at this!'

"And up went her skirts to a point between knee and waist
(remember that this little scene occurred fifty-three years ago),
revealing drenched stockings and underwear. I am unable to

say what would have happened next, had not the door opened at this juncture, permitting the entrance of Colonel Blood's older brother, George . . ."

Bennie Tucker's later recollections of the famed sisters in full bloom are in general antagonistic, for reasons he thought justified—and it will be seen why—but occasionally he permitted himself to praise, not to sneer:

"Victoria and Tennessee were fond of money, but not miserly. They spent freely when they had the means. On several occasions I was the guest of the family at Delmonico dinners, and was entertained lavishly. This hospitality was never returned in kind, largely because I had not the means. I am absolutely sure that Victoria's love for me was thoroughly sincere and disinterested. She had little or nothing to gain by it. I was too unsophisticated to offer her a fruit or a flower or a jewel or a scarf, and she never gave me the slightest hint that such testimonials were expected of a lover. She received from me nothing but affectionate admiration and steadfast devotion, and with that she seemed to be content."

How important Bennie's role was, in an amatory way, is not known; but he tells, perhaps unwittingly, of his services as a mere messenger boy. While Bennie was living in New York he stayed with the Claflin family constantly, from ten in the morning to ten or later at night ("meal hours generally excepted," he delicately adds). He describes the clan as living "in a condition of Bohemian disorder," and tells of his numerous trips to the corner saloon, armed with a large pitcher from the washstand, to "rush the growler." And, though Victoria was his idol, he had a difficult time fending off sister Tennessee:

"One afternoon, when I was walking uptown with Victoria from the office, she said to me suddenly, 'Tennie is going to love you this afternoon.'

"I looked at her wonderingly. 'But,' I said, 'I don't care to have her.'

" 'Oh, don't say that,' she answered. 'Nobody can love me who doesn't love Tennie.'

"Not liking to be impaled upon either horn of so perplexing a dilemma, I resolved to make at least a temporary escape. As we were nearing the apartment, I found an excuse for leaving her, and did not go back. The next day, when I saw her, no reference was made to the matter.

"Tennie herself, however, gave me numerous hints and opportunities. For instance, she once asked me to take off her shoes and put on her slippers. Seeing her motive, I became confused, and tried to put the right slipper on the left foot. She laughed at my stupidity, and at the same time seemed a little vexed. On another occasion, when I was going out for the beer, she accompanied me. On the way she managed to suggest, though I forget in what way, the possibility that some night we might sleep together.

" 'Are you in earnest about that?' I asked.

" 'Why, yes, Bennie, of course. Do you think that I wouldn't do a little thing like that for you?' "

. 16 .

Early in August, 1874, Victoria, Tennessee and Colonel Blood were arrested on the complaint of a Mrs. A. M. Thurman of

Brooklyn, who charged she had deposited on May 26, 1871,
$400 in government bonds with the Woodhull & Claflin broker-
age firm, and could not get them back.

Victoria testified in court that the money had been invested
and, unfortunately, lost. She had warned Mrs. Thurman against
speculating. It was believed pressure was brought to bear on
Mrs. Thurman, from somewhere, by someone, for the case soon
was mysteriously dropped.

Soon afterward, a large party hired suites on the *Lafayette*
and sailed in style for Havre. Victoria told reporters at the pier
that she was taking her husband, Tennessee, her mother, and
her daughter Zulu on a tour of France, and that she was paying
all expenses, as a "present" to her family. Unmentioned was a
sixth member of the group, Bennie Tucker, who was going
along for the ride.

There were a good many alert observers who wondered how
Vicky was able to finance this "present" to her family. Simple
arithmetic showed that her normal income would not have permitted such an expensive excursion. And who was this "someone," who had compelled the inconsolable Mrs. Thurman to
drop her case against Victoria? Obviously, this "someone" had
the most vital interest to prevent a lawsuit which would have
kept Vicky in the city, who yearned to put an ocean between
him and herself, to get rid of her embarrassing presence, no
matter the cost. These same alert observers, who had followed
the Beecher story with the closest attention, did not have to
strain their imagination too much to identify the Great Unknown who sent The Woodhull on vacation.

. 17 .

While Vicky and entourage were on the high seas, the Beecher Investigation Committee continued to sit and hear evidence. Theodore Tilton appeared before the body and swore the Reverend Beecher had committed adultery with his dear wife, Lib. The informal probe was attended with the greatest interest by the public.

At this hearing, General Benjamin F. Tracy, one of the many counsels representing Beecher, asked Tilton if he had ever had improper relations or criminal intercourse with one Victoria C. Woodhull, or with one Tennie C. Claflin, both of whom were now residents of Paris.

Tilton refused to make a categorical denial, though he implied that his answers, if made, would be in the negative.

General Tracy then stated that servants of the Woodhull household were prepared to vouch for the truth of the first accusation, and that a hotelkeeper in Winsted, Connecticut, would swear to the second.

Tilton again refused to affirm or deny. He evidently feared that Victoria had been bribed by the Beecher forces and therefore could not be trusted to support his side of the argument. At this time the newspapers were full of parodies of Theodore's poem, "Sir Marmaduke's Musings," and it is likely that Tilton believed in the warning words of the anonymous ditty, "Sir Sinbad's Advice":

> Trust not to woman — she can smile,
> And raise the devil all the while:

Or, like Vic Woodhull, can beguile
  With Free Love's new philosophy.

O! cling not then, as fondly on
The flowers or earth around thee strewn—
Vic says: "They'll do to sport upon,
  But never to love fervently."

In his testimony (of course he was not answerable to the
laws of perjury in this informal hearing) Tilton said he was
convinced of his wife's infidelity because Lib herself had told
him of her many "irregularities" with the brawny Reverend.
He recalled two specific instances in which the two had indulged in rather extreme fondling, right before his eyes. The
first was when he had caught the minister groping with his
hand "slyly, very slyly" under his wife's dress.

"What part of her person did he touch?" General Tracy
asked calmly, as if the incident might happen to any man's
wife.

"Her ankles and lower limbs."

"Not above the knee?"

"No," replied Tilton, and then said: "If he had, he probably
would have been struck."

Having settled this fine point, Tilton added thoughtfully,
amidst rising titters:

"It was a question in my mind whether a minister could consider that a proper sort of caress."

The second time he became somewhat suspicious, Tilton
continued, was on coming home unexpectedly and finding the
bedchamber door locked. This puzzled him, as Lib, when she
took naps, never resorted to such absurd precautions. Tilton
went on:

"I knocked at the door and Elizabeth came. I was surprised

that it was locked. She was surprised at finding me. Mr. Beecher was sitting in a red plush rocking chair, a sort of Ottaman chair—with his vest unbuttoned, and his face colored like a rose when I saw him."

Beecher himself did not testify. Instead he submitted an interminable statement in which he rhapsodized about his love of God and small children and his innocence, and lamented over his persecution. As for Victoria C. Woodhull, he scarcely knew her—he had met her but three times in his life. As he recalled it, the only time he had talked to her at length was one evening in Mr. Tilton's house. He had consented to meet her solely because his sister Isabella regarded The Woodhull as "Joan of Arc with a vision of the Virgin Mary."

"I went in, and after some conversation down in the parlor I went upstairs into the famous boudoir-room, where she sat waiting," the Reverend declared in his deposition, "and, like a spider to a fly, she rushed to me on my entrance and reached out both her hands with the utmost earnestness, and said how rejoiced she was to see me. I talked with her about five minutes and then went downstairs."

Five weeks after the start of the informal hearing, on August 27, the Committee found its pastor not only was non-adulterous, but that he "has never committed any unchaste or improper acts with Mrs. Tilton." The verdict of the hand-picked Committee surprised no one, and least of all The Reverend Henry Ward Beecher.

Seemingly, this complete vindication put an end to the matter; actually, Beecher's troubles were only beginning. To the newspapers which were convinced of the preacher's guilt, the investigation was a whitewash. Those favoring Beecher were prone to condemn his original accuser, Victoria, as being responsible for the mess. In the eyes of the Brooklyn EAGLE, which blew hot and cold depending on how it felt about The

Woodhull, she was "that notorious drab" and "arch priestess of Priapus." The curious took to their dictionaries to learn Priapus was the god of the phallus. Pamphlets were issued decrying "The wicked Woodhull," and flatly calling her "Queen of the Whores," and Beecher himself was quoted as publicly labeling the sisters "The two prostitutes," and Victoria in particular as a "sexually morbid monomaniac."

"Leo," the New York correspondent for the Chicago JOURNAL, was outspoken as he wired his newspaper:

"From the day of her arrival in this city she [Woodhull] has been on the make. That she holds the reputation of many an unfortunate in the hollow of her hand is undoubtedly true, and that she will soon commence the process of skinning the cat is beyond doubt."

It was the undocumented belief of the JOURNAL reporter that thanks to The Woodhull's "baneful magnetism" the Beecher secret had been wormed from the Suffragists who were familiar with the situation. He said these ladies found "there was no resisting her" because "They rode with her, lunched with her, when they could, slept with her, and she in turn pumped them until they were as dry as punk."

Another person who pondered on the "strange fascination" Victoria held for various women was the Reverend George H. Beecher, one of Henry Ward's brothers. He mused publicly on the subject in a letter to the Brooklyn EAGLE, the "she" being Isabella Beecher Hooker:

"She was devotedly attached to Mrs. Woodhull, and has never withdrawn from her. The strange fascination which this remarkable woman possessed over her is evinced, among other things, by the letter which she wrote to Mrs. Woodhull about the time of her nomination by the Free Love wing of the Woman Suffrage Convention—'My Darling Queen' and proceeding in the same language."

Victoria C. Woodhull often was accused of sleeping with men, many men, but this is one of the rare instances where she was covertly accused of Lesbianism.

· 18 ·

The only account available about Victoria's trip to France is found in the reminiscences of Bennie Tucker in old age. They concern mostly his virtuous attempts to defend himself against the amorous onslaughts of Tennessee. According to Bennie (after describing his alleged seduction in Boston he has become strangely silent about Victoria as his sexual partner), it started during the opening days of their ocean voyage:

"On no other occasion, during my acquaintanceship with Victoria, did I ever see her in a state of angry excitement. One night, after I had gone to bed, Tennie came into my cabin holding a bottle of whiskey, which she was endeavoring to open. Just then Victoria happened along, and, at the sight of Tennie thus engaged, went into a panic. She begged and implored and threatened and wrung her hands, in the hope of inducing Tennie to desist. But all in vain. Evidently it was not the first time that Victoria had seen Tennie with a bottle of whiskey, and scenes of the past remained vivid in her memory."

The party stayed at the luxurious Grand Hotel in Paris. In between tours of the art galleries, sessions in cafés and bistros and inspections of the ravages that remained from the struggle of the Commune against the besieging army of Versailles, Bennie, so he claimed, was hard put to repel the insinuating Tennessee. For, no sooner had they settled down in the city than she pursued him anew:

"Victoria and the Colonel had one room. Tennie and her mother and Zulu had the room adjoining. My own room was about a hundred feet away. Probably the others felt a little crowded. At any rate, Tennie entered my room one afternoon, and, looking about, remarked:

" 'Why, Bennie, your bed is plenty big enough for two, isn't it?'

"I allowed for the accuracy of her estimate, but refused to take the hint."

At any rate, as Bennie put it, the travelers returned to New York and astounded the ship reporters by refusing to comment on the whitewash verdict given by the Beecher Investigation Committee. The astonishment of the press was further increased when, in January, 1875, Victoria appeared and behaved in what can only be described as a notoriously *un*sensational way in the celebrated suit brought by Theodore Tilton against Henry Ward Beecher.

· 19 ·

Tilton's suit started belatedly, years after the preacher's alleged affair with his wife Lib, and then only after Beecher had accused Tilton of blackmail and forgery, immorality and insanity. Theodore charged alienation of his wife's affections and criminal libel, asking $100,000 to compensate for his grief.

This, perhaps the most famous trial in American history, was thoroughly covered then and later in thousands upon thousands of newspaper and magazine articles, books and pamphlets. It was a trial running for half a year with testimony of a million and more words filling three thousand printed pages, and was followed with greater interest through the land than any other spicy and exciting episode of the day—the prosecution of Tweed and his Ring, the Crédit Mobilier scandal, the adultery trial of the Reverend Isaac S. Kalloch in Boston which almost rivaled Beecher's in its national reverberations, the exposure of the Whiskey Ring, and the conviction of Stokes for the murder of Jim Fisk, Jr. It is considered but briefly here, and mainly through Victoria's connection with the case.

The Woodhull appeared in Brooklyn City Court on May 12. She had been subpoenaed by the brilliant battery of defense lawyers, William M. Evarts, Benjamin F. Tracy, John K. Porter, and "Tearful Tommy" Shearman. Beecher's counsels merely wanted her to produce billets-doux written by Tilton, which they hoped might be discrediting to him. They did not wish to put her on the stand as a witness. It was the hope of Tilton's attorneys, a galaxy of legal lights including William A. Beach, General Robert Pryor, William Fullerton, and Judge Samuel D. Morris, that she would testify, and thus be subject to cross-examination.

"A loud murmur ran through the court, and all eyes were turned in the direction of that person, who modestly seated herself in a rear chair," the TIMES said, somewhat contemptuously, describing Victoria's entrance. Beecher's attorneys asked her kindly to produce the letters Tilton had written her. This The Woodhull refused to do, without a direct order from the court.

Tilton's lawyers objected to having the notes entered as evidence unless Victoria were put in the witness box.

During the argument, Victoria stepped over to Fullerton and Evarts and made it plain that she preferred to produce the letters rather than take the stand. As the TIMES described the scene:

"There was a sudden upheaval of people in the gallery and around the edges of the main floor, to get a better sight of her. Victoria took another step forward and said, in a low clear voice, mid the most profound silence, that she had only a few unimportant letters written by Mr. Tilton to herself. They were nothing in the least discreditable, either to herself or to the gentleman. She had been several times imprisoned for publishing his scandal, and her office had been ransacked and some of her private correspondence carried off."

With this explanation, she handed over a large morocco pocketbook to "Tearful Tommy" Shearman and Fullerton. The rival attorneys eagerly scanned the letters, but they were found to be valueless to either side.

Victoria's reluctance to stir up trouble against the divine-defendant prompted newspapers openly to speculate that she had been "bought off," by someone, and not by Theodore Tilton.

This was Vicky's only appearance in court (though both parties feared she later might "find" the private correspondence she had "lost"), and it was anticlimactical enough; yet her name popped up, red-herring style, throughout the case.

Beecher and Tilton each were disdainful in their references to Victoria, each speaking scornfully of her "low associates," and so it came as a surprise to everyone when a list of frequenters to her salon was placed on the record. The public long had been led to believe that Victoria's home was visited only by prostitutes, Free Lovers, members of the underworld and the *canaille;*

that no man of respectability or decency would dare be seen in her company. But testimony revealed that Victoria's receptions were not entirely unlike those that took place in Mme. Roland's famous salon in Paris. Among the prominent individuals who willingly sat at Victoria's feet during these soirées, charmed by her wisdom and wit, were:

TRIBUNE editor Jacob Whitelaw Reid (as the TIMES gleefully noted, placing his name at the top of the roster); William Orter, President of Western Union; General Hillier, Grant's Chief of Staff; General J. H. Hammond, Sherman's Chief of Staff; banker Henry Clews, Albert Brisbane, The Reverend Octavius Brooks Frothingham, A. F. Wilmarth, President of the Home Fire Insurance Co.; T. J. S. Flint, President of the Continental Bank; T. J. Durant, Vice-President of the Union Pacific; Jesse Wheelock, President of the Stock Exchange Board; Josiah Warren and Josiah Cummings. Newspaper readers were stunned at the idea of such celebrities communing, even in a conversational way, with The Woodhull.

Tilton repudiated Victoria in his testimony. He had done her favors, to quiet her, to protect his wife, and to protect Beecher. "I wish distinctly to say to the jury that my relationship with Mrs. Woodhull was a foolish one and a wrong one, as the event has justified, and I do not ask any man to defend me, but I say here before God that Mr. Beecher is as much responsible for my connection with Mrs. Woodhull as I am myself."

Many people were mystified by Tilton's words. Did he mean to imply that Beecher should be convicted not only for his own adultery, but for Tilton's as well, having practically forced him into his love affair with The Woodhull?

The defense lawyers then put on the stand two of Victoria's Negro servants, Lucy Giles and Jim Woodley, who testified to the presence of a "sofa-bed" in the parlor of the Claflin home, upon which, to their knowledge, Victoria and Tilton had wres-

tled vigorously for at least two nights. Tilton denied ever seeing
such a bed. He also could not remember ever drinking champagne with The Woodhull, or of riding with her to the beach
and the woods. His memory was refreshed by the direct refutation of a number of defense witnesses.

It was now the turn of the famed William M. Evarts,
Beecher's attorney, to read a love poem written by Tilton, generally understood to have been addressed to Victoria when
their romance was at its height. Theodore blushed as Evarts
recited the lyrical gem which was titled "French without a Master." The lawyer intoned with great gusto, accompanied by fur-
tive snickers from the courtroom audience, which soon swelled
into laughs. There is space here for only the last verse of this
epic:

> Sweetheart, no! You cannot go!
> Let me sit and hold you so.
> Adam did the same to Eve!
> *Aimer, aimer, c'est a vivre.*

Theodore never recovered from the humiliation of having his
composition read aloud and reprinted in the newspapers, and
years later, when he was living in seclusion in Paris, it was
noted that he shuddered convulsively when the verses were
mentioned.

The highlight of the case came, of course, when the great
man himself, The Reverend Henry Ward Beecher, made his
appearance. There were 179,000 people living in Brooklyn in
1874 and it seemed as if almost all of them were gathered outside the Supreme Court Building. The Man of God always drew
a crowd, whether it be in his Plymouth Church pulpit or elsewhere.

Beecher made his entrance in much the same style as a movie

star or a TV personality does today. He doffed his broad-brimmed farmer's hat to the throng, he blew kisses at the spectators, and he repeatedly threw his hands aloft and clenched his fists, as might a present-day prize fighter. He was greeted with tremendous cheers but their volume was matched by a thundering roll of boos. The men in the street had already made up their minds as to Beecher's guilt or innocence and no matter what testimony he gave, they would not change their partisan views.

Beecher's adherents had festooned the courtroom and hallways with lilies, the symbol of purity, and when he had been sworn in and took the stand he carried the motif further. He sniffed delicately at a bouquet of wild violets, the emblem of modesty, which he held in his hand.

In the pulpit, the Reverend preached a muscular sort of Christianity, popularized later by Billy Sunday, and his frothy orations, punctuated by platform acrobatics, impressed the people of that age. He was particularly effective in showering down imprecations on some obscure Biblical character who had sinned in one way or another. This, as he found out the instant he was seated in the confines of the witness chair, was far easier than explaining away his own private peccadillos.

Frank and open and honest-appearing in the pulpit, he was the very incarnation of evasiveness on the witness stand. On 894 different occasions—by actual count—Beecher could "not remember" or could "not recollect" or "did not know." His was an ordeal, for attorney Fullerton spent four full days in a penetrating cross-examination, giving no rest to the wilted divine. When he was dismissed and left the courthouse there were no waves at the populace, no doffing of the hat or arms outflung to heaven. Sweating, feverish, he was in too much of a hurry to get home and into the comforting quiet of his bed.

· 20 ·

The trial ended two hundred and twelve days after it started, on June 24, 1875. Porter took five days in summing up, Evarts took eight. His opponent Beach, who had criticized Evarts for delaying the case by unnecessary oratory, consumed ten days for his summation. The jury went out and, before it came in, cast fifty-two ballots. On the final one, the jurors were deadlocked at nine to three in favor of the defendant, Beecher.

The jury disagreement was regarded as a victory by both sides. The case never was retried, and the criminal libel suit was dropped by Tilton; both opponents had had enough. In the eyes of many citizens, Beecher was guilty. The TIMES and SUN thought so, and the latter gave seven reasons why, but most of the other New York journals favored the Brooklyn pastor. Whether or not he was guilty, his reputation was damaged, while Tilton's was permanently ruined. To Beecher's friends, who were vociferous in defending him, he was a slandered, Christlike creature. Whatever the truth, his trial was a severe blow to the Protestant ministry. And even today, nearly a century later, the question of the divine's guilt or innocence is, to some people, a fighting matter.

. 21 .

Mrs. Stanton was disgusted with Tilton's repudiation of his one-time mistress. "Theodore Tilton need not have shirked an acknowledgment of his association with Mrs. Woodhull," she told the Newark CALL. "Victoria Woodhull's acquaintance would be refining to any man . . . She has faced and dared men to call her names that would make men shudder, while she chucked principle, like medicine, down their throats." This was eulogy indeed, for the many suffrage leaders were jealous of one another, and each had her eye on the history books that were to be written.

Victoria, who usually was quick to take umbrage at even fancied insults, at first was peculiarly calm about Tilton's betrayal. She seemed willing to forgive and forget. "No matter how inconsiderately Theodore Tilton has treated himself—not me—in regard to his relations to me, I forgive him heartily all his intended harm," she humbly told a reporter.

After she had turned the cheek, however, she evidently thought things over and became once again her usual self. The HERALD's former columnist now told her side of the story in an article titled "Whom the Gods Destroy: Theodore Tilton," which the HERALD published. Among other things, she condemned Tilton for switching his allegiance—for deserting Victoria C. Woodhull in her campaign to become President of the United States to support Horace Greeley, just because Greeley had promised him a post in the Cabinet. Then came the cutting paragraph:

"That he now regards his action as having been 'foolish and wrong' I have no reason to disbelieve, but the attempts to make Mr. Beecher equally responsible . . . a little schoolboy's snivelling—'He made me do it; if it hadn't been for him I shouldn't have done it'—ought to make him a laughing stock. I have said before that I believed that Mr. Tilton would make quite a man if he should live to grow up."

What few people could have thought possible had happened: The Woodhull had come to the defense of the Reverend Henry Ward Beecher, against her former lover.

. 22 .

The Free Lovers, Spiritualists, Suffragettes and assorted radicals who had rallied under the Woodhull banner were startled the next day when they read Vicky's open letter to the HERALD deploring publication of her story and claiming she had neither wanted nor permitted it to be printed. And the words that followed threw her adherents into downright consternation:

"But on the verge of its publication I remembered how, when they had cast me into prison and turned the whole world so much against me that . . . in the grated cell, before our iron bed, upon that stone floor, my darling sister and my angel kneeled with me, and how, as we prayed our cell was lighted up with spirit-light, and the power of Heaven overshadowed us, while a still small voice whispered comfort to our troubled souls, assuring us that help would come."

To the radicals, who in the main were irreligious, this was

blasphemy in reverse, and they were aghast. But that was not all, for, as Victoria continued:

"I remembered all this and also how wondrously it had been verified, and then with the proofs of the article in my hands, I went before the throne of grace and asked that Jesus come and show me the right. And He did come and He said: 'Stay thy hand, my child. All these things are committed to my charge. In the fulness of time all hidden things shall be revealed and you shall be justified where now you stand condemned. Wait!'"

Vicky's followers began to wonder. When Demosthenes had appeared before her, practically in the flesh, and had given her guidance they had been understanding. When Napoleon had instructed her what to do (his Empress Josephine also had chatted with Victoria) there had been no undue comment, and there was the same indulgent attitude when Alexander the Great had come on the scene to give Victoria some sound Macedonian advice. "Your body shall never know corruption," Alexander had confided, and The Woodhull in turn had relayed the message to her breathless lecture audiences. But now—when Jesus Christ in person introduced himself to have a long chummy talk with Victoria in Ludlow Street Jail—there were many who thought that this was too much.

The reporters, who could not imagine the lively and always-merry Tennessee in the role of a penitent kneeling on a cold stone floor, asked her to corroborate the truth of the Deity's visit. Tennessee said she had been asleep at the time.

· **23** ·

Victoria's "Tried as by Fire" lecture was her last radical pronouncement. Her interest in Spiritualism was vanishing, and with it her prominence in the movement, and she was more and more careful not to extol the glories of Free Love. It is not known why she changed her mind on these matters, but it is just likely that she had exhausted their possibilities, and knew it. It may have been at this point that she realized her militant fight against Respectability was lost. Since she was a creature of extremes, there was only one other way open to her. She now set out to do with the same vehemence and vigor what was seemingly incompatible with her character and background: She started to climb the steep slope leading to the goal at the summit—Respectability.

As the months slipped by she drew away from Colonel Blood, to whom the idea of anything religious was preposterous beyond discussion, and began to lean on her husband's inveterate enemy, mother Roxy. As old age crept up on Roxy she became more and more devout. She turned away from her old faith in Spiritualism and was received into the Catholic Church.

In time Victoria was to flirt with the Catholic Church, but to flirt only. However, it was evident to the perplexed readers of the WEEKLY and to her listeners on the lecture circuit that religion of some kind had gotten into her blood. Many of the erstwhile faithful suspected she was trying to form a new sect, with Victoria C. Woodhull as chief Deity. A majority of the WEEKLY readers regarded her abandonment of her former principles with distaste and referred to her as "Mrs. Judas," and the journal began to lose circulation, and money. On the other hand, the so-called "Christian element" and the "better people" of the country, so long her enemies, viewed her "conversion" with distrust. The Woodhull began to lose what old friends she had, and she gained no new ones.

· 24 ·

Much of Victoria's time late in 1875 and early in 1876 was taken by lecture tours and she crisscrossed the country talking on the subject of "Breaking the Seals." This was a plea for people to become purer, and a *defense* of the noble institution of marriage. The speech was published in pamphlet form by the WEEKLY but it did not sell well. (Victoria's list of publications was mounting: In 1873 her "Elixir of Life: Why Do We Die?" was printed, and in 1874 "The Scarecrows of Sexual Slavery"; but now she kept these works off the market.)

On the tour Vicky found people did not hate her, or love her, with their former fervor, though there were still many curious who were eager to see the once notorious Woodhull and willing to pay for the privilege; and it was a living.

Colonel Blood's influence over Victoria was definitely on the wane and she left him behind in New York, taking with her on the long jaunts mother Roxy, Tennessee, and daughter Zulu, who now was fifteen. Before starting her speech proper, Victoria would read several verses from the Scripture, and thereafter

she would hand her well-worn Bible to mama Roxy. Zulu would
entertain with Shakespearean readings, provided the passages
were pure, and Tennessee would recite poetry—good clean poetry. Newspapermen, remembering the flamboyant Tennessee
of happier days, did not think she had assimilated as much
purity as sister Victoria, but they noted she tried to subdue her
boisterous traits and to act less familiarly around men, no
longer edging close to them as she talked. She tried hard, but it
was plain her heart was not in it.

Now there were many suspicious and cynical individuals,
particularly among newspapermen, who believed Vicky's sudden desertion of Sin was merely a surface manifestation. These
skeptics pointed out that the sisters once again were close to
bankruptcy, and recalled the repeated begging appeals in the
WEEKLY, "to the generosity of the friends of true reform not to
withhold any pecuniary aid that they can constantly offer us in
this crisis." They also pointed at the open letter addressed to
Commodore Vanderbilt, wherein the sisters suggested that he
again become their "patron saint," open once more his fat
purse and keep Victoria "Queen in the domain of the affections, where so long she has been subject only." But, alas, old
Vanderbilt had given up spooks, he was eighty-one and less
susceptible to the potency of the siren call. He ignored the letter, or perhaps never was permitted to see it. It was only then,
so claimed the carpers, that opportunistic Victoria with her
characteristic verve, and Tennessee with great reluctance,
"turned square." These beliefs were widespread.

Then came the final blow to the most loyal of Victoria's followers. Each issue of the WEEKLY became cluttered up with
references to the Seventh Angel, Elisha, Hiddekel, Gihon,
Moses, and Malachai, and the readers deserted en masse to the
Crucible, edited by Moses Hull, a radical magazine which
kept its radical keel. Two valuable WEEKLY editors, Stephen

Pearl Andrews and Dr. Joseph Treat, went over to the *Crucible*. The Woodhull, whose right hand once used to display sparkling diamond rings and now clasped the Holy Bible, was derided in the *Crucible* for her "Search the Scriptures for The Truth" lecture she was giving, mostly in small towns; she was termed a "traitor," a "female Jesuit," and sneered at as "St. Victoria."

The press obtained by lecturer Victoria was good—but it was also apathetic. The Watertown, New York, DISPATCH commended her "deep-seated religious enthusiasm" and let it go at that. The Albany POST thought "her faith in her errors [is] so great that she becomes a power at once dangerous and fascinating," but the newspaper did not think the story was worth more than a few buried lines. "She made many friends in Kokomo and removed a false prejudice that had long been entertained against her," the Kokomo, Indiana, DISPATCH noted, and surely this prompted the question back in the big town, New York: What does The Woodhull want to do, make friends in Kokomo? "Not the least remarkable of the revolution wrought in the sentiments, feelings and conduct of the people of this country, and in the public press," said the Washington GAZETTE, "is that which has taken place in respect to Mrs. Victoria Woodhull." This was a nice little notice, but a few years before the name of Victoria C. Woodhull had been bannerlined on her visit to Washington, and, now that she was gripped with purity, the lecture hall was almost empty. There had been a time when the newspapers had jumped on her, heels first, belaboring her with stories covering columns and bringing attendant publicity, and the lecture halls had been jammed. Now. . . .

· 25 ·

In 1876 Victoria once and for all severed all ties with three of her former great loves: Spiritualism, Free Love, and husband Colonel James H. Blood. She did not, however, disavow woman's suffrage, but in this field she was losing authority. Mrs. Stanton publicly revoked a prophecy made earlier, that in the future histories of feminine emancipation, the name of Victoria C. Woodhull would shine.

The final break with the Spiritualists came when the WEEKLY printed a series of articles ridiculing materializations, manifestations, "Paraffin hands," and other occult mysteries. It is presumed that Tennessee, with her first-hand knowledge of the shadowy arts, wrote the exposé.

Victoria said good-by forever to Free Love in the June 10, 1876 issue of the WEEKLY. She insisted, in an open letter to what few readers she had left, that Victoria C. Woodhull never actually had been a supporter of Free Love, and that an examination of her record would show she always had been a sincere advocate of "the sanctity of marriage," as expounded in the Holy Book. Some people had been led to think that "I do not believe in marriage relations." This impression was quite erroneous:

"It is I who believe in the institution as a divine provision, but law alone cannot make it divine. There must be honesty, purity, intelligence, goodness. Nor do I believe in the loose system of divorces now so much in vogue. To me, this business is as reprehensible as the promiscuousness that runs riot in the land."

There were WEEKLY enthusiasts of long standing who gagged on reading these words, but, as they gagged, Victoria hurried to Boston where her pronouncement, for a change, had been given prominence in the newspapers. She followed up her letter by an explanation that the Free Love she had supported —*if* she had—was an altogether different kind than was commonly thought of. Victoria patiently elucidated:

"The *love* of God is *free* to all," ergo the expression, Free Love.

The Woodhull explained further:

"God is love, and Love is God." That is what Free Love meant to her, and always had. "Your abominable lust I abhor, and God's intelligent love I adore," she added, driving the point home in unintended rhyme.

The final break with her husband came in September, 1876. Three years before Vicky had publicly declared: "There is my lover; but when I cease to love him, I will leave him. . . ." The time had come. Despite her antipathy to "the loose system of divorces now so much in vogue," the Supreme Court of Kings County on September 18 granted her an absolute divorce, giving Victoria the right to remarry, denying that privilege to Blood. The grounds were adultery. Victoria professed to be quite shocked at what had happened to her marriage. She produced a witness who swore he had accompanied the Colonel to a house of prostitution. Blood did not deny the charge or fight the suit, and as long as he lived he never was heard to lift his voice against Victoria C. Woodhull.

· 26 ·

Vicky and Tennessee lived between lecture dates in quiet fashion at 75 East Tenth Street, only a door away from a church. They were selective when it came to choosing their friends, being careful to snub the "old crowd," and yet for some reason the Stuyvesants, Kimballs, Fishes, and other aristocratic families in their neighborhood did not seem to want to associate with them. They found, however, that their newly acquired piety brought them favor from an old foe—the law. At the request of the United States District Attorney, orders of *nolle prosequi* were entered to quash old indictments against Victoria and Tennessee for sending obscene literature through the mails. Two similar joint indictments, and another in a state court, were also *nolle prossed*. Now that the hullabaloo over the Beecher case was dying down, people began to think perhaps the sisters' sins had not been so great after all and that, as a pamphlet on the scandal put it, "It was that wicked Woodhull who blabbed on the streets [only] what had been whispered on the housetops."

The action of the District Attorney was welcome and comforting, and yet Victoria was not happy, for she found people did not flock to lectures on Purity with the same zest as they did to those on Sin. Lectures now were the only source of income for the Claflin family (which as usual was supported by The Woodhull) for, when Victoria printed the open letter about her undying belief in the sanctity of marriage, so many

WEEKLY readers canceled their subscriptions that the journal was forced to suspend publication.

This was the third, and final, suspension of the WEEKLY. Under Victoria's editorship the newspaper had run for slightly more than six years, from May 14, 1870, through June 10, 1876, with the exception of two intervals, both in 1872. Today, the files of this stimulating journal may be consulted in many libraries in this country, and, of course in Moscow.

Hard times loomed for the Claflin clan, and its burdens were not lightened when Dr. Joseph Treat published a pamphlet, "Beecher, Tilton, Woodhull: the Creation of Society." Dr. Treat, a former editor of the WEEKLY, had been among the most vociferous in denouncing the new religious trend of the journal. His pamphlet, which was as vicious and libelous as any ever printed (it will be considered more fully later), accused Vicky and Tennessee of every imaginable crime against morality, except incest. Treat was arrested on the charge of malicious libel, on the complaint of Victoria, Tennessee, and Colonel Blood, but was released on bail, and curiously enough there was no effort made to bring him to trial. Meantime, the spicy booklet sold tremendously.

This was the nadir in the lives of Victoria C. Woodhull and Tennessee Claflin. But their opportunity to make a new career, in a new country, was not far removed.

. 27 .

In January, 1877, old Commodore Vanderbilt, probably the wealthiest man in the country, died. The publication of his will was awaited with consuming interest. Who would get the money?—estimated at about $100,000,000. Two months after his death the will was made known.

At the reading of the will Vanderbilt's children smiled contentedly (this was before it was disclosed that their brother William Henry, Vanderbilt's favorite son, was to inherit ninety-seven per cent of the fortune) when the lawyer of the state droned on that Tennessee Claflin had been bequeathed a painting, and nothing more, and that Victoria C. Woodhull had been forgotten. Their gaiety was understandable, for the painting, "Aurora," a life-sized Venus with a few wisps of gauze around her middle and a Cupid wearing nothing but wings, had been given to Vanderbilt by Tennessee herself six years before. It was a bauble valued at but $2,000.

There was consternation on all sides, however, when it was announced that the Commodore had set aside certain large sums to be used for carrying on the noble work in Spiritualism —under the trusteeship and supervision of Victoria and Tennessee.

As it turned out, no one was satisfied.

Vanderbilt's two daughters and his second son refused to be content with splitting three per cent of the estate left them, amounting to a mere $3,000,000. They filed suit to annul the will. To their dismay, they found along with them Victoria C. Woodhull and Tennessee Claflin.

The sisters explained that it was sweet and thoughtful of the old Commodore to leave them funds for furthering the cause of Spiritualism—and of course they would obey his wishes and spend the allotted sum—but, actually, they felt insulted. They did not think the cash *left* them for Spiritualistic purposes was enough to make any impression on the dull and stupid bourgeois minds of the community, but luckily they happened to remember that Vanderbilt owed them a good deal of money, and they were willing to use the cash *due* them from the multi-millionaire to put the fantasmagoric faith across. (To some people it was quite a spectacle to see Victoria's interest revive in a cult whose priestess she was no more.) Victoria and Tennessee said they had consulted one of the best lawyers in town, who had drawn up papers, and so they would sue. They did not, however, immediately file suit.

The editor of the New York TIMES sent a reporter to interview the sisters, and the next day, May 13, his findings appeared in a column-long story. The Woodhull and Tennessee had hit the headlines again.

The interview took place in another of a series of homes occupied by the Claflins over the years, in the parlor of a brownstone house on Forty-seventh Street, off Fifth Avenue.

"Among Mr. William H. Vanderbilt's recent annoyances has been the presentation of a claim by Tennie C. Claflin upon Commodore Vanderbilt's estate for an indefinite amount, stated as 'over $100,000,' or in other words, '$70,000 with compound interest," the reporter's story started off.

The TIMES said he was shown the papers which would be filed—the next day—unless the claim was paid. The documents revealed that in the fall of 1871 Tennessee, the great and good friend of the old magnate, had called on him at his office on Fourth Street and handed him $10,000, a spare amount that she had come across, somehow, somewhere. She asked Vanderbilt to use the sum to speculate in stocks of his own New York Central and Hudson River railroads. Tennessee had requested that he keep the accumulated profits handy for her. She would call for them later.

In the spring of 1873, Tennessee and Victoria happened to be temporarily short of spending money. Suddenly, they remembered the sum on deposit with the Commodore. They had forgotten about it, completely forgotten. Tennessee sent her sis-

ter, Mrs. Miles (who was ready to testify under oath in court as
to the truth of the transaction), to pick up the money. The
Commodore was loath to relinquish the sum, which, he allegedly said, now amounted to $70,000, with profits. Vanderbilt
explained to Mrs. Miles that he had promised their old mother,
Roxy, who had besought him on bended knees, that he would
not hand over the money unless the sisters pledged themselves
to buy a home for her which would be as fine as any in New
York. Mama Roxy was prepared to swear this was true in court,
if a legal proceeding were necessary.

What with the numerous excitements in their lives, Vicky
and Tennessee no longer thought about the $70,000 that was
theirs. And then, some time in the fall of 1874, they had remembered it again. They called on the Commodore but he said
that, times being what they were, the money would be in safer
hands if they would leave it on deposit with him. The sisters
said they agreed, having full confidence in Vanderbilt's good
intentions and superior monetary wisdom.

That, said the sisters, was their story, and they were reluctant to publicize the facts of their absurd absent-mindedness.
The TIMES reporter's comment here was:

"Mrs. Woodhull and Miss Claflin protested yes that they had
no wish to give the matter publicity, but at the same time they
rattled off the details with a vigor that scarcely gave them
breathing space."

Vicky explained that this loan on deposit was not an isolated
example of the "fatherly interest [he had taken] in them ever
since." She and Tennessee often had left money with the Commodore to speculate on margin, and that Victoria herself had
had as much as $17,000 in his trust at one time. Vanderbilt
often had told them he intended to leave them half a million
dollars—a minimum—in his will. The sisters believed that he
had done just that, per his promise, but, inasmuch as they were

denied access to his private papers, they were helpless to en-
force its payment. Therefore, reluctantly and after prayer, they
had come to the conclusion that they were forced to sue.

The reporter asked if the sisters had any receipts or account-
ings for the money they had deposited with the Commodore.

No, they replied haughtily. That was not the way the three
did business. They trusted Vanderbilt and Vanderbilt trusted
them.

Surely the sisters knew, the newspaperman ventured, that the
Commodore had been getting on in age, and had they been
wise to entrust such a large sum of money to a person who
surely did not have many more years to live?

"At that time," said Tennessee, changing the subject somewhat abruptly, "he thought I only wanted my $10,000 back,
with simple interest." She sighed, and added, in a measure
enigmatically, "There were some facts that I knew, and that he
did not wish to be made public."

After probate of the will, Tennessee continued briskly, William H. Vanderbilt had sent a gentleman to see her to ask what
she would take in settlement of the claim. He had hinted that
$14,000 or $15,000 was a nice round sum, but Tennessee had
told him she would listen to no such deal. All she wanted was
her money back—the $70,000 which, with interest, would
amount to somewhere around $100,000, she had not figured
out the exact sum. Tennessee said the suit would be filed in
court the following day if a settlement was not effected. She was
awaiting the return of one of her lawyers, who had gone to the
Britannic to talk to William H. Vanderbilt, who was sailing for
Europe that afternoon.

"Understand," said Tennessee, "that Mr. Vanderbilt has
never denied the justice of the claim, but he hopes to force me
to accept anything he chooses to give, knowing that I am poor.

A man with his money is well able to settle any time, and I consider it a shame that we have been compelled to wait."

Victoria shushed her sister. She thought William H. Vanderbilt undoubtedly was a man of integrity who would live up to his obligations, but "We have been prevented from going to Europe," she pointed out. "We have had the papers ready to sign for over six months by which we would have been enjoying a profitable series of lecture engagements on the other side. We have lost over $100,000 by the delay already."

"If I had taken my $10,000 and interest," Tennessee put in, "I would have been paid long ago. But Mr. Vanderbilt will have to pay eventually. I have too much proof. I have over one hundred witnesses."

As the newspaperman jotted down her words, Tennessee added, significantly:

"If I was to tell you all I know, it would be worse than the Beecher case."

"It would make a splendid sensation article for the newspapers," The Woodhull interrupted, "if we gave you the reasons why Commodore Vanderbilt took such an interest in a paper that expressed the most radical of views, but our lips are sealed."

As the TIMES man left the house a cab drew up, a man got out and was ushered inside. The reporter returned to the stoop and was told the visitor was the sisters' attorney, who had returned from his interview with Mr. Vanderbilt, but neither Victoria nor Tennessee would comment on it, except to explain it was favorable to them. But again they said that they intended to begin suit the following day unless their honest and just claim was paid.

. 28 .

Exactly what did and what did not happen is not known, for the principals on both sides of this threatened lawsuit never revealed the details of what many people suggested was a "transaction."

This much is certain—

William H. Vanderbilt silenced his brother by presenting him with an income on $1,000,000 placed in escrow, in addition to his inheritance. He silenced his two sisters by giving each of them an additional $500,000.

As for Victoria and Tennessee:

Though known to be virtually penniless early in 1877, in the summer of that year they sailed for England, hiring servants and in a fine flourish four double cabins. They were questioned by ship reporters as to what had happened to the suit which they never had filed, but, as Vicky had mentioned to the TIMES man and as she now repeated, their "lips were sealed."

And, once arrived in Britain, Victoria and Tennessee rented a mansion at 8 Gilston Road, in fashionable West Brompton, a suburb of London.

Operation Virtue

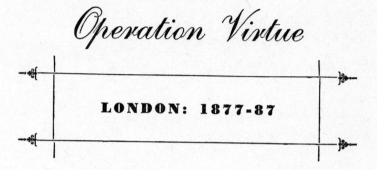

LONDON: 1877-87

. 1 .

It was hardly to be expected that Her Britannic Majesty, Queen Victoria, would send a delegation of Dukes to greet her namesake from across the sea, or that she would insist that the American Victoria dash straight from the boat at Southampton to Buckingham Palace; nonetheless, the sisters were disappointed at their reception upon arrival in England. When Vicky stepped onto the pier and glanced around expectantly, she found not a single reporter to interview her. Not a single reporter to interview the supreme orator, the standard-bearer of suffrage, the first woman to be given an official hearing before Congress, the only woman in United States history to be a Presidential candidate!

It was rather discouraging, and this discourtesy, or perhaps it was thoughtlessness on the part of the press and the Old Lady of Windsor, moved Victoria to act in characteristic fashion. As soon as she and Tennessee had settled in their West Brompton flat near Kensington she announced she would carry on her work in England by giving the orations which had so stirred the entire American nation. She did not want any personal publicity; she just felt it her duty to speak to the English people.

The Woodhull's debut was made in St. James's Hall in December, 1877. The London correspondent of THE NEW YORK TIMES predicted a sellout and he knew the reason why: "People want to see what a great American orator is like, specially when the speaker is a woman, and more specially when she is supposed to speak publicly on subjects which never enter the thoughts of decent and respectable women."

The reporter shuddered in print at Victoria's chosen subject —"The Human Body: The Temple of God." He confided to his American readers that "travelled Englishmen and women know that the women of the United States are not in the habit of talking about the human body in miscellaneous company in a way that would bring the blush to the cheek of her average British sister," and he predicted that "Mrs. Woodhull will come to grief between the Scylla of prurient curiosity and the Charybdis of current philosophy."

The newspaperman was wrong. Though the awful words, "the human body," indeed were spoken aloud by Vicky, her listeners soon felt they had been cheated, for instead of a daring, radical speech such as was her reputation to give in "the States," the talk was mild and decent. Victoria merely pleaded with English mothers to enlighten their children, to tell them where babies came from. "Those who went to St. James's Hall to hear something nasty, came away disappointed," the TIMES man recorded, "because she didn't go far enough." The reporter felt that Victoria had betrayed him.

English editors gave little space to the talk, but back in America it was like the old days. Newspapers told of the notorious Woodhull's attempt to form a British following and they wondered how long it would be before she announced her candidacy to run for the Queen's job. And back in London the same TIMES man prophesied the awful type of person Victoria would attract to her lectures and to her boudoir:

"Mrs. Woodhull will be sure to receive many letters and have many callers. I venture to predict that her correspondents will not be philosophers, nor her callers respectable women. There are a set of weak-backed sneaks in London who devote their wretched lives to running down women, to Argyle orgies, to the study of indecent pictures. They will be curious about Mrs. Woodhull. She is a rather good-looking woman, and she has circulated her picture."

This might indicate to the casual reader that Victoria had distributed pornographic pictures of herself. Actually, posters showing a three-quarter profile, with chaste religious mottos underneath, had been put in shop windows to advertise her lecture. But the journalist continued with his harsh predictions:

"Roués in search of a new sensation will call on her in the disguise of a philosopher. Over-educated young women will be among her visitors. She will attract just the sort of people who used to go to Khan's Museum of Anatomical Figures . . . the flippant, the morbid, unhealthy people who come under the special care of the Society for the Prevention of Vice will be Mrs. Woodhull's chief patrons."

This correspondent, as events were to prove, was not much of a seer. For among Victoria's visitors backstage after a lecture was a man three years her junior at thirty-six, a man of impeccable antecedents, very rich, finely educated, and regarded as one of the most eligible bachelors among the gentry of England. His name was John Biddulph Martin, Esq. He was a partner of Martin and Martin in Lombard Street, the oldest banking house in Britain, older even than the Bank of England. Mr. Martin asked permission—and quickly received it—to call upon Victoria. This tall, bearded, handsome banker, a graduate of Harrow and of Exeter College at Oxford had the poise of a well-bred gentleman, backed by wealth and prestige, and yet he had never married. He always had been firmly tied to—in a phrase of the times—his mother's apron strings. Now his astonished friends saw that he seemed gripped, as so many males before him had described it, by Vicky's "peculiar fascination." Victoria's caller hardly was a "roué" or a "weak-backed sneak." He moved in court circles and, it is safe to assume, never had been inside Khan's Museum of Anatomical Figures. John Biddulph Martin, Esq. was more likely to be seen at St. George's Hospital, where he was a life governor, or at the Charing Cross and Royal Orthopaedic Hospitals, or at the Society for the Promotion of Hellenic Studies where he served as Treasurer.

The wags of course would have their little joke. They suggested that Mr. Martin in his last-mentioned capacity perhaps had met Vicky's old chum, Demosthenes, and had been told to get in touch with her.

. 2 .

Reuben Buckman Claflin and his wife Roxanna had been left behind in New York, apparently for a good reason. The dispute over old Vanderbilt's will had flared up again. One-eyed Buck appeared in court and it was plain he was out to make trouble. He testified that the Commodore had wanted to marry his daughter Tennessee, and that he had witnesses to prove it. The judge quickly excluded the remainder of his testimony owing to possible disclosures bordering on indecency, and court was at once adjourned.

What happened then can only be guessed at. The next day father Buck announced the Claflin clan had no demands to make on the Vanderbilt estate and that he did not wish to testify further. Somehow, things had been settled to the satisfaction of all parties concerned.

His mission completed, old Buck decided to go abroad, and it was noticed he seemed unusually well stocked with cash. In London, Victoria and Tennessee announced that their father, Dr. R. Buckman Claflin, the rich and respected and retired judge, would visit them. Just why a judge should sport a doctor's degree was not explained. It was also announced that despite all the pressure brought to bear on him by prominent citizens of the city and state of New York, Dr. Claflin had refused to run for the United States Senate. He appreciated the honor of being elected to that august body, but it was more important that he see his beloved daughters.

The sisters also recalled for those uninformed in matters of their genealogy that their father was the direct and only living descendant of King Robert III of Scotland, 1340-1406. Accompanying Dr. R. Buckman Claflin on his voyage to England would be his wife, Roxanna Hummel Claflin, well known to high society in New York, and who herself was a direct descendant of the famous Hummels of Germany, and, through that distinguished family, of Charlemagne, whose pedigree was such as to need no comment.

· 3 ·

Bennie Tucker, the teen-age intimate of Victoria, had no love for the sisters when, as a near-octogenarian, he wrote his memoirs, yet he was forced to admit that:

"However unpleasant and disappointing may be the truth about Victoria and Tennessee, it is equally true that for years they were victims of the abominable liars. Blackmailers beset them continually . . ."

Victoria and Tennessee often were accused themselves of blackmail, and, though the evidence at times seemed damning, the charges never were proven in court. But there is little doubt that, as Tucker said, they themselves were blackmailed. A clear case for this can be established in the pamphlet, mentioned earlier, which was published in New York by Dr. Joseph Treat. Now, strangely enough, a reprint of the pamphlet began to circulate in London.

Treat, a former editor of WOODHULL & CLAFLIN'S WEEKLY, declared that he had turned against Victoria when she "got religion." He issued a booklet that even the callous newspapers of that age would not reprint because of its below-the-belt attack on the Claflin sisters. The full title of this sixteen-page pamphlet (spoken of before) was "Beecher, Tilton, Woodhull, The Creation of Society: All Four of Them, Exposed, and if possible Reformed, and Forgiven, in Dr. Treat's Celebrated Letter to Victoria C. Woodhull."

Treat declared his words had been written originally for publication in the WEEKLY but that the sisters had refused to print "any such revelations about themselves." Inasmuch as their "friends and subscribers have a right to know the truth about you," Treat had decided to issue the pamphlet himself, for the sake of establishing The Truth.

The good doctor appeared in the role of a frustrated lover as his story got under way. He confessed that, in his many years of fighting for Social Freedom:

". . . I idealized you as the embodiment of that principle, since *it* was my very self, you stand to me as one sacred and holy, and the very room in which I sat and wrote was transfigured every time you entered it, and the very sound of your voice heard through open doors thrilled every fiber of my being. Though we were nothing to each other, and both knew never could be, I was ready to die for Social Freedom, and why should I not give myself to you?"

Hurrying over the inescapable fact that he was not permitted to give himself to Vicky, Treat then leveled a series of wild and unsubstantiated and undocumented charges against her. He vowed as to the truth of the following accusations:

That, in return for the courtesy of Mr. James Kiernan of Brooklyn, who supplied bail when the sisters were on trial for circulating obscene literature, Victoria and Tennessee both and at the same time went to bed with the gentleman.

That the Reverend Henry Ward Beecher secured Victoria's silence during his civil suit trial by giving her $10,000 hush money.

That Tennessee's lovers were legion, her two favorites being Johnnie Green, city editor of the New York SUN, and Mr. Maxwell the broker, who once gave her $700 for sexual services rendered.

That when Victoria had had enough of Theodore Tilton's embraces she promptly took on top of her naked body one Mr. Machado, broker, of 53 New-Street.

That Mrs. Polly Sparr, a Claflin sister, acted as pimp for another sister, the ill-fated Utica Brooker.

That Treat himself had, at Victoria's instigation, written, carried and delivered notes appointing an assignation for Utica at The Woodhull's home.

That a son of another Claflin sister, Mrs. Margaret Ann Miles, had supported two women at one time, even though he was afflicted with a "private disease," and that Victoria and Tennessee had been proud of the little fellow, who was only twenty.

That when the sisters were campaigning against gambling in the WEEKLY they had been daily devotees of the "policy strip" in the rear of Clute's brokerage office at 205 Broadway.

That Colonel Blood wrote all of Victoria's speeches and also penned every one of her private notes to lovers.

That when Victoria traveled to Chicago to give her "Scarecrows of Sexual Freedom" lecture, she slept in a berth with a prominent Boston businessman, and when he asked what she charged, Victoria said $200, and the man paid up.

That . . . and so on, and so on.

Those were some of the choice accusations made by Dr. Treat. The pornographic pamphlet sold well at ten cents a copy, with Treat receiving a windfall. Eventually, he was hailed in court on the complaint of Victoria, Tennessee, and Colonel Blood, charged with malicious and obscene libel, and held in $1,500 bail for trial.

The months rolled by, and then the years, but no move was made to try Treat, who was demanding that he either be prosecuted or his bail money refunded. Then, on June 27, 1879, the sisters through their lawyers quietly dropped the case, three years after publication of the libelous pamphlet, for reasons best known to themselves.

Editors in the United States now began to speculate as to why the suit had been dropped, and this afforded them the opportunity of reviewing the lurid careers of the sisters. More and more rumors began to circulate in England about the notoriety of the American visitors. Libel laws being what they were then, and are today, in that country (where Coke originated the peculiar doctrine pertaining to libel: "The greater the truth, the greater the libel"), the newspapers were cautious in their comment. But American newspapers were distributed in England and the friends of John Biddulph Martin wondered if he had read about the strange life of his good friend, Victoria C. Woodhull.

. **4** .

Victoria made many attempts to be accepted by English society but, though backed by Mr. Martin and certain of his friends, she was cold-shouldered everywhere. It was difficult enough at the time for *any* American to be accepted in society (Bertrand Russell has recalled that a Duke at a garden party fingered his mother's skirts and bellowed: "I want to see if they are dirty, because I hear you only associate with dirty radicals and dirty Americans") and so Victoria found that because of the tar of her newspaper reputation the ambition was not likely to be realized. There were certain prominent people who were adamant when it came to accepting her; and, as will be seen, what at first was a stubborn antagonism later turned into a bitter and vindictive enmity.

Unable to stem what she called "the stored-up venom" of American editors, The Woodhull booked some lecture dates and delivered a series of talks extolling the nobility of Womanhood, in the hope of swinging public opinion in her favor. The English found the talks so nice and ladylike, and so boring.

Victoria then turned to the British press to spread what she called the truth about her career, lest they in the future should become interested in her past. The TRAVELLER printed an article on the "Martyr Woman," and it turned out that this spotless character had for unexplained reasons been subject to extortion and blackmail all her life. "A more unsoiled woman does not walk the face of the earth," asserted the magazine. It was revealed that only the grace of The Almighty Himself had prevented Victoria from committing suicide: "Three times did she stray to the river, but the mighty impulse of a million prayers ascending to the angels stayed her footsteps," somberly recorded the TRAVELLER. It was generally assumed the American visitor had paid to have the article published.

That was not all. Vicky wrote a long letter to the respected LONDON COURT JOURNAL, a letter most remarkable considering that the gist of her speeches had been printed thousands of times in hundreds of newspapers in the United States, and could be easily checked by anyone who took the trouble to do so. This letter, a complete repudiation of her life to date, was dated December 29, 1880, and bore the heading MRS. VICTORIA WOODHULL'S VINDICATION.

To those who might be ignorant of her abilities, Victoria modestly informed them she was a public personality "whose career as a successful platform speaker was unprecedented." She condemned various unnamed "unscrupulous and corrupt minds" and the "outpouring of calumny which was to assail my reputation." She railed against certain "cancerous tongues wagging gleefully with insinuations—direct accusations there

are none—calculated to be befoul an unsullied reputation and
an honored name—a name which I had flattered myself should
have long survived my mortal destiny."

Victoria's task, as she saw it, was to vindicate her "womanly
honour." To do this, she first explained away her connection
with Free Love. It was simple enough:

> "My name has been most unrighteously associated with
> what is known by the name of 'Free Love.' No viler an
> aspiration was ever uttered. No greater outrage could be
> inflicted on a woman. No deeper harm could be done to
> an innocent."

Victoria the innocent said that once upon a time she was the
"ostensible" editor of an unnamed journal in New York, which
of course was WOODHULL & CLAFLIN'S WEEKLY. Pulling all
the stops, she went on to explain what happened:

> And here, Sir, it behooves me to mention the manner
> in which my name first got mixed up in connection with
> a small section of the American community called 'Free
> Lovists,' for whom, ever since I became acquainted with
> their principles, I have entertained the profoundest ab-
> horrence.
>
> For several years I was the ostensible editor of a New
> York journal, the main object of which was the elevation
> of woman, politically, morally and religiously. I did my
> best to conduct the paper and keep it true to the purposes
> with which it set out. It happened, however, I could not
> always read and select the contributions sent me for in-
> sertion therein. My lecture engagements in distant part of
> the States, sometimes extending over one hundred nights,
> prevented such rigid supervision, or, indeed any super-
> vision at all. Still, I had not the slightest apprehension
> that any matter should find its way into the columns of

my journal calculated to lower its tone or taint its character. But it was not so.

Articles favoring Free Love appeared without my knowledge, which startled the readers of my hitherto spotless print. But the evil done did not rest here. I became inculpated as though I was morally responsible for utterances and doctrines which I loathe and abhor from the depths of my inmost being.

I now openly avow, with all the earnestness of righteous indignation, that during no part of my life did I favour Free Love even tacitly.

I only wish that this honest unreserved declaration, which, through your kindness I am enabled to make, would exonerate me from any degree of responsibility in the matter, silence serpent tongues, and clear my reputation from the slur which ignorant, unthoughtful or vindictive persons have cast upon it, reckless of the result.

This letter, when cabled to the United States, sent guffawing editors scurrying to the clippings, and naturally extracts of Victoria's many defiant speeches touting Free Love were reprinted. But in London there must have been many readers of the COURT JOURNAL who were mystified, for they had seen nothing against Victoria C. Woodhull in the English press. Undoubtedly the letter struck home in one quarter, however, in fashionable Overbury Court, where lived John Biddulph Martin, Esq., and indeed there were many who thought the words were addressed only to this strait-laced gentleman. In any case, Mr. Martin was seen more and more in the company of the charming visitor, and there were reports that an engagement would be announced.

"As long as I live there will be no engagement," Mr. Martin's aged mother supposedly declared. The authority for this statement is weak; an American newspaper quoted her as saying so.

Whether or not it was true, that is what happened. **And Mrs. Mary Ann Martin was to live for six more years.**

. 5 .

Meantime, Victoria had entered the political lists again, making her second bid to become President of the United States. (She had not run in 1876, a year when she was occupied in discarding Spiritualism, Free Love, and Colonel Blood and had a variety of other troubles to attend to.) Victoria announced early in 1880 that she had been cheated out of office eight years before through corruption of the bosses and by ballot-box juggling, but that this time she hoped and believed she would win. She intended to hire thousands of women watchers who would guard the polls on Election Day and see to it that the votes cast for her would be recorded.

Her campaign was run rather differently from that of other Presidential nominees. Those candidates stumped the United States. Victoria remained in England and conducted her campaign by remote control, but she was active enough in showering her native country with pamphlets extolling her Presidential qualities. Evidently she was somewhat dubious as to the efficacy of such tactics, however, for shortly before Election Day she stated that if she lost, which after all was in the realm of possibility, she would enter the 1884 race with greater vigor. She would spend the intervening four years in planning the perfect campaign, and, when election time came, she would make a whirlwind tour of the United States to permit the

voters to see her in the flesh. Victoria added that she was prepared to spend hundreds of thousands to gain certain victory in
1884. It was not specified whether this meant dollars or
pounds.

Victoria's pessimism was justified, for after the ballots had
been counted the results were:

James A. Garfield, Republican	4,449,053 votes
Winfield S. Hancock, Democrat	4,442,035 votes
James E. Weaver, Greenbacker	308,578 votes
Victoria C. Woodhull	0 votes

· 6 ·

As American newspapers speculated on The Woodhull's
chances of making a stunning catch in London, they noted that
sister Tennessee had not been idle either, matrimonially speaking. It was reported that she had snared an old man twice her
age, one of the richest men in all England with a fortune running into the millions—and this time it indubitably was
pounds, not dollars—and that a wedding was imminent.

All this was true, except for two minor facts: the marriage
was not to take place immediately, and, as Tennessee indignantly pointed out, the beau was *not* twice her age. He was
sixty-three, and Tennessee was thirty-five.

There was no doubt but that the luck of the Claflin sisters
had changed since their departure from New York. A letter
written by Tennessee to Francisco de Martin, a friend of the

family, reveals the full extent of her happiness. Tennessee's letter read in part:

"It was poverty and the terrible maelstrom of hell that surrounded us, but thank God we have escaped from that bad man Blood, but since we have been in this blessed old country we have been blessed. I am now engaged to be married to a gentleman who is richer than Vanderbilt and titled, and who worships his precious treasure, and Victoria will be married in a few weeks to one of the richest and into one of the noblest families. . . ."

Tennessee erred in saying that Victoria would be "married in a few weeks," but her boast of being engaged to a fabulously rich man was true. He was Francis Cook, a widower. Cook, however, was not titled at that time (he was the Viscount of Montserrat by courtesy of the King of Portugal, which did not count for much in England)—but that could come later.

Cook was an astute merchant. He had secured a monopoly on the importation of Indian shawls after Queen Victoria had shown a preference for them, and they became the rage, and he soon had quadrupled the immense fortune left him by his father, a retailer of linens. Cook lived in a mansion on the Thames, Doughty House, where he had a private art collection conservatively valued at two million pounds.

Tennessee now moved from her residence in West Brompton into a luxurious flat, splendidly named 47, Emperor's Gate, Cromwell Road, in a most fashionable quarter of London. She often entertained Cook there, and when she found that he was mildly interested in Spiritualism, she stepped back into the fantasmic world she had forsaken a few years before. Soon Tennessee was informing her wealthy admirer that the wraiths watching over him in the heavens above had come to her and imparted some advice—some very sound advice. Francis Cook should marry Tennessee Claflin, for his own good.

Mr. Cook was willing and his children, who were about Tennessee's age, liked their prospective stepmother. There were other relatives, however, who were inclined to view the matter in a decidedly antagonistic light, and so five years were to pass before Tennessee was to marry the millionaire, who by that time had reached the age of sixty-eight, presumably old enough to know his own mind.

. 7 .

In her vindication printed in the LONDON COURT JOURNAL, Victoria had promised the English public:

"In further justification of my innocence it is my intent to republish my journal at once. There in full particulars shall be given the manner in which articles got into WOODHULL & CLAFLIN'S WEEKLY bearing my signature. Those articles I utterly repudiate, more especially the one known as 'The Beecher Article.'"

Thirteen months passed before Victoria got around to issuing the paper, per her pledge. This time it was called WOODHULL & CLAFLIN'S JOURNAL, not WEEKLY, and there were no reprints of articles bearing her signature. Instead, the JOURNAL told the British people how its "ostensible editor" had been slandered and mistreated by the vulgar Americans.

The JOURNAL appealed to "the whole press of the world to aid us in unearthing those vile traducers who are wanton with our good name, which, though nothing to them is to us our all, dearer than life itself," but it was clear to what few readers the magazine had that the chief traducer had already been un-earthed: he was ex-husband Colonel James H. Blood.

Blood was excoriated for standing silently by at a time when Dr. Joseph Treat, "the vile mendacious vendor," sold his "malicious, obscene and scurrilous pamphlets" in the streets of New York. This referred to the "Beecher, Tilton, Woodhull" booklet mentioned earlier. It was insinuated that Blood was not only pleased with its publication but had supplied Treat with some juicy details. Blood, who should have been the gentleman and acted as his wife's protector, had not wanted to sue, and it was only when Victoria herself had obtained the indictment that the miscreant Treat was tried in court—to be found insane.

Several pertinent facts were omitted in this new and strange interpretation of what had actually happened. For instance, it was Blood himself who acted as co-complainant with Victoria and Tennessee in the legal action brought against Treat. And Treat, as we have seen, was never tried, let alone found insane. Victoria's "refutation," however, was necessary because the odious Treat pamphlet was being sold in London.

Perhaps Victoria's JOURNAL might have done well in the United States, but in England its few readers were apathetic. They did not know what the excitement was all about. As no one felt compelled to buy the tract, it was distributed free. And so it was that the Volume I, Number 1 issue of WOODHULL & CLAFLIN'S JOURNAL, published January 29, 1881, was the first and last printed. Vicky found, instead, a sounding board in an evening paper, of sorts, called the CUCKOO. People said it definitely was.

The CUCKOO, as editor Edmund Yates proudly pointed out, had the same number of pages as the famed PALL MALL GAZETTE (but the GAZETTE carried eight fat columns to the page, while the tabloid CUCKOO carried two) and on its staff were great writers who chronicled the doings in court and town, theater and sports. (Difficult as it would have been for Vicky to visualize at the time, there was a CUCKOO staff member who would be recognized as an even greater writer than she, who would achieve a notoriety that was to make her own reputation seem saintly by comparison—his name was Oscar Wilde.) The CUCKOO, however, was a consistent money-loser until into the breech stepped Victoria, possibly with the financial help of the rich banker, John Biddulph Martin, Esq.

Someone, anyway, pumped money into the dying journal, for it continued to publish, and its issues became chockful of apologies for the reputed dark past of Victoria C. Woodhull. The stories concerning her were touchingly headlined:

TRUTH CRUSHED TO THE EARTH
OH NO, IT COULD NOT BE!
THIS FAIREST, PUREST, NOBLEST BORN

Here is part of a sample article giving Victoria's own explanation once again, but this time with variations, of how she had been tricked, of how she had unjustly become known to the world as the Queen of Free Lovers:

"About twenty-five years ago a moral leprosy broke out in New York City. A Free Love club was founded, the direct objects of which were for a time hidden from the public. By and by it was discovered that members of this strange organization repudiated the marriage tie—in fact were the most pronounced opponents of normality.

"To such length did they carry their vile practices that the civil authorities were induced to interrupt their nightly orgies. This publicity broke up the club. It did not, however, sweep away the contagious impurity from the land.

"The high priest of Free-Lovism entertained advanced

views upon wedlock. Taking mean advantage of Mrs. Woodhull's long absence from New York City, he had opportunities
for airing his monstrous doctrines and uttering his blasphe-
mous sentiments.

"Mrs. Woodhull, who started her journal in 1870, was made
the scapegoat of the others' evil doings. She was arrested and
imprisoned as ostensible conductor of the print in which it was
attempted to pollute the fountain of public morality. Nor are we
surprised at this issue, seeing that one contributor, Stephen
Pearl Andrews—the high priest of debauchery—actually had
the audacity and unblushing effrontery to affix Mrs. Woodhull's
signature to his filthy effusions.

"But, it will be asked, why did Mrs. Woodhull keep silent?

"The answer is simple and satisfactory.

"She acted thus to exculpate her husband Colonel Blood,
who was the responsible editor and who was threatened with
lynching by an exasperated public. When the whirlpool of public astonishment and approbation reached her—the scapegoat
of others' enormities—her hands were tied, for personal feelings restrained her. She shielded him who should have been as
a right arm between her and the outer world. . . ."

"Cuckoo! Cuckoo!" chortled American editors as they reprinted this tidbit. Americans in London who were familiar
with the career of Victoria C. Woodhull were astonished at this
version. English readers, who could not figure out what was
going on, were equally astonished. But the astonishment of all
turned to disgust when the CUCKOO through an anonymous correspondent painted the depths of depravity of her husband,
Colonel Blood. The honest-to-God "true story" about Victoria's
illness in 1873 was revealed, the illness from which, as we have
seen, she recovered overnight. The tale, which proved to be a
boomerang, was this:

"It will be known to many of her friends that some years ago Mrs. Woodhull was in precarious health, failing day by day, many persons expecting her death. She has since discovered that she was near being the victim of poisoning. Mrs. Woodhull was treated by an eminent American physician as a pronounced poisoning case . . ."

Newspapermen in the United States found Colonel Blood living in near-poverty in Portland, Maine, still boosting Spiritualism, Free Love and Hypnotism. He was asked to comment on his alleged attempt to poison his wife. Colonel Blood's answer was dignified and restrained. He said he was following Victoria's career in England with all good wishes and had sent a life subscription to her new journal (not knowing that the magazine had suspended publication after one issue). He added that never had he commented adversely on The Woodhull, nor did he intend to do so now, or in the future.

As for the CUCKOO, it lost $25,000 of somebody's money in six weeks and was sold for a few hundred pounds to James Davis, proprietor of PAN. The CUCKOO is remembered today only because Oscar Wilde slept there.

Victoria had been away from her native United States for four years when, in 1881, she decided to revisit her homeland. She said good-by to Mr. Martin at Southampton and sailed aboard the *Gallia*, accompanied by mother Roxy, Tennessee, and daughter Zulu, and was greeted by large numbers of reporters when the steamship docked in New York on November 26.

The newspapermen noticed that Roxy had aged, that Tennessee had put on a little weight, though her figure was still good, that Zulu had grown up to be an unpretty girl, but that "Mrs. Woodhull has not changed in appearance since she made her home here, but talks more eloquently perhaps than she did then."

Victoria first was asked if she intended to reinstate her libel suit against Dr. Joseph Treat, as his pamphlet was still being hawked in the streets of New York.

Victoria replied, "My reception in England, especially among the higher classes, was very flattering."

She was asked if she would see ex-husband Colonel Blood, who happened to be in the city.

Victoria replied that she found "the English a whole-hearted, generous people," and that, when you came down to it, the citizens of France, Spain, Germany, Switzerland, and indeed those of the whole continent, Russia included, were graciously cheering her name. This made her feel humble.

She was asked if she would marry the wealthy English banker, Mr. Martin.

Victoria replied that everywhere she traveled she had been pleasantly received, and that she had come to America to arrange for an extensive lecture tour.

She was asked to comment on the death of her old friend at eighty-seven, Lucretia Mott, the grand old lady of suffrage.

The reporters now were given a straight answer. Victoria replied that Lucretia Mott had been of valuable assistance to her in the fight for suffrage.

One journalist told Victoria his office had just received a romantic story from Britain which revealed a secret—that the aristocratic Lord Colin Campbell, son of the Duke of Argyle, would marry a Miss Blood. Was this her daughter, Zulu Blood?

The question momentarily seemed to stun Victoria, and also daughter Zulu. Then it was evident from Victoria's chagrined expression that someone, somehow, had let the cat out of the bag. Victoria reluctantly admitted that, yes it was true, her twenty-year-old Zulu was the bride-to-be of Lord Colin Campbell, member of the famed Campbell clan of Scotland, but she refused to answer further questions about the romance and abruptly ended the interview.

The next day THE NEW YORK TIMES in its story about the visitor said:

"She takes deep interest in the proposed stage career of her daughter. This is the young lady published far and wide as the intended bride of Lord Colin Campbell, brother of the Marquis of Lorne."

To her New York friends Victoria confided that, there was no doubt about it, Zulu's engagement to Colin Campbell was a lucky strike. Victoria liked to open a copy of DEBRETT'S and read the social qualifications of her intended son-in-law. The young man's father, the Duke of Argyle, was also Marquess of Lorne and Kentyre, Lord Lorne, Earl of Campbell and Cowall, Viscount Lochow and Glingle, and Baron Sundrage of England. The son was a darling. The old Duke was a jolly fellow, one could not help but adore him; he was high up on the list to inherit the throne. Zulu was marrying into an *old* family. The Dukedom had been created in 1701, the title of Lord as far back as 1445, 436 years ago.

Zulu described herself as very happy, but shyly refused to say more. Victoria told reporters that she, too, was happy because of another honor that had been bestowed on her. At last her great work for suffrage had been recognized in the United

States with the founding of Claflin University in South Carolina. Victoria told reporters that, as they knew well, her maiden name was Claflin, and she was considering sending Zulu to the school for a few months before she got married. One noble gesture deserved another.

Alas, the storm soon broke.

It was disclosed in London that, true, Colin Campbell was to marry Miss Blood, but that she "was not the daughter of the American adventuress." She was Miss Gertrude Elizabeth Blood, daughter of Mr. Edward Maghlin Blood, a gentleman of high standing in English society.

And the dean of Claflin University in Orangeburg, South Carolina, hastened to announce that the school was not named after any kin of Victoria C. Woodhull. It had been founded in 1869, before the Claflin sisters had become abominably notorious.

As the cuckoo might have headlined it, AH, CRUEL BLOW! The Woodhull morosely decided to return to England. Once she had complained that it was enough to confound a lady, the way newspapers hounded her. Now that the reporters had been fooled, they left her alone. She was labeled a "back number," best to be forgotten and ignored. Once, the name of Victoria C. Woodhull, the bewitching Lady Broker, had been on everyone's lips, but now another beauty, Lillian Russell, was the rage. There was a vague similarity between the two. Lillian Russell was promiscuous in her love affairs, but the details never reached print, and she was accepted everywhere. Victoria had married twice, and was now angling for a third husband, and she was sneered at as a multiple-divorcée. The actress had many spouses, no one knew exactly how many, but when it was asked, "Why do so many people marry Lillian Russell?" there were merely good-natured laughs, not jibes.

When Victoria sailed, no reporters interviewed her at the

pier. But on reaching England she was greeted at the dock with deference and affection, not by newspapermen—but by John Biddulph Martin, Esq.

. **9** .

John Biddulph Martin had entered the banking firm of his family, Martin and Martin, in 1863, at a time when Victoria was living in squalor in Chicago with her alcoholic first husband, Dr. Canning Woodhull. Most other London bankers did not move in the highest circles of society because they dealt on the side in mercantile speculation and so were tainted with "trade." Martin and Martin never stooped so low because the firm had a reputation to conserve. The Martin business had been carried on in Lombard Street continuously since the reign of Edward IV in the fifteenth century.

Honors came easily to John Biddulph Martin. He was honorary Treasurer of the Statistical Society of Paris, Treasurer of the International Statistical Society, a member of the Council of the Society of Arts, and President of the Statistical and Economic Section of the British Association for the Advancement of Science. In short, Martin loved figures, as well as Victoria C. Woodhull. He contributed many papers on currency and banking to the JOURNAL of the Bankers' Institute. His essay, "Our Gold Coinage," published in 1882, proved of practical aid in the reform of gold currency. He loved to write on "the wear and tear" of gold coins, and his "History, Functions and Fluctuations of the Bank Note Circulation" enjoyed a vogue among those who were interested in the subject.

There were many in London who wondered why John Biddulph Martin, Esq., with such a conservative background, was so peculiarly fascinated by Victoria. What did this fastidious banker, who shied away from publicity, see in a woman who felt called upon to defend her reputation in the newspapers, and of whose real past he knew virtually nothing? Perhaps it is safe to say that Mr. Martin's was not too inquisitive a nature, and that he was content to believe what he saw with his own eyes. What he saw was a strikingly beautiful woman, even in middle age, proud and of a bold turn of mind, a brilliant speaker, which he was not, intellectually his equal, and quite unlike anyone he had ever met.

There were others who wondered why Victoria C. Woodhull was attracted by such a stolid person as Mr. Martin, after having been married to Dr. Canning Woodhull, a shiftless alcoholic, and Colonel James H. Blood, a fiery radical.

Victoria herself candidly explained why she was so captivated by Martin. It was quite logical, quite simple. Mr. Martin was a banker. In London. Victoria had been a banker. In New York. That was their bond.

There were some who thought this an oversimplification. Martin was a handsome man and surely must have measured up to her aesthetic standards. He was shy and pliable and in almost every way temperamentally her opposite; he was someone easy to handle. Money was important to her, but she thought primarily in terms of a security she had never had. It must be remembered that she always was and had been the provider for her large family. Most important of all, perhaps, Martin was a man of social standing and satisfied her yearning for respectability, the same respectability she had set out to destroy and now wanted for herself. And, too, the chances are she was genuinely fond of the man.

Eventually, the two told their closest friends that it was true, they intended to marry. They were engaged but would have to postpone their nuptials because of the old-womanish, stubborn resistance of one Mrs. Mary Ann Martin, owner of a silver cord. The mother threatened to disown, and, worse, to disinherit him if he married his American sweetheart. And Mrs. Martin lived on and on.

· 10 ·

True to her promise, Victoria proclaimed she would for the third time become a candidate to be President of the United States. This time, she said, all political portents pointed to sure victory.

There were many English gentlemen in circles frequented by Mr. Martin who were horrified at the thought of one's wife running for public office, and particularly when she always lost. Martin seemed to like the idea, however. After all, it was the Presidency. A big job, in a big country.

There had been a time when Victoria called upon the Communists of her day to support her in Presidential campaigning. Now, in 1883, it appeared she was backed by a group on the other side of the fence. Victoria issued a "Woodhull Manifesto" to her followers across the Atlantic, and elsewhere:

"This call goes out from England issued by Victoria C. Woodhull, supported by British capitalists."

The Manifesto summoned "the people of all Europe, America and all the world [to] rally round her standard and support her in her right to represent and to work for the people of America," though how the citizens outside the United States were supposed to cast their votes for an American was not explained.

There followed the ringing appeal:

"Upon receipt of this call, let every city, town and village in all Europe, and in every state and territory in America, by public announcement, summon their meetings, pass resolutions, appoint delegates, take minutes of such meetings, and send the same to the secretary of this call, to be put in form and to be used as campaign material."

The Woodhull Manifesto was sent to editors in the United States and attached to it was a proof sheet of an article said to have appeared originally in THE CALL of Paris. This was a plea for Americans to elect Victoria C. Woodhull President because of her supreme fitness for the job, and was labeled as Most Important, because of the world-wide reputation of its author, Victor Hugo. After many newspapers had risen to the bait it was discovered (the pity of it!) that Victor Hugo's recommendation had been forged. Exactly who forged it was anybody's guess.

There was, surprisingly enough, a surge of response from American citizens, and mailbags stuffed with letters were delivered to Victoria's political headquarters at 32 Thistle Grove, South Kensington. This was because of an announcement in the Manifesto that a three-day convention would be held in St. James's Hall, Piccadilly, to nominate Victoria as Presidential candidate, and that all delegates would have their steamer passage as well as all expenses for their visit paid by Woodhull backers, those English capitalists.

There were thousands of Americans who, visualizing a free trip to London and back, wrote Victoria enthusiastically in support of her campaign. We are behind you, hurry and send the tickets, they cried. It appeared that St. James's Hall would be packed, come convention time.

Victoria promised in her Manifesto that she "is again ready, with all her wonted devotion to her country and to the cause of humanity, to take this work upon herself and give unreservedly all her strength, enthusiasm and all the wealth she has accumulated, to the result of this election."

These were splendid words, but it is sad to relate that the delegates, with-all-expenses-paid, never met in convention, for no convention was held.

. 11 .

The mother of John Biddulph Martin was in failing health and so the wedding of the loving couple seemed not far distant. Then, to Mr. Martin's dismay, to Victoria's consternation, to the horror of Tennessee, who was also trying to establish her respectability, and to the hilarious cackles of their enemies, there appeared in one of the best-known magazines in the world a serialized novel. The *Cornhill Magazine* published *The Siege of Paris,* by the American writer Henry James.

The parallel between the career and character of Nancy Headway, the heroine of Henry James's story, and Victoria C. Woodhull was all too apparent. The plot was this:

Nancy Headway is a wild and unfledged American beauty who has been married and divorced a number of times. "I'm known from Chicago to San Francisco, if not personally, at least by reputation," James has her declare. Nancy is an adventuress from out of the West, with a lurid past, but, as James explains, she "had become a great critic and handled many of the productions of the age with a bold, free hand."

Nancy goes to New York to conquer the city by her personal charm, and for a while she succeeds, but her notorious past catches up with her and she is snubbed by society. She travels to London, driven by ambition to turn the tables on her traducers by making a top-drawer marriage. She attracts to her, in spider-fashion, Sir Arthur Demesne. He is a Tory, wealthy and conservative, and moves in the rarefied atmosphere of British aristocracy, but he is a weak and colorless individual. Sir Arthur's greatest interest is in statistics and economics.

From here on, Nancy's exertions as a social climber are an approximation of The Woodhull's own strivings toward respectability, but in the end James's heroine triumphs and is married to the baronet. She takes a minor place in society and, though regarded as a celebrity of a scandalous sort with an unmentionable past, is accepted in some circles because of her charm and magnetism.

A reporter from Joseph Pulitzer's New York WORLD interviewed a close friend of Henry James, and this was the gossipy story printed in the newspaper:

"I understand you had a noted model for your heroine in your new novel, 'The Siege of Paris,' " remarked an American lady to Mr. Henry James.

"Nobody has a right to say the character is actually drawn from life," answered the novelist, laughing as he spoke. Notwithstanding this quasi-denial it is an open secret that the heroine referred to is the well known American, Mrs. Victoria C. Woodhull.

The "Siege of Paris" is one of James' latest works. It

> describes the intrigues of a scheming widow whose past
> reputation will not bear investigation. A young nobleman
> falls desperately in love with her, but his mother will not
> listen to his proposal to marry her. Finally the Lord's
> mother dies and the marriage takes place. . . .

After the *Siege of Paris* appeared in *Cornhill Magazine* it
was published as a book in Great Britain and the United States.
The chuckles over Victoria's discomfiture were plentiful, but,
just like the fictional Nancy Headway, she was to have the last
laugh. For, seven months after Henry James had married off his
"heroine," the novelist's plot came true. On October 1, 1883,
shortly after the death of Mrs. Mary Ann Martin, her son took
as his wife Victoria C. Woodhull in a private ceremony attended only by close friends. Six years had elapsed since the
two had met.

"It is quite a mistake to suppose that most of the Americans
who marry Englishmen are rich," the WORLD of London stated
in that year of 1883. This at least was true of the marriage of
Victoria. She brought her husband nothing but a dubious past.
He brought Vicky money and an impeccable background.

. **12** .

Victoria pointed out to one and all that the Nancy Headway in
Henry James's novel was a person of obscure antecedents. So,
she explained, the character could not very well have been
modeled after her, not with *her* family tree. The pedigree was
double-barreled, the lineage on both sides of her family being

aristocratic. She was descended on her mother's side from the Hummels of royal blood in Germany—but of course the Hummels flourished centuries before Germany was known as Germany—and on her father's side from various excellent kings of Scotland and England. There were others outside of royalty in the family tree too, for both branches were shot full of illustrious personages. Take one example: the blue-blooded Alexander Hamilton, first Secretary of the Treasury of the United States, was an ancestor. (This was an unfortunate selection, as Hamilton was a bastard.)

The Woodhull issued a brochure said to have been documented and authenticated by four prominent genealogists, all unnamed, thus baring her ancestral background for the whole world to see. The pedigree ran something like this:

Once upon a time, years and years ago, there was a man named John Dandridge.

John Dandridge had two daughters, *viz.*, Anna and Martha.

Now, jumping back to the fourteenth century, there was a King and his name was Robert III of Scotland, and, a little later on there was another King, and his name was James I of England.

Among the descendants of these two kings were the Dukes of Hamilton. And among the descendants of the Dukes of Hamilton was a fellow named Thomas Hamilton.

Thomas Hamilton married the first Dandridge daughter, Anne.

Their grandson was Dr. R. Buckman Claflin, the father of Victoria Claflin Woodhull Martin and Tennessee Claflin.

That took care of Victoria's pedigree. Now—and here was a surprise!—it seemed that Victoria and her new husband were related, in a distant sort of a way.

Because, once upon a time there was a man named George Washington. George Washington married Martha Dandridge, the second daughter of John Dandridge.

Penelope Dandridge [just who she was, no one will ever know] married Michael Biddulph.

Michael Biddulph's grandson, John Biddulph Martin, Esq., married Victoria C. Woodhull.

The brochure was mailed to editors of American and English newspapers and magazines, sent to libraries, and distributed free to any who desired to have it as a keepsake. The pedigree of course is a complete concoction, except for the fact that Washington did marry Martha Dandridge Custis. Actually, old Buck Claflin's ancestors were poor Irish emigrants, and Roxy's father was a German-Jewish peddler.

. 13 .

Victoria moved out of her West Brompton house, husband Martin left his diggings in Overbury Court, and the two moved into a roomy but somewhat somber mansion at 17 Hyde Park Gate. Once a visitor entered the front door he found himself in a hall adorned with marble busts in niches. He walked upstairs to the drawing room and there was a huge white bearskin rug on the floor. Scattered around were Martin's statistical trophies, framed letters and commendations, and against a background of purple velvet there was a silver statue of Nike. Nike had the body of Nike, but the face was that of Victoria. Everywhere there was expensive bric-a-brac, so much in fashion. It was quite a place, Victoria's American friends admiringly told her. She knew that, but, it wasn't the White House.

For, after the 1884 elections in the United States, it was clear Victoria would have to remain with Nike at 17 Hyde Park Gate. The campaign had been spirited—it had been a six-way race, and for the first time The Woodhull faced another woman as a competitor. She was an old compatriot, Mrs. Belva A. Lockwood, a Suffragette nominated to run for the high office by the very party Victoria had founded, the Woman's National Equal Rights Party. It was a consolation that Mrs. Lockwood did not poll any more votes than Victoria, though the over-all returns were discouraging. Again the American public had been finicky. The results were:

Grover Cleveland, Democrat	4,911,017 votes
James G. Blaine, Republican	4,848,334 votes
Benjamin F. Butler, Greenbacker	175,370 votes
John P. St. John, Prohibitionist	150,369 votes
Belva A. Lockwood, Equal Rights	0 votes
Victoria C. Woodhull	0 votes

Chagrined at her poor showing (though actually her votes had not fallen off from any cast in past elections), Victoria announced that she might not run again in 1888. This was not a threat. There was a chance she might change her mind.

. 14 .

There was good news on the other side of the sisterly fence, however, for the romance between Tennessee and old Francis Cook was blooming. Tennessee confided to her friends she was fascinated by the man, terribly in love with him, in fact. He was now sixty-seven, but lively for his age. Tennessee said the two would marry, but she was frank about it: The old boy might take a year or two to make up his mind.

There was no doubt about it, Tennessee was being courted (the envious said she did the courting) by a highly eligible wooer. Her sister's husband, John Biddulph Martin, had a place in society, and a million dollars or so. Francis Cook did not move in high circles, for after all his father had been a linen-draper and when one came right down to it that was what *he* was too, but he was worth more than twenty million dollars, and that, as Tennessee put it, was the nicest thing about him.

The trouble was that there were some people, relatives of Cook's and sundry busybodies, who opposed the marriage. They spread all sorts of tales about the background of Tennessee and her sister Victoria. The situation was further complicated by the damnable way in which irreverent American editors handled the sacred matter of nuptials. These editors chortled, not in privacy but in black print as they described the romance as a vulgar May-and-December affair, inspired, on Tennessee's part, by greed.

When such stories were printed, however, the editors usually wished Tennessee happy fishing in her quest for a rich husband. Victoria seldom earned the good wishes of the press in any of her enterprises, but editors always had a warm spot in their hearts for the friendly, easy-going Tennessee. They pointed out it might be just another example of a smart Yankee putting it over on the bumbling Englishman. And they shook their heads wonderingly in print at the possibility that the raffish Tennessee might become Lady Cook, for old Francis Cook had made so many handsome contributions to causes favored by Queen Victoria (a cause, to her, was erecting a statue of her dead husband Albert) that it was believed he would be rewarded with a knighthood, at the very least.

. 15 .

In the spring of 1885 Victoria again visited her native country. Tennessee stayed home to be with Cook, for they were getting along nicely and a prolonged absence might have broken the spell, but Vicky's husband Martin and daughter Zulu tagged along.

To Mr. Martin's amazement, the reporters who met them at the pier and the friends they encountered later in the city, all addressed his wife, Mrs. Martin, as Victoria Woodhull. What was worse, John Biddulph Martin, Esq., famous in England for being the head man of the country's oldest bank, famous for his many published works on currency, his treatises on statistics and his lofty position in society, was boorishly referred to in an offhand way as "*Mr.* Woodhull"!

Mr. Martin quickly decided they should sail at once for a

civilized land, and Victoria was inclined to agree with him, for her reception by the press was irksome. The reporters derisively asked her, in front of Martin, if she intended to run for President again, and there were mocking queries about her pal Victor Hugo and about Zulu marrying young Colin Campbell.

The Martins scarcely had settled down in a hotel suite when there was an incident that caused Victoria's husband to have the luggage packed. A newspaper described Victoria as "that contemptible scut." Mr. Martin considered horsewhipping the editor, but was dissuaded when it was pointed out that slander by American newspapers meant nothing. (True; Dana of the SUN called Pulitzer of the WORLD "a bastard swindler" in print, and Pulitzer countered by describing Dana as "an unmitigated scoundrel," and later on the two had dinner together.) So Victoria, Martin, and Zulu returned posthaste to London, and a few weeks later a spiteful interview about The Woodhull appeared in the WORLD with an American who fancied himself a gentleman:

> I went over on the *Oregon* with a party of friends . . . We saw a good deal of an old lady travelling with her daughter and a niece . . . and before we reached the other side the old lady presented her cards to me, as well as to my companions, and invited us to call upon her in London.
>
> The cards simply read, "Mrs. J. B. Martin" and of course I had no idea who that lady was. I, however, thought I would call once, for you know a man can call anywhere.
>
> I went to the address given, and was ushered into a beautiful parlor. The walls were covered with valuable paintings, and all around were scattered gold and silver cups and medals . . . Shortly after, a handsome woman entered the room and advanced toward me. Her face was

strangely familiar, though I could not place it for a moment.

"I believe I have met you before," said Mrs. Martin, advancing. "I am an American. Before I was married my name was Victoria Woodhull."

I was never more taken aback in my life . . . After leaving Mrs. Martin's house I went to see a lady who occupied a high social position in the American colony and related my adventure. She was much entertained and begged me to return some time, telling me that everyone was eager to hear all about the family affairs though no lady cared to venture in the house.

The smug New Yorker who permitted this petty interview to be published did not explain why The Woodhull's face had seemed "familiar," as he presumably had met her on board ship, nor why Victoria on ship was an old lady and in her home a handsome woman. For Vicky, who cherished being presented at the Court of St. James's, it meant that her hopes, if not blasted, had to be postponed because the incident was reprinted in a London sheet. What must have vexed her even more was that she, the seductive Victoria, had been called an old lady as she approached forty-seven.

· 16 ·

Now old Francis Cook's serenity was upset when the career of his lady love, Tennessee, was reviewed in the American press, all because of an unseemly squabble between two of her sisters in New York, Mrs. Margaret Ann Miles and Mrs. Polly Sparr.

Tennessee with a lordly gesture had sent some oil paintings to Mrs. Miles. Among the lot was the "Aurora" originally given by Tennessee to Commodore Vanderbilt and bequeathed back to her in his will. Mrs. Sparr was outraged at such favoritism. She claimed "Aurora" as her own, saying Tennessee had intended to give it to her. Sister Margaret Ann refused to give up the treasure. A deputy sheriff called and seized the painting. Mrs. Sparr at once took it to Kerrigan's auction rooms on Willoughby Street, put it up for sale, and the story was in the newspapers.

Mrs. Miles went to court and denounced her sister as a thief. Mrs. Sparr filed a countersuit, describing her sister as a lewd slattern. Finally, due to the intercession of Victoria, who pointed out that the wrangling and ensuing publicity was not helping Tennessee in her all-important task of marrying one of the richest men in England, the case was dropped by mutual consent.

. 17 .

Victoria's castle in Spain had hove in sight when John Biddulph Martin attended her 1877 lecture in St. James's Hall. Tennessee's came into view, in the literal sense of the phrase, when she met Francis Cook, for he owned one of the most famous castles in Europe, though in Portugal, not Spain. And now, in October, 1885, the London correspondent of THE NEW YORK TIMES cabled the astonishing news across the Atlantic:

"The sisters, so well known in America, have fallen on their feet. Mrs. Woodhull made a stroke when she became Mrs. Martin, wife of the head of the firm of Martin & Co. [*sic*] in Lombard Street, and Tennessee is much envied as the wife of Francis Cook . . ."

It was true. On October 1, 1885, forty-four years after his first marriage, the Viscount of Montserrat, known in England as the incredibly rich Francis Cook, took another wife. Tennessee, aged forty, was described as a spinster.

The ceremony in Kensington was attended by hundreds of guests who were lavishly entertained, in contrast to the quiet wedding of Victoria and Martin. Tennessee moved into Doughty House high on the Thames in Richmond, Surrey, and along with her trotted mother Roxy. Father Buck, a doddering oldster of eighty-nine, was left with Victoria at 17 Hyde Park Gate.

Tennessee now began to live in great style. Gone and forgotten were the distant New York days when, as she once said, she struggled to support her "deadheads" in cramped quarters. Doughty House was a showplace, an imposing stone and brick structure built in 1751 with all of the appurtenances thought necessary at the time—a paved courtyard, a fountain, a cottage on the grounds, a wrought-iron staircase, cherubs littering the garden and, naturally, a lily pond.

It was enough to confound the moralists, American newspapers noted. When the Claflin sisters had left the United States an awful and shabby existence had been predicted for them; yet now they were wives of two of Britain's wealthiest men.

The career and riches of old Francis Cook were reviewed at length and the story made good copy:

Francis Cook was born in 1817, the second of seven children. His father's firm, which Cook was to make the largest of its kind in the United Kingdom, was located at 21-23 St. Paul's Churchyard. Acting both as manufacturer and importer, the company built up an immense trade throughout the world by selling silk, woolen, and cotton goods.

Francis Cook started to work for the concern, which became known as Cook and Son after his father made him a partner, and when the father died in 1869 he, the eldest of the family after the death of his brother, was left the bulk of a fortune of two million pounds—the equivalent to about ten million dollars.

Cook had married for the first time in 1841—four years before Tennessee was born—and his children were about her age. The title of Viscount of Montserrat was conferred on him by King Luiz of Portugal in 1864, at a time when the girlish Tennessee was traveling through the United States in a medicine show. He earned the distinction of Viscount (which is below an earl or count and above a baron) by spending half a million pounds near Cintra on the Portuguese seacoast, bringing prosperity to a district which had fallen into decay. He had purchased there in 1856 the palace and castle of Montserrat, said by some travelers to be the most desirable country seat in Europe. The estate once had been owned by William Beckford, who wrote the oriental fantasy, *Vathek*, and was immortalized for its beauty by Byron in "Childe Harold's Pilgrimage." Cook restored the gardens, known for their magnificence, and added a few square miles to the original property.

The palace-castle of Montserrat was a grand showplace, but Cook's pride, and indeed the pride of England, was the art gallery which he established in Doughty House, his country estate. The pictures alone in the collection were valued at two million pounds. In Doughty House there also were other collections, antique rings, Italian majolica, bronzes, ivories, tapestries, and statuary.

Americans were awed as they read about the wealth of Francis Cook, and it was hard to believe that Tennessee, who had hurriedly left New York for London under suspicion of blackmail less than eight years before, now could stroll, in her own home, through a private gallery of art unrivaled in England and the world. The collection contained nearly five hundred paintings and most of the famed old masters were represented. But the New York GRAPHIC, which could inject a note of lubricity even when describing a funeral, mustered moral indignation as it described one picture hanging on the walls of Doughty House, right out in the open where decent and God-fearing people could see it. The GRAPHIC professed to believe that this painting, which was of Diane de Poitiers, the Duchess of Valentinois who was the mistress of Henry II of France, should be locked deep in the trunk where the dirty books were hidden. The portrait, by François Clouet, showed the King's paramour nude to the waist, with breasts outflung and nipples erect, and with a come-quickly look in her eyes. Horrible! The GRAPHIC demanded the picture be removed, but England did not listen.

. **18** .

As the year 1885 came to a close, there died within six weeks' time two men whom Victoria alternately adored and despised. The death of one, father Buck Claflin in November, was accompanied by outpourings of grief; the demise of the other in December, Victoria's ex-husband, Colonel James H. Blood, was unmentioned and unmourned in the Martin and Cook households.

Victoria's own feelings about the peculiar behavior of her
father had been frankly described to Theodore Tilton, who, in
his *Golden Age* biography of The Woodhull wrote:

"The father, at times a Mephistopheles, waits until the inspiration of cunning overmasters his parental instinct, and, watching for the moment when his ill word to a stranger will blight
their [Victoria's and Tennessee's] business schemes, drops in
upon some capitalist where money is in their hands, lodges an
indictment against his own flesh and blood, takes out his hand-
kerchief to hide a few well-feigned tears, claps his hands with
an unfelt agony, hobbles off smiling sardonically at the mischief he has done, and the next day he repents his wickedness."

According to the doctor's certificate, father Claflin at eighty-
nine simply had died of old age. According to Victoria, he
would have lived on and on, had it not been for the New York
WORLD. The SUN in New York printed a bitter, explanatory
note from Victoria:

> Sir:
>
> My father, Reuben B. Claflin, died of grief caused by
> the malicious libel published in the *World* of October
> 25th. Has not our family suffered enough? Please insert
> this notice for our heart-broken family.
>
> Victoria Claflin Martin

It is unlikely that old Buck died from shame after reading
about the visit of the anonymous New Yorker to Victoria's
London house, for, long senile, he had been prostrated for more
than a year by paralytic strokes.

The father of the Claflin clan was given a quiet funeral; Victoria and Tennessee said they would wear black for a few
months, and that seemed to be the end of the matter. But there
was a strange aftermath. It had happened before to the sisters
that when a family member died—Utica Brooker, Dr. Benja-

min Sparr, Dr. Canning Woodhull—someone had spread rumors that the deaths were not by natural causes. Now, an anonymous letter was posted to Mansion House, the residence of the Lord Mayor of London. The note, signed "Justice," found its way into the newspapers. It read, in part:

> A mysterious death occurred on the nineteenth of November of a much respected and honored citizen by the name of Reuben B. Claflin. His papers were spirited away as well as the will that is known to have been made by him, including money and bonds. His death was sudden. His sickness and burial was very mysterious. It would be well to have this matter investigated at once by the proper authorities, as delay may defeat the ends of justice.

Victoria and her husband, accused by inference of euthanasia or worse, inasmuch as old Claflin had died in their home, hired detectives to track down the author of the malicious note and posted a reward for the apprehension and conviction of the slanderer. Then suddenly the hunt was called off. It was believed that mother Roxy, who was in her dotage and acted increasingly more irrational, had, though she could not write, for reasons known only to herself managed to have the message sent. Now it began to dawn on the sisters just who it was that had inspired similar rumors in the past. Soon after, Roxy, an octogenarian, conveniently passed away and one source of the sisters' difficulties ceased.

After leaving New York the Claflin family had used Colonel James H. Blood as a public whipping boy to explain away any derelictions blamed on them, but as long as he lived he never was heard to attack his wife. Bennie Tucker, who knew the Colonel well, wrote that "I always found Colonel Blood to be an honest, whole-souled, open-hearted, open-handed, generous gentleman." Victoria viewed her ex-husband differently.

After Colonel Blood had been divorced from Victoria he had fallen into obscurity, and, no matter how he tried, he never again could attract public attention. He ran a stand at Coney Island and tried his hand at odd business jobs, but failed. An old friend, Frank Fogg, gave him an editorial post on a little country weekly in Maine. Then he drifted up and down New England, practicing Hypnotism, preaching Free Love, touting Vegetarianism, trying to cure the sick with "Spiritual Healing." Early in 1885 he married again, though forbidden to do so by court decree. His bride was the mother of Frank Fogg, who was a man his own age. The widow had money and she financed an expedition to mine gold in Africa. Colonel Blood believed he would make a fortune.

Instead, the Colonel, at the head of a party cutting its way through the jungle in the British Gold Coast, was stricken by "the fever." A few days later he died, aged only forty-eight, and was buried in that faraway land.

When the news reached his wife in the United States, she had the body exhumed and shipped to Brooklyn. There he was put to rest once more. The second Mrs. Blood and her son, friend Frank Fogg, were the only mourners at the grave. No flowers were sent, no minister attended the rites. There was scant mention of his death in the newspapers, which were no longer interested in the once fiery and controversial Colonel. And there were no condolences sent by his one-time wife, who, living in London, had put disturbing thoughts of the past out of her mind.

· 19 ·

The year 1886 got under way auspiciously for the forty-year-old Tennessee. "Dr. Claflin, of Iowa, who is here," the London correspondent of THE NEW YORK TIMES cabled his newspaper, referring to Hebern Claflin, the youngest brother of the sisters and another member of the family who appropriated the title of doctor, "swells with pride over his sister, Lady Cook. . . ."

The news, so welcome to the Cooks, who were members of "the trade," was true. A few days after his sixty-ninth birthday Francis Cook was elected Fellow in the Society of Arts, and on March 16 he was made a baronet by Queen Victoria, and so became Sir Francis Cook. It was well known that Cook had been aiming for a title somewhere between a knight, whose rank is not hereditary, and a baron, with its privilege of being addressed as Lord. The baronetcy conferred upon him fell in between. Baronets are commoners with a hereditary title. Tennessee had for some time been experimenting with her name. She had called herself T. Celeste Cook, and Tennie C. Cook, and then Celestia Cook. She tried using her Portuguese title, the Viscountess of Montserrat, but the British sniffed at such foreign ennoblements, so she dropped it. Now she did not need to search further. Lady Cook had a fine ring to it. "A far cry, indeed, from Homer, Ohio," observed a Cleveland newspaper.

The honor accorded to Cook was hardly unexpected. It came five months after he had taken eighty thousand pounds from his bank account and founded Alexandra House in Kensington Gore, where lady students in music and art were tutored free of charge. The name was a tribute to the then Princess of Wales. Cook paid off, so the Queen paid off in return with the baronetcy.

It is possible that Vicky, who had always been recognized as *the* Claflin sister, resented the idea of Tennessee becoming a Lady, a real English Lady, but then new honors came to the Martins as well. John Biddulph Martin contributed many articles on currency and banking to economic magazines. The history of his venerable firm, titled *The Grasshoppers in Lombard Street,* was received graciously by critics, and is used today as a reference work. Husband Martin served as President of the Royal Statistical Society, was founder and Treasurer of the British Economic Association, Treasurer of the International Institute, and honorary Treasurer of the Bankers' Institute. He was in demand for talks on currency in Europe and America, and less and less was he known by his Yankee cognomen, "Mr. Woodhull." It was thought for a while that he would receive a knighthood, but this never came to pass.

The kudos bestowed on Mr. Martin was most pleasing to Victoria, but then there was a scandal, one of those dreadful scandals followed so avidly by the London papers and the American press, involving a relative of hers but eventually dragging in the unsullied name of Victoria C. Woodhull. It happened in October, 1886, and strangely enough there was a man named Martin who figured in the case. He was not related to Victoria's husband; he was a Spaniard, the respected Fernando de Francisco Martin, Chancellor to the Consul-General of Spain in New York and Secretary of the Spanish Naval Commission.

Victoria's sister, Mrs. Polly Sparr, had always had a special talent for creating embarrassing situations and making the most of them, to the horror of her relatives. In the late 1850's she had married Ross Burns, but her life with him was unhappy, for the man appeared to have no future. Polly deserted Burns, leaving in his care their one-year-old daughter, Rosa, and went to live in Cincinnati. There, in 1860, she met Dr. Benjamin Sparr, who wanted to marry her. Luckily, so she explained later, at the same time a letter reached her from Kansas saying that Ross Burns had died. Polly and her father, Buck, wrote to inquire further about it, but that was during the days of the John Brown troubles and the mails were irregular. So Polly went ahead and became Mrs. Sparr.

Ross Burns, it turned out, was very much alive, and he went on to become a rich man and to carve a political career for himself, becoming Lieutenant-Governor of Kentucky. At the age of fifteen his daughter, Rosa, married a Charles Farlan and the marriage was quite a success until it was discovered that Farlan had neglected to divorce another wife. Farlan decamped, leaving Rosa pregnant and destitute, and he was never heard from again. At this juncture, however, Ross Burns died just in time to leave Rosa a fortune of $40,000. When Polly Sparr heard the news she hastened to invite daughter Rosa back into the bosom of the family.

Rosa did not get along with Polly, whom she regarded as an unmotherly soul. She was attracted to Fernando de Francisco Martin, an elderly man, almost three times as old as herself. Rosa described him, with remarkable candor, as someone who was "a friend and more than a father." Rosa moved from her mother's wing and went to live with Martin in his Thirtieth Street house, taking her inheritance with her.

Early in 1886 Rosa died. When her will was probated it was found that she had left all of her legacy to Martin, and nothing to her mother. Mrs. Polly Sparr was outraged. She sued in Surrogate Court to set aside the will. She claimed that her loving daughter had promised to leave her the money, and that Rosa had died following an abortion which Martin had insisted upon. The body was exhumed, an autopsy held, and the charge found unproved.

In the suit that followed, the names of Victoria and Tennessee, Rosa's aunts, were tossed around with abandon by both litigants. Martin testified that Victoria and Tennessee had told him years before about their niece and had asked if he knew of some kind man who would like to take care of such a young and pretty girl. Martin said he then had attended some Free Love meetings held in Victoria's "Psyche Salon" on Twenty-third Street, and was horrified at the way Sex was so freely discussed in front of little Rosa—so horrified in fact that he had taken Rosa away from the den of iniquity to his own bed, for her own protection.

Polly Sparr was equally harsh when considering her sisters. Before she was called on to give evidence she told a HERALD reporter:

"What about the club Mrs. Woodhull started in Twenty-third Street? She had to foster Free Love. Just because my sisters were public characters, people pitched into their club. Free Love and social clubs, indeed!"

The newspaperman asked Polly about reports that she herself was a Psyche Club habituée and about the rumor that she was a bigamist. "I've got the marriage certificates of both my husbands," she replied, missing the point, "and I was honorably and legally married, let them say what they will."

It is not known whether Polly was assured beforehand that Victoria and Tennessee would support her in the suit; in any event, when she testified under oath she was careful not to defame her sisters, particularly in one interchange:

Q. Did you not publicly charge Victoria Woodhull and Tennessee Claflin, your sisters, with murdering Dr. Sparr when he was found dead in a hotel in 1871?

A. I did not.

The lawyers of Fernando de Francisco Martin then introduced as evidence newspaper clippings showing that Polly had accused her celebrated sisters of murdering her husband and robbing him of $5,000, and that an investigation had found the charges unwarranted. Moreover, they put in the record a letter written to "Dear Mr. de Martin and the two Rosas" (Martin also had a young and pretty stepdaughter surnamed Rosa living with him). This letter was unsigned but was accepted as evidence because of the return address on the envelope: "T. Claflin, 47, Emperor's Gate, Cromwell Road, London, England." Martin's attorneys attempted to show by this letter, which was dated Sunday, November 7, 1880, that before their spectacular marriages Victoria and Tennessee had openly approved of Martin living in sin with their young niece. The message read, in part:

"How glad I would be to see you and dear Rosa. If you will come over and bring your daughter and Rosa I will send you three tickets for over and back and while here it won't cost you a penny, and you may better your prospects for you may rest assured, if I could aid to brighten your future, Victoria and I will do so, for I am satisfied that you have taken good care of Rosa and that you love her and she loves you."

After this, the case was immediately settled out of court, but the newspapers delighted in reminding their readers that the now respected Lady Cook, a baronet's wife, and Mrs. Martin, a banker's wife, only a few years before had invited as their guest in London the elderly individual who lived with their teen-age niece in unsanctified circumstances, to say nothing of a beautiful and young stepdaughter.

John Biddulph Martin was so angry that he wrote a letter to the editor of the New York HERALD. He said he was considering

suing somebody for libel, that he was certain as to the innocence of his wife, whose name was being thus besmirched, and
then added:

"Referring to reports of the case of Sparr vs. de Martin that
recently appeared in your columns, it is impossible to remain
silent or to refute *seriatim* the innumerable falsehoods and ma-
lignantly libellous statements and insinuations that have been
directed in that law suit against my wife, Victoria Woodhull
Martin.

"They originated, to our certain knowledge, in personal malice. They have been revived in certain false evidence in the said
law suits; and they are now being re-echoed in the more
unprincipled portion of the London press. I can only stigmatise
them, one and all, as infamous falsehoods."

This letter was not written in the style of a man at home in
the field of statistics and, also, Mr. Martin always referred to
his wife as Mrs. J. B. Martin or Mrs. John Biddulph Martin,
but never as Mrs. Victoria Woodhull Martin. The letter points
to the hand of Victoria, and it was not to be the last of its kind
supposedly written by husband Martin. And there never was
any suit for libel.

· 20 ·

In October, 1886, a visitor arrived in England. His previous
trip to the British Isles had been made twenty-three years before, when he was merely famous. Now he was famous and notorious, for he was the Reverend Henry Ward Beecher. When

he lectured in London he was greeted by thousands, for many people regarded him as the greatest living American, but it is safe to assume that Victoria C. Woodhull was not among his admirers. Questioned as to his opinion of Mrs. Martin, Beecher shrugged and dismissed her as an inconsequential blackmailer. When he returned to his homeland, New York bay was crowded with saluting vessels, and the bands played "Hail to the Chief" as he stepped on the pier. The following March he was stricken with paralysis and died soon afterward. His death was widely mourned, particularly so by Mark Twain, but his sorrow was of a different nature. The publishing house which Twain owned had given Beecher a $5,000 advance to write his autobiography. Three weeks later the Reverend was dead and Twain found himself with an unfinished manuscript and a paper loss which he estimated at $100,000.

The Fruits of
Respectability

ENGLAND: 1888-1927

. 1 .

Early in 1888, correspondents in London sent a routine paragraph to their New York newspapers. The Woodhall sisters, those notorious Americans, had been arrested on a charge of having swindled the late John Gill of Manhattan out of a large sum of money. In a decision handed down by a British court, American authorities were permitted to secure extradition of one of the sisters to stand trial.

This item sent the reporters hurrying to the clippings in the morgues, and the paragraph was rewritten and expanded to make column-length stories. There was much speculation as to which of the Woodhull sisters had been brought to dock. Most editors were inclined to think it was Victoria, and said so. They pointed out that, inasmuch as Victoria had announced she would run again in the fall Presidential election, this would be the first instance in history when a candidate for the office would at the same time be tried as a thief.

On hearing the news, Vicky, in Paris with Martin, who was to make a speech before some international bankers and Tennessee, who was vacationing in Sir Francis' palace near Lisbon, were aghast. They sent vehement, protesting cables to New York.

Eventually the newspapers apologized: it had been a misunderstanding. The sisters arrested were named Woodhall, not Woodhull, and their first names were Alice and Harriet. As is always the case, the acknowledgments of error were made in a terse paragraph buried deep in the back pages.

This example of what would later become known as yellow journalism was nothing when compared to the indignity suffered by Victoria and Tennessee at the hands of what they believed should have been members of their own set.

John Biddulph Martin, who was President of the Athletic Club in London, announced that its members would give a banquet for their wives. A spokesman of a clique high up in the social world that was determined never to speak, even by way of introduction, to what it considered the two American adventuresses, let it be known that all decent people would boycott the dinner if it were attended by Victoria and Tennessee. The boycott did not come off, but there was not a single lady who dared sit at the large table reserved by Mrs. Martin and Lady Cook, or to approach it with the usual social greetings. The sisters sat there scarlet-faced, surrounded only by men, but they were *gentlemen.*

. 2 .

The news that the Americans had been put in social Coventry was soon discussed in the drawing rooms, and Victoria and Tennessee reacted characteristically by launching a counter-attack. They realized the futility of preventing American newspapers from rehashing certain unsavory episodes in their careers, but they saw a chance of suppressing unfavorable items in the British press, where the laws of libel were stringently enforced. So the sisters started a Campaign to Educate the People to The Truth.

This amazing personal crusade was to extend over the years, and during that time there was an avalanche of newspaper and magazine articles, pamphlets and full-length books, all extolling the purity of the two Claflin sisters. The pamphlets and books were sent to the leading libraries in Britain and the United States, and even as far away as Australia, where they may be read today. The proofs of newspaper and magazine articles, together with a selected list of pamphlets, were mailed to editors everywhere. What was left was put on sale, and, when unsold, was given away, to anyone.

The output of this material was staggering in quantity. Much of it presumably was written by Victoria and Tennessee, some by authors who signed pen names to these effusions. There were carefully excerpted speeches made by the two Claflins in their New York heyday, with the pruned versions being presented as originals; there were articles merely stretching the

truth, and there were some which were downright forgeries.
Only a few choice stories will be considered here:

The "reprint" of an article that allegedly appeared in the
New York SUN of June, 1876, praised the sisters for their unimpeachable background and for their conduct in fighting the
valiant battle for Suffrage. This not only was a forgery, but an
inept forgery, as the article, supposedly published in 1876,
mentioned that in 1877 Victoria and Tennessee left New York
for London.

A pamphlet, "The Alchemy of Matrimony," reminded all
readers of the royal blood coursing through the Claflin veins.
The lineage of mama Roxy ("It is but natural the ladies revere
such a mother") was played down, but it was pointed out that
papa Buck ("He was tendered many political positions, which
he invariably declined, preferring the serenity of private life")
was the scion of "one of the oldest and most aristocratic houses
in England." The pamphlet asserted that "No one of their ancestry ever was a drunkard, a convict or a pauper," a statement
wrong on all three counts and a curious kind of defense by any
standard.

Victoria issued another pamphlet in which she said she had
never supported Free Love. There had been a misunderstanding, somewhere. What she *had* supported had been "Stirpiculture." And "Stirpiculture" was merely the breeding of special
stocks or races, by bringing together the best blood—a doctrine
Hitler and the Nazis preached half a century later. Unmentioned was Victoria's own definition of Stirpiculture, given
in WOODHULL & CLAFLIN'S WEEKLY of November 2, 1872:
"Stirpiculture, or the scientific propagation and cultivation of
the human animal, demands free love or freedom of the varied
union of the sexes."

A tract selling for ten cents, "One Moral Standard For All," written by one M. F. Darwin, explained how the sisters had been incarcerated in a New York jail only because they dared openly to support woman's suffrage.

A bulky booklet called "A Page of American History, 1870-76," quoted from a long poem supposedly written in 1873 by the famed bard, William Cullen Bryant, in his New York EVENING POST with a rousing salute to Victoria:

> The much-dreaded 'naked truth' has reached
> The public ear through the silver-tongued
> Woodhull, the brave.

Victoria was so enchanted with Bryant's tribute to her genius that she had it published many times over. Unfortunately, however, it later was revealed that Bryant never wrote the free verse encomium and it never appeared in the EVENING POST, or in any other paper, in 1873, or in any other year.

To give the English people an idea of the innocent little journal they had published in New York, Victoria and Tennessee issued a "sample copy" of the old WEEKLY. Actually, it was of course no reprint. It was newly written, consisting of delicate, ladylike appeals to American women to stand up for their rights.

There were many more such publications: "Brief Sketches of the Life of Victoria Woodhull (Mrs. J. B. Martin)"; "Paradise Found"; "Pharmacy of the Soul"; "Aristocracy of Blood"; "A Fragmentary Record of the Work Done in America, 1871-2"; "Some Thoughts about America"; all of which presumably were written by Victoria. Among the works supposedly presenting the true story of Victoria and Tennessee and their careers by other, and unprejudiced, authors were: "A Great Reformer: Victoria C. Woodhull Martin," by Anony-

mous, "History in Biography," by Henry E. Branch; and
"Synopsis of the Lives of Victoria C. Woodhull and Tennessee
Claflin," by G. S. Darewin.

Victoria devoted so much energy to putting out all these publications that her fourth campaign to become President of the
United States (for the unpredictable woman had changed her
mind again) sorely suffered. She admitted that, frankly, she
had given so little time to running for office that it was doubtful
if she would be elected. Vicky was right. Cleveland received the
popular vote, Harrison got the electoral vote and became President, and Victoria's counted ballots were the usual number cast
for her. The results of the 1888 race were:

Benjamin Harrison, Republican:	5,440,216 votes.
Grover Cleveland, Democrat:	5,538,233 votes.
Clinton B. Fisk, Prohibitionist:	249,506 votes.
Alson J. Streeter, Union Labor:	146,935 votes.
Victoria C. Woodhull:	0 votes.

. 3 .

Victoria and Tennessee knew the people who snubbed them.
They were always women, never men, social she-wolves who
saw the two sisters as interlopers, and, to make it worse, American interlopers who were trying to break into their tight-knit
ranks. Being snobs, perhaps they were justified, for that was
exactly what Victoria and Tennessee were trying to do. But
there was no justification for the malicious offensive taken by a

certain few of the clique. *Their* identity was not known, otherwise they would have been denounced by the sisters. It may seem incredible that these persons (or perhaps one person) would be so vindictive over the years as to spend large sums of money to discredit the American intruders, but the record shows this is what happened. And it is not so incredible when one considers the nature of these enemies.

Victoria and Tennessee were violent partisans of violent causes, causes which demanded a change, and, as always was the case in history—and still is—when you disturb the status quo you make violent enemies. Victoria particularly upset the Philistines, outraged the rulers of society and confounded the mealy-mouthed moralists because she was so effective in undermining their dogmas. As Gerald W. Johnson wrote so perceptively about Victoria:

"She attacked and seriously damaged several of our most pompous and venerated frauds, including the double standard, the legal ascendancy of the male, and Pecksniffian religion. . . . It was the belief of the righteous, which they had done their best to translate into action, that she should have been dressed in a yellow robe and incinerated in an auto-da-fé."

So the terrible sisters had to be punished for their heresies. And here, as happened so often before, the Claflin women abetted their own enemies.

It is astonishing to contemplate that Victoria and Tennessee, brilliant in their own fashion and having achieved wealth and a name known in two hemispheres, were both obsessed with explaining away their past actions and had absolutely no sense of proportion or self-preservation when it came to keeping what they had fought to get. If they had only left well enough alone, they might have had peace and quiet. But that was apparently more than they could bear, and so the flood of self-justification continued.

This time it was Tennessee who asked for trouble, and she got it. She distributed a passage from one of her books that had been published in New York in 1871, *Constitutional Equality: The Right of Women,* and declared that her words, printed in the United States eighteen years before, stood on their own in the England of her day. The passage was:

"There are thousands upon thousands in this country who hate us with an inveterate hatred; who think us the personification of everything that is bad, who honestly believe that no fate could be too cruel for us to endure, and yet not one of these people, *of their own knowledge,* know a single fact to justify their convictions."

The italics were Tennessee's, and the challenge was accepted. The shadow enemies of the sisters hired copyists in New York to dig deep into the old files of the WEEKLY, and into the newspapers, and to obtain interviews with their antagonists in America. These documents were incorporated into pamphlets and sent to prominent individuals. Usually the words of the sisters were reprinted out of context—as if their actual utterances were not damning enough—and they proved horrifying to the leaders of London's social world. There it could be read in merciless type: The rampage of mama Roxy, Utica's habitual drunkenness, Tennessee's admission in court that she had acted the humbug for years to support her "deadheads," the continual rows between all the Claflin sisters and relatives, Victoria's defiant admissions on public platforms that she was a Free Lover, and proud of it, her statement that when fresh out of Ludlow Street Jail she had put her "body in the gap" to raise money for the WEEKLY. The dignified and socially correct John Biddulph Martin was brutally informed in print what his two predecessor-husbands had been like. Colonel Blood was described as a shady medicine showman with many aliases, who had married Victoria two years after he had lived with her as man and wife. There were the old stories of husband Dr. Woodhull and his constant delirium tremens, of Victoria living for years with two husbands in the same house, and perhaps in the same bedroom. Theodore Tilton was named as authority for the last charge, being quoted in a passage from his *Golden Age* biography of The Woodhull.

Tilton when questioned by newspapermen said he only had polished (with his rare-sparkling-old-wine phrases) the biography, which was written by Victoria and her husband, Blood, and for whose truth they had vouched. Destroyed by the Beecher scandal, his marriage broken, Tilton had gone to Paris, where he lived in poverty for twenty-five years, drinking too much, playing chess and writing poetry until he died, and, though he must have been tempted, for he needed the money, refusing to write his memories of Victoria C. Woodhull.

One of the defamatory pamphlets, "The Sexual Problem," which was quite a title in itself in Victorian days, was so obnoxious that Sir Francis Cook, who perhaps adored his wife but who never felt moved to defend her in public, for the first and last time openly protested. He joined Mr. Martin in taking an advertisement in the London TIMES in January, 1890. Proof sheets were drawn and sent to all American and English editors. The advertisement read:

£1,000 REWARD

Mr. John B. Martin and Sir Francis Cook will pay the sum of ONE THOUSAND STERLING to anyone who shall reveal the names of the person or persons concerned in the conspiracy to defame their wives, Victoria C. Woodhull, now Mrs. John B. Martin, and Miss Tennie Claflin, now Lady Cook, and who shall give such evidence as shall secure a conviction.

TWENTY POUNDS will be paid by the above mentioned gentlemen for the names of the author and printer of an obscure and libellous leaflet entitled, "The Sexual Problem," that has recently been circulating in England . . .

TWENTY POUNDS also will be paid by the above named gentlemen for the names in any paper, issued in England, that has published a recent libel against their wives.

Though one thousand pounds was a considerable amount of money, no informer stepped forward and talked.

. 4 .

When word reached Victoria and Tennessee that the revengeful clique had sent investigators to the Midwest, and particularly to Ottawa, Illinois, where the sisters once had lived, and that the sleuths were said to be questioning old settlers about the Claflin clan's past, they decided it would be best to carry on the fight in the United States. They rushed to Southhampton and took the fastest steamer to New York, and along with them went Mr. Martin and Zulu. Sir Francis Cook begged off—he never fancied being interviewed even by the genteel newspapermen of Britain—and went vacationing at his Montserrat palace.

The reporters who boarded the *Trave* in New York bay on April 25, 1890, saw that the wealthy ladies had brought one hundred pieces of luggage with them, and they noted, too, that the once lovely Claflin sisters were aging. After all The Woodhull was nearing her fifty-second birthday, Tennessee her forty-fifth.

"Lady Cook and myself had hoped that our return home

would be unknown," Vicky announced as Mr. Martin retreated to the background. Little credence was given to these words, however, for she seemed willing enough to talk, though her statements were somewhat conflicting.

"I have come over here with my husband and Lady Cook on a pleasure trip and not bent on libel suits," Victoria told a TRIBUNE man. But to the TIMES reporter she disclosed that their visit "had to do with recent publications of an unpleasant nature."

The TRIBUNE representative wanted to know if they had been annoyed much by blackmailers. "A large number of letters were sent us, but they did not annoy us," replied Victoria.

The distinguished English visitors were asked if they had any comment to make on the current activities of their old acquaintance, Anthony Comstock, who was upset because a photograph of a naked statue was being displayed in a New York shop window. (Comstock would soon threaten to sue dealers in athletic goods because they were advertising, with illustrations, men's elastic supporters; and to bring into court a person who sold a reproduction of a painting, "A Gunner Aboard the *Yankee*," in which could be detected, if one had keen sight, a sailor completely nude, about half an inch high.) Victoria did not care to discuss Mr. Comstock, who, she said, was at times accomplishing good work.

Victoria informed her interviewers that she would be staying at 142 West Seventieth Street, with her sister, Mrs. Denis W. O'Halloran (Margaret Ann Miles, who had remarried and become friends again with The Woodhull), where she would be available to the press. She warned them to be on the alert for libelous stories which were being fabricated and spread to defame her good name. "The press in this country is generous," she declared. "I have confidence in American manhood, and know that I shall be vindicated."

Victoria's faith in the generosity of the press undoubtedly was severely shaken when the Brooklyn EAGLE splashed over its front page the history of two notorious "adventuresses," i.e., Victoria C. Woodhull, alias Mrs. J. B. Martin, and Tennessee Claflin, alias Lady Cook.

The story, which was ghost-written, appeared under the signature of Inspector Thomas E. Byrnes, a tough Irishman who later became New York's Chief of Police and acquired a smelly reputation. Byrnes reviewed the careers of the two sisters, and he was most unflattering. He seemed to remember them as little better than common streetwalkers who were in jail more than out of it. Other newspapers picked up the EAGLE story.

"I will incur any inconvenience to obtain justice and redress," solemnly announced John Biddulph Martin. "It is not a question of damages. No damages, however exemplary, would be any satisfaction for injuries that cannot be measured by dollars."

Mr. Martin and Victoria went to police headquarters to have a talk with Inspector Byrnes. They demanded that he refute his accusations. "I am a public official and any statement I make I may be held responsible for," he coldly informed his visitors. "And you have the courts to which you can have recourse, of course."

Victoria and husband departed quietly. They were questioned outside by the ever-present newspapermen. "Inspector Byrnes assured us solemnly that he never gave out the facts coupled with the names of the Woodhull-Claflin sisters, and that he had no evidence," Vicky told them. "The Inspector has made a manly reparation and that is all I can ask at his hands," she went on. "He confessed that he knows nothing about my past life and that the use of his name has been unwarranted."

Inspector Byrnes was surprised when he heard this. He denied the story and said that he was willing to face any libel suit that might be filed. He had had a witness to the talk, and he insisted that Victoria merely rambled on about the injustice being done her fair name and tried to give him some pamphlets to read.

Bewildered, but not too much so, the reporters returned to Victoria. Victoria explained that Byrnes had made a "manly apology," and that ended the matter. "For years I have been exposed to the merciless and devilish malignity of an enemy," she continued. "Marked newspapers have been sent to English newspapers, banks, friends and leading scientists, to destroy our reputation."

The reporters wanted to know who this mysterious enemy was. Victoria said she did not know. Then she remarked, her voice choked:

"My little girl [meaning Zulu, aged twenty-nine] said to me this morning, 'Mama, if these men continue to attack you, we will die together in each other's arms, down in the East River.'"

The reporters were not much interested in Zulu's reactions. They wanted to know if Victoria intended to sue the Inspector.

"No, by no means," she answered. "Such a case might take years. I might be dead when the case was closed."

What did she intend to do to obtain the "justice and redress" demanded by Mr. Martin?

"I shall appeal to the newspapers for fair treatment and through them to the people," declared Victoria. "My court shall be in the public press and its readers shall judge of the attacks which have been made upon my reputation these many years."

. 5 .

"The newspapers! Sir, they are the most villainous, licentious, abominable, infernal—Not that I ever read them! No, I make it a rule never to look into a newspaper."

This feeling, expressed by Sheridan in *The Critic*, surely was shared by Mr. Martin, for, only a few days after Victoria had made her wish that the American press be her court and the readers her judge, such an opportunity came. Authorities in Ottawa, Illinois, announced that an old indictment against Tennessee, charging manslaughter and fraud, had been revived. Lady Cook was branded a fugitive from justice. Officials said they had been searching for her since June, 1864, for twenty-six long years, when she had fled from Ottawa on receiving the news that a grand jury had returned the indictment.

Ottawa authorities, eager at the chance of getting their names in the big city newspapers, obligingly disclosed why Tennessee had been indicted, though actually the event had happened so long before that none of the town officials were now alive. The facts, if true, were damaging. "Doctor" Buck Claflin and his troupe, consisting of Roxy, Victoria, and seventeen-year-old Tennessee, had arrived in Ottawa in 1863, rented a hotel, the Fox River House, and turned it into a cure-all cancer emporium. Claflin's advertisements "guaranteed cures" for quite a number of ailments—"fever sores, home diseases, scrofula, piles, sore eyes, heart and liver complaints, female weaknesses, consumption, inflammatory rheumatism, asthma, neuralgia, sick headaches, dropsy in the chest, and fits in vari-

ous forms." Doc Claflin's temple of health also advertised itself
as qualified to give neophytes full instructions in a "Cult of
Love," but the Midwesterners had not been sufficiently sophis-
ticated to make this a paying proposition. The medical end of
the business had been the moneymaker. Cancer was the Doc's
specialty. The disease, so puzzling to many physicians, was an
open book to him, for he had a remedy no one else knew about.
"Cancers killed and extracted, root and branch in from ten to
forty-eight hours without instrument, pain, or the use of chloro-
form, simply by applying a mild salve of the Doctor's own
make," Buck advertised in the Ottawa FREE TRADER.

It developed later that this "mild salve" was a mustard plaster.

Not that Doc Claflin was dogmatic when it came to curing
cancer with his mild salve. Sometimes Tennessee would wipe
away the ailment without the use of medicine, by going into
spiritualistic trances or by hypnotizing the patients; yet, in the
long run, the mustard plaster was relied on, as it seemed to
bring better results. And then, one day early in June, 1864, an
indictment was returned by the grand jury to the Circuit Court
of La Salle County. The document charged that Tennessee
Claflin had applied deleterious and caustic drugs to one Re-
becca Howe in an effort to cure the disease known as cancer,
that the patient languished and, on June 7, had died.

Here was the aftermath of this event that occurred twenty-six
years before, according to the story as printed in 1864 in the
FREE TRADER:

"Miss Tennessee Claflin, clairvoyant, doctress, &c., whose
ability to perform miracles in the way of wonderful cures has
been somewhat largely advertised in the local press hereabouts
for the last six months and who had opened a 'magnetic infirmary' at the Old Fox House in Ottawa Center, suddenly disappeared about a week ago.

"There are said to have been some fifteen patients in her 'infirmary' two weeks ago, all of whom she had 'paroled' except four who were too sick to leave. These were cancer cases, and were literally deserted, having no notice of her intention to leave them. They were in the most horrible condition and were taken charge of by humane persons in the vicinity. . . ."

Why seventeen-year-old Tennessee had been indicted instead of Buck Claflin, the entrepreneur, was not known. Why the indictment was revived so many years later—whether because of the itch of a politician to make news, or because of the antagonism of Midwest inlanders to a titled British lady—was not clarified either. But it all made embarrassing reading to Lady Cook and to the husband of her dear sister, Mr. John Biddulph Martin, Esq.

There was more to come. After the furore over the Ottawa story had somewhat died down, the editors of leading newspapers in the country were given (by persons unknown, or whose identity was kept secret) a documented article giving the true history of the Claflin sisters and family. The story, unearthed by ferrets who evidently had spent months in digging up information, was this:

It was not quite correct that Reuben Buckman Claflin and wife Roxy were of distinguished ancestry, their veins bubbling over with royal blue blood. Buck was born in Sandisfield, Massachusetts, the son of an Irish deadbeat, and had started out in life as a common stableman. He was one-eyed, known as a rough-and-tumble fighter, and was always on the go. Buck became a roving horse trader and then settled in Homer, Ohio, in 1844, when Victoria was six and Roxy was carrying Tennessee. Homer's citizens at first suspected Buck of counterfeiting, but nothing was done about it. After his gristmill, which was heavily insured, burned down he was accused of arson. When he protested his innocence he was given the benefit of doubt and not prosecuted, but he was ordered to leave town. Buck and family left the next day.

For years Claflin and his troupe toured the Midwest as a patent-medicine show, and in such surroundings Victoria and Tennessee had grown up. Roxy, who had been a servant in a Pennsylvania household before her marriage, was, though illiterate, an adept at Spiritualism, and she had taught the art to her growing young daughters. After fleeing from Ottawa following Tennessee's indictment, the family went to Cincinnati and set up in business—"Tennessee Claflin and Victoria Woodhull, Clairvoyants"—with Father Buck pocketing all the profits. Later they were run out of town, so the article claimed, and in 1866 moved to a new field, Chicago. There, so read the old handbills, "Miss Tennessee The Wonderful Child Has Established a Magnetic Infirmary at No. 265 Wabash Avenue." At this juncture one John Bartels popped up at a seance and shouted that Tennessee was no child—she was his wife. Bartels, who claimed later he was given hush money, then disappeared and was never heard from again.

So much for Tennessee. Now it was Victoria's turn.

At the age of fourteen and one-half Victoria had married Dr. Canning Woodhull, but had left him upon meeting Colonel James H. Blood, alias J. H. Harvey, or perhaps his real name was Harvey—no one knew. They had traveled together in a medicine show, with Victoria, who was known as Madam Harvey, telling fortunes and giving Spiritualistic seances. A newspaper story printed two decades before, at a time when Victoria was becoming well known, was quoted. According to the Cleveland LEADER:

"Her career as a trance-physician in Cincinnati, her brazen immodesty as a stock speculator in Wall Street, and her open, shameless effrontery with which she has paraded her name in circus-bill types at the head of her newspaper as candidate of the Cosmo-Political party for the Presidency in 1872—all this has proclaimed her as a vain, immodest, unsexed woman, with whom respectable people should have as little to do as possible. . . . At Cincinnati, years ago, she was the same brazen snaky adventuress that she now is."

The details of Victoria's and Tennessee's life in New York were more familiar to newspaper readers. Once more the alleged facts of their careers were paraded in terrifying array— from Free Love to communism to attempted blackmail and imprisonment on various charges, to Vanderbilt's contested will and their sudden departure for England. And in the end, of course, there was the story of how, after years of perseverance, they had managed to corner rich and respected husbands.

Newspaper devotees found all of this entertaining reading indeed, but John Biddulph Martin, Esq., his wife and Lady Cook did not. They quickly gathered their one hundred pieces of baggage and, after almost inaudibly informing the press that the defamations were preposterous and unfounded, sailed for quiet England. No libel suits were filed.

. 6 .

Just the bare mention that Lady Cook had once been indicted in the United States for manslaughter and fraud was cautiously printed by London newspapers. Nevertheless, Tennessee launched a campaign to retrieve her reputation by establishing herself in the eyes of the English press and people as a public-spirited philanthropist. It took years of hard work and hard money but in the end she succeeded.

First, Tennessee announced she was founding a Home for Wayward Girls in Richmond (this meant a home for prostitutes, or as it was more hopefully phrased at the time, for *reformed* prostitutes), and she added that she would donate several thousand more pounds to Alexandra House. The money was given to the charitable institution and royal thanks from the royal throne itself was gratefully received. But the Home for Wayward Girls fell through. This was because of the parallel drawn by the venomous members of the clique opposing Tennessee and Victoria.

They recalled the undeniable fact that Theodora, the notorious wife of Emperor Justinian, who was too much of a whore even for the broad-minded citizens of the fifth century, had founded a similar home in Constantinople in a futile attempt to atone for her misspent youth.

It was in the staging of public exhibitions of the famed Cook collection of paintings that Tennessee gradually managed to erase the curse of the Ottawa indictment and to become recognized as a benefactor of the nation. The Cooks were generous. Their gallery in Doughty House was open to students and visitors, and was frequented by connoisseurs, among them Bernard Berenson, with Tennessee often escorting the art lovers about. The pictures were shown elsewhere in Great Britain and abroad without the customary admittance fee. The collection was shown to the people of France, Germany, Italy, Portugal, Spain, and Holland (fifty years later the citizens of the United States were to see it), and usually Lady Cook acted as hostess for the absent Maecenas, Sir Francis. Tennessee's magnanimity and graciousness were extolled everywhere, and with time her troubles in "the States" were overshadowed and gradually forgotten.

Sir Francis and Tennessee were in truth public benefactors
in permitting the pictures to be shown to almost anyone, almost
anywhere—a gesture unusual at the time. The collection,
formed under the direction of Sir James C. Robinson, later the
Purveyor of Her Majesty's Pictures, was recognized as being
unrivaled by any other private gallery. Sir Francis Cook was
lavish when it came to acquiring masterpieces. (He knew a
bargain, too, or perhaps Robinson did, for in 1875 the latter
purchased at public auction Hubert van Eyck's "The Three
Maries at the Tomb" for three hundred and fifty pounds, which
was sold in 1951 for $450,000, and another time he brought off
a sensational coup, buying two Fra Filippo Lippis for twenty-
eight pounds apiece!) Of course, the provocative nude of
Diane de Poitiers by François Clouet was the eye-catcher and
eye-opener for the general public, but, to the art student, the
connoisseur and critic there were among Cook's five hundred
paintings many masterpieces of unique beauty. Tennessee's
setting, if not her background, was completely authentic. The
collection included such masterpieces as:

Raphael's "Saint Jerome Punishing the Heretic Sabini-
anus," a portrait begun by Giorgione and finished by Titian,
circa 1641, Rembrandt's famed portrait of his son Titus, and
another of Tobit and his wife, Fra Filippo Lippi's "The Adora-
tion of the Magi," bought for 735 pounds, Velasquez' "Old
Woman Cooking Eggs," Hans Holbein the Elder's "Portrait of
A Lady in a Yellow Dress," Dürer's "The Procession to Cal-
vary," Rubens' "Portrait of a Gentleman," Van Dyck's "The
Betrayal of Christ," Pieter De Hoogh's "A Company of Ladies
and Cavaliers in a Room," Gainsborough's "A Young Lady
Seated in a Landscape," Turner's "The Windmill and Lock,"
in addition to various works by Murillo, Ribera, Claude, Pous-
sin, Lorenzo Monaco, Benozzo Gozzoli, Gabriel Metsu, Sebasti-
ano del Piombo, and other well-known masters. In addition to

the paintings there were also collections of Italian majolica, bronzes, sculptures, miniatures, and old Continental ecclesiastical plate.

. 7 .

John Biddulph Martin, his wife and Lady Cook bounced back to the United States in 1892—after all, it was a Presidential campaign year, and this time Victoria announced she was determined to win—but they postponed their visit until an unpleasant lawsuit had been settled in New York.

Two decades before, when the sisters were being harassed by authorities because of the Beecher scandal, Edward MacKinley had served as one of their attorneys. Victoria and Tennessee, then near-bankrupts, had promised to pay his fee later. MacKinley now was suing for his bill, $10,000. He claimed the sisters had often said they would pay him, but, though his former clients were among the wealthiest women in England, in twenty years he had not received a cent.

It was a matter of court record that MacKinley had served as counsel for the sisters, and in the trial that followed it was not denied that the money was owed the lawyer. Instead, the counsel for Victoria and Tennessee, the aptly named Treadwell Cleveland, tried to prove that (1) MacKinley had never been qualified to practice law, and (2) if he had been, he never had received more than $100 a case in his life. Treadwell Cleveland put before the court a deposition from William F. Howe, the splendiferous member of the Howe and Hummel firm which had represented the sisters, to the effect that he alone had acted as counsel and that MacKinley had never figured in the case. (Howe soon after was disbarred, though not for this particular act of perjury.)

MacKinley's attorney, suitably named Robert Birdseye, produced John H. Shields, a clerk in the Circuit Court who in 1872 had accepted bail from the sisters, and he testified that MacKinley had been their lawyer. William H. Gardner, the deputy warden of Ludlow Street Jail—the same man who two decades earlier had sympathetically presented Victoria and Tennessee with a copy of Pope's poems when they were incarcerated, but who was now in a less helpful mood—swore that MacKinley had been their lawyer. Millard F. Sparr, the son of sister Polly, took the stand, and, true to the tradition that members of the Claflin family testified against each other in lawsuits, said he remembered his aunts' conferring with MacKinley in Victoria's home.

After eight days of listening to the evidence the jurors retired. At first they were unable to reach an agreement, but, after hours of consideration, returned their verdict. It was in favor of Victoria Woodhull Martin and Lady Tennessee Cook, defendants. Even the sisters were stunned.

. 8 .

The MacKinley suit started January 12, 1892, and ended on the 19th. Victoria and Tennessee arrived in New York a decent interval after, on February 22. Before they stepped onto the pier, Mrs. Margaret Ann O'Halloran, one of the Claflin sisters, informed the newspapermen that Lady Cook and Mrs. Martin had decided to found and endow in New York a Home for Old and Needy Journalists. It was evident that she thought the news would make the reporters ecstatically happy. Why, they probably would live there some day.

"My sisters have received a good deal of attention from the New York press at one time or another," Mrs. O'Halloran declared, and the newspapermen agreed as one that the statement certainly was true, "but they are returning good for evil." Mrs. O'Halloran said she hoped the reporters would receive the English visitors graciously. The "heaping-coals-on-fire" idea was out as far as Victoria and Tennessee were concerned, she disclosed, for the sisters had but the kindliest of feelings toward the working press. Mrs. O'Halloran also revealed that the sisters would live in the United States for the rest of their lives and establish a magazine which would be conducted on the lines of the old WOODHULL & CLAFLIN'S WEEKLY.

The reporters who clustered around Victoria at wharfside saw that, though still beautiful, she was aging. She seemed somehow not the dashing and vicacious creature they remembered. Veteran journalists noted another change. Before, Victoria always had what was described in the phrase of the times as a roving eye. She liked to talk to and flirt with husky young men, even those from the hated press corps if no one else was available. Now, approaching the age of fifty-four, she completely ignored all these handsome specimens.

It clearly was a case of going from men to menopause.

Despite Mrs. O'Halloran's suggestion, the newspapermen were in no mood to be respectful. They resented the idea of a Home for Old and Needy Journalists, for then as today there never was a newspaperman who thought he ever would be Needy or Old. The reporters gathered around the visitors like gadflies with their stinging questions. They wanted to know why their friend, MacKinley, who *was* old and needy, had not been paid for acting as counsel for the sisters during their "Beecher troubles." Victoria said she had never heard of the man. She was asked bitterly about this Home for Old and Needy Journalists she was planning. Victoria was puzzled. She had never heard of such an idea. When Mrs. O'Halloran's words were repeated to her she said that she did not intend to establish such a poorhouse, but that she and Tennessee did plan to contribute handsomely to the Press Club treasury. She thought one thousand pounds would be a nice round sum.

Victoria was asked about the new magazine she meant to publish, the one patterned after the WEEKLY. There had been a misunderstanding, The Woodhull slowly replied. It would not be *exactly* like the old WEEKLY. Queried as to whether she still held Presidential ambitions, Victoria said, simply:

"I have come back to ask my people to put me in the White House. I only care for it so far as it will give me the power to inaugurate a system of education which will waken people to the responsibility of creating a race of gods instead of inferior human beings who encumber the face of the earth today. It is my destiny to work out the salvation of my country."

The reporters doubted if Victoria was appealing to the common denominator of American politics, but they printed her words.

Unfortunately, due to the bustle of events that followed, for after all Victoria was busy running for the Presidency, she forgot all about the promised contribution of one thousand pounds to the Press Club. All her energy was devoted to the campaign. The old standbys, the Victoria Leagues, were resurrected and there rose the popular demand that Victoria Woodhull Martin run for the highest office in the land. To make it official, a National Convention of Victoria Leagues was held in the Willard

Hotel in Washington, which was estimated by newspapers to have cost someone, undoubtedly Mr. Martin, $50,000. Fifty delegates were present, with all expenses paid, and they knew their minds. They unanimously nominated Victoria as candidate for President. Mrs. Mary L. Stowe of Wisconsin was chosen to run as Vice-President.

Victoria appeared surprised at being so honored, but she accepted the nomination with dignity. She promised that, upon being elected chief executive of the nation, her first act of office would be to revise the Constitution to her own taste. Remembering the royal blood coursing in her veins (and at the same time disremembering her old communist teachings) she deplored the fact that so many ruffianly aliens had the right to vote. She said she would see to it that all legislation passed by Congress would be for the benefit of the human race, but that immigrants would be denied the right of ballot. An amendment to the Constitution would take care of the problem.

The newspapers were jocose in reporting this, her fifth, try for the Presidency. Victoria had entered the race every four years with the exception of the year 1876—a record unequaled then and later by any woman in the world, dead or alive. "The humors of the campaign are already turning up," THE NEW YORK TIMES remarked unkindly. "Victoria Woodhull Martin has nominated herself for President."

The contest that followed was one of the closest and most spirited Victoria ever participated in. The results were:

Grover Cleveland, Democrat:	5,556,918 votes.
Benjamin Harrison, Republican:	5,176,108 votes.
James B. Weaver, Populist:	1,041,028 votes.
John Bidwell, Prohibitionist:	264,133 votes.
Victoria Woodhull Martin:	0 votes.

Victoria was so disgusted by the apathy and stupidity of the American electorate that she announced she never again would run for President.

She never did, either.

What is more, from the low-tariff era of Grover Cleveland to the corn-pone days of Lyndon Johnson three-quarters of a century has passed by and no woman has run for President.

Victoria had stumped vigorously for five campaigns and had gained a total vote through all those years of—nothing. (Norman Thomas was to surpass this record later on, with six unsuccessful tries at the Presidency, but at least he did accumulate a considerable vote when he ran.)

One is left to conjecture why Victoria, a woman of uncommon intelligence, so persistently pursued such an unobtainable goal, because she knew that, as a woman, she was specifically barred from holding the high office. Perhaps her first campaign was justified because it drew national attention to the crusade for women's rights. But what about the other four? The complete folly of the enterprise, with its attendant ridicule and humiliation, cannot merely be explained by her desire for personal publicity. Perhaps here we enter into the realm of the fixed idea, into the "blind spot" area, and it is a tribute to her vitality that this neurosis did not destroy the core of her personality.

. **9** .

As promised, The Woodhull established a magazine in New York, and, as she said, it was not *exactly* like the old WEEKLY.

The journal was called the HUMANITARIAN. It was to be long-lived and seldom-read. Whereas the old WEEKLY had numbered its subscribers in the thousands, hitting a 20,000 peak, the HUMANITARIAN had but a few hundred readers, and there was a reason: the HUMANITARIAN was dull. The magazine's contributors seldom were professional writers but mostly ultra-respectable—such as Cardinal Vaughan, Archbishop Ireland, Archdeacon Farrar (however, Enoch Arnold Bennett, as he was known then, made an early appearance in print in the journal). The HUMANITARIAN was packed with pseudo-philosophical ideas, with columns upon columns recording for posterity Mr. Martin's dissertations on statistics, but most of all it served through the years as a personal organ for Victoria, to defend herself, to have herself glorified by others, to reproduce old pamphlets which she thought suitable for pure minds, and to reprint what complimentary notices could be found in newspapers twenty years earlier in her New York days. Issue after issue contained half-tone photographs of Victoria, those which were not retouched having been taken decades before when she was young and lovely.

The trials and tribulations Victoria C. Woodhull experienced during her life were implied in the familiar quotation from *Hiawatha* printed on the cover of the magazine. It read (and the reader was supposed to be alert enough to substitute "she" for "he"):

> How he lived and toiled and suffered
> That the tribes of men might prosper
> That he might advance his people . . .

There was other poetry, too. "Two Women" concerned first the unnamed and possibly unknown leader of the clique determined to ostracize Victoria. This poem, supposedly written by

The Woodhull herself, painted this picture of the shadowy enemy:

> I know the one and one is chaste
> As cold as the snow on a winter waste;
> Stainless ever in act and thought
> (As a man born dumb in speech errs not)
> But she has malice toward her time,
> A cruel tongue and a jealous mind.
> Void of pity and full of greed —
> She judges the world by her narrow creed —
> A breeder of quarrels, a breeder of hate,
> Yet she holds the key to society's gate.

Then, in contrast, Victoria herself was described:

> The other woman with a heart of flame
> Went mad for a love that marred her name
> And out of the grave of her martyred faith
> She rose like a soul that had passed through death.
> Her aim is noble, her pity so broad
> It covers the world like the mercy of God.
> A healer of discord, a saviour of woe,
> Peace follows her footsteps wherever she goes.
> The worthier life, too, no doubt,
> But society locks her out.

Editorial headquarters for the HUMANITARIAN were rented at 302 West Seventy-second Street and the magazine was published at 20 Vesey Street. Victoria was listed as its editor, with Zulu as associate editor, but most of the work was done by Dr. Charles Stuart Welles, who had married Mrs. O'Halloran's daughter, Ella. Money was spent lavishly to produce a fine magazine, typographically speaking, and it was estimated that the project cost John Biddulph Martin more than $100,000.

The HUMANITARIAN was put out intermittently from its July 1892 issue until December, 1901, when it died a nine-year-old stillborn child. Its lackluster volumes may be found today in many American and British libraries, presented with the compliments of Victoria Woodhull Martin, Editor.

· 10 ·

Victoria decided to show her husband the country. They first visited Chicago, and news of their impending arrival was sent ahead to the press. Tennessee did not care to make the trip, and understandably so, for Ottawa was only a few miles from Chicago.

The newspapers in the Illinois metropolis were singularly unimpressed by the visit of the distinguished couple. They preferred to remember Victoria not as the editor of the pure HUMANITARIAN but of the wicked WEEKLY. The reporters wanted to know if Mrs. Martin had any comment to make on the indictment still in force against sister Tennessee. Mrs. Martin ignored the question. The couple no sooner had settled down in their hotel suite than the MAIL printed a short article recalling the Midwest adventures of Victoria and Tennessee. The story was insinuating, though not particularly vicious, yet John Biddulph Martin was outraged, again. He obtained a warrant for the arrest of the MAIL editor on a charge of criminal libel. He also asked for $100,000 damages, pledging to spend an equal sum, if necessary, to convict the dirty dog.

Far from being intimidated, the MAIL barked back:

"If this notorious adventuress had remained in the obscurity of her London life, certainly the MAIL would have had no word to say about her, but when she has the effrontery to come to Chicago, it is different. This woman, known to be a bad character, remembered in police and detective circles in this city, has the hard gall to talk about regenerating and educating the American people. Victoria Woodhull and Tennessee Claflin expose this country to contempt and ridicule by their absurd but offensive impudence; they need but to have their records exhibited to drive them back where they belong."

This was strong stuff, but there was more to come. The MAIL delved again into the Midwestern career of the sisters, and the Ottawa indictment was reproduced in full for its readers. A new item was added to this rehashed saga— the alleged fact that Madame Tennessee had conducted a whorehouse in Cincinnati.

Aghast, Mr. Martin announced he would fight the case to the bitter end, and would if necessary establish residence in Chicago so as to personally push it through the red tape of court procedure.

The MAIL in reply informed Mr. Martin that it was prepared to produce evidence, *new* evidence, in court "to make him the laughing stock of everyone who knows anything about the record of the royal and noble family into which he has entered." Go ahead and file another libel suit against us, the newspaper taunted.

A few days later, the Martins left Chicago for New York, picked up Tennessee and quietly boarded a steamer for England. In Chicago, the MAIL asked dismissal of the suit pending in Circuit Court and its motion was granted because of want of prosecution.

. 11 .

John Biddulph Martin, Esq., had no luck with his Chicago suit, but, once back in London, he was successful in browbeating the British Museum, no less. It was brought to his attention that among the million and more books in the Museum was a copy of *The Beecher-Tilton Scandal,* merely one of hundreds of books published on the case. This particular volume contained, as did practically all concerning the scandal, Vicky's light-hearted confession that Tilton had been her "devoted lover," and that any woman on earth who could not love this Apollo incarnate was "dead to all sweeter impulses of nature."

Martin sternly informed British Museum officials that the book slandered his wife, and so he intended to sue. Unlike the Chicago MAIL, the Museum backed down. The institution never in its long life had been threatened with such a suit and it was feared that a precedent might be established. The trustees bowed low to Mr. Martin, begged his pardon, withdrew the offensive book from its shelf, and locked it up in the safe reserved for pornographic literature. Mr. Martin was appeased, but he warned Museum officials that if, in the future, any such similar slanderous volumes became accessible to readers, he would seek satisfaction in the courts.

Early in 1893 Victoria announced to the British press that she would go on a lecture tour of England, Scotland, Wales and Ireland, and possibly to the dominions overseas, talking on "Humanitarian Government." Her first scheduled appearance was to be in St. James's Hall, where she had made her English debut sixteen years before and had met Mr. Martin.

Victoria did lecture in St. James's but it was a most unpromising beginning of an effort to resume her career as a public speaker. The attendance was sparse and her prosy message was received with indifference.

Her lecture tour through the Empire was canceled. Victoria explained that the people of the United States, her native land, were clamoring to hear her, and had to be given preference. She and husband Martin sailed for New York, but they did not linger in the city. They went to, of all cities, Chicago. Victoria did not lecture there, though. Mr. Martin had been appointed one of the British Commissioners to the World's Fair. Chicago was anxious for the exposition to be a success (and it was, thanks to the twitchy belly of Little Egypt, the hootchie-cootchie dancer), and so Commissioner Martin was greeted with deference, as was his wife, and even by the MAIL.

After the Fair, the Martins returned to New York where they planned to spend the winter. Victoria felt she had restrained herself long enough. In Chicago she had been regarded as the wife of the World's Fair Commissioner John Biddulph Martin, and not as Victoria C. Woodhull. She now announced she would embark on a lecture tour which would extend from New York to the Pacific Coast and include the deep South on the way back. Her first speech was held in New York's Carnegie Hall. Victoria talked on her pet topic, "The Scientific Propagation of the Human Race," otherwise known as stirpiculture. The lecture was a distinct failure. The listeners were bored— Victoria wanted to breed a Godlike perfect race by means of planned cohabitation, with the best people sleeping with only the best people—and they found, too, that the once flamelike oratorical genius was now just another old-fashioned lecturer, with the once-celebrated beauty now wearing spectacles.

Three days after the Carnegie Hall fiasco there appeared a discreet note in the theatrical gossip section of the TIMES: "Departure of Mrs. Victoria Woodhull on the *New York* yesterday was a general surprise. She had announced she would deliver a number of lectures . . . she quit because her husband feared impairment of health."

Back in London, Victoria decided to employ the pen instead of the larynx, and here, too, her efforts were more convulsive than convincing. Another batch of booklets streamed out, each commending her past life and condemning "the shameful efforts to besmirch" her reputation. She would have been most dismayed to know that the New York Public Library promptly filed these pamphlets under the heading "Free Love."

But she was not alone in defending herself. At her side was Tennessee, whose output was equally formidable. Among the literary products Tennessee gave to the world were: "Lady Cook on the Evils of Society and Their Remedies," "Who Rules?" "The Primrose Path," "Illegitimacy," "The Life and History of the now Lady Cook," *Talks and Essays* in four volumes (later condensed to two), *Essays on Social Topics,* and *The Beginning of the Battle*. None of these are readable by any standards.

John Biddulph Martin, Esq., got into the act too, publishing *Silver Census,* on statistics, naturally, but this volume sold for hard cash; Victoria's and Tennessee's books were given away.

The sisterly campaign was, as usual, augmented by other books and pamphlets ostensibly written by unbiased authors. Only two of these fabrications will be considered here.

The regally titled "Two Noble Women, Nobly Planned" was a reprint of an article in the MODERN REVIEW of April, 1893, by one Madeleine Legge. The two noble women, nobly planned, happened to be Victoria and Tennessee. It was revealed that the sisters' joint motto was: *Pacem Hominibus*

Habe, Bellum cum Vitiis—They were at Peace with Men and at War with Vices. The booklet carried many flattering pictures of Victoria and Tennessee, taken more than twenty years before, although the sisters were still regarded as beautiful, considering their age, and had no need to resort to this form of trickery, and it was intended to clear them of the dastardly accusation that they had been Free Lovers. "They never alluded to 'Free Love' in writing or speech from the moment they began their benevolent propaganda on behalf of their sex to the present day!" The exclamation point belongs to "Madeleine Legge."

Brief Sketches of the Life of Victoria Woodhull (Mrs. J. B. Martin) was published in July, 1893. The Library of Congress in Washington registered its free copy as being received in fairly fast time, on November 15. The "Sketches" are notable for a study of Victoria's palm by "Cheiro, the Palmist"—he found it to be quite a hand—and also for a poem, the last stanza of which read:

> Victoria, see us bending low
>   While dawns the critical ninety-three.
> The royal banners, forward go
>   To hail thy bright Epiphany.

Another chapter of "Sketches" was called "Victoria Woodhull: A Memory," written by "A Church of England Clergyman," who modestly remained anonymous. "She openeth her mouth with wisdom," the divine started off, "and in her tongue is the law of kindness—Prov. xxxi, 26." It seemed that the Church of England clergyman first had called on Victoria fourteen years before, but "the memory of that event is fresh . . . her sheer physical beauty surpassed only by her higher charm of conversation." It was indicated, perhaps unwittingly, that the Man of God was unable to get any words into the conversation himself: "I cannot recollect what we talked about, but I recollect it was very difficult to talk at all." "She may yet be the first woman President of the United States," the Reverend disclosed.

Still another section of "Sketches" was signed by one Roslyn D'Onston, but the identity of this individual with the incredible name was not revealed. Roslyn found Mrs. Martin "nervous like a racehorse, [at fifty-five] beautiful beyond dispute, but it is a mystic beauty." The author was interested most in Victoria's blue blood. "She is the daughter of Mr. Claflin of Sandersfield, Massachusetts, who was the grandson of Thomas Hamilton . . . the direct descendant in straight line from Robert I (Robert Bruce) of Scotland," Roslyn revealed.

. **12** .

Early in 1894, one year after the British Museum had been forced to remove the "slanderous book," the vigilant Mr. Martin discovered that the institution had two volumes of a similar obnoxious nature on its shelves. They were Tilton's biographical sketch of Victoria and *The Beecher-Tilton Scandal . . . with Mrs. Woodhull's Statement.* As Mr. Martin had threatened, he sued.

The suit of Martin and uxor (wife) v. the Trustees of the British Museum was started on Feburary 24—the first libel case ever brought and tried in court against the historic institution. The uxor declared herself "damaged" by the display of these books, and seemed to think that the trustees, among whom were the Archbishop of Canterbury and other church dignitaries, members of the Cabinet and numerous prominent lay individuals, had gone out of their way to persecute her.

The case was heard in the High Court of Justice before Sir Frederick Pollock (whose correspondence with Justice Oliver Wendell Holmes was to be published five decades later). The legal talent retained by each side was of the highest caliber. The complainants were represented by Sir Richard Webster, Q.C., who later became Lord Alverstone. The Museum trustees were defended by the formidable and brilliant Sir Charles Russell, Q.C., later Lord Russell of Killowen, who was a trustee himself. Both opposing counsels eventually became Lord Chief Justices of Great Britain.

The trial, which was closely followed not only by the general public but by librarians throughout the world, who feared that a dangerous precedent might be established, continued for five days. Much of the time was consumed by the cross-examination of Victoria, a skillful and devastating performance by Sir Charles Russell. But before that, Sir Richard Webster described his client to the court. Mrs. Martin, he said solemnly, had felt compelled to clear her spotless reputation. The two books which the Museum had made available to the public (and which were being freely circulated in other British and American libraries) had accused her of immorality. This stemmed from the fact that, as Sir Richard lightly put it, Victoria had taken "a strong view" of the Beecher-Tilton "imbroglio."

When Sir Charles Russell put Victoria on the stand he was alternately suave and savage, polite and sneering, as befitted the most adept cross-examiner in England. *Had* she ever been guilty of immorality? Gracious, no! replied Victoria. She had been constantly before the American public from 1870 to 1877, and during all that time not one single charge had been made against her character.

Sir Charles moved in to demolish this strange assertion with keen questions, but Victoria, as the London TIMES said, branched off into a variety of subjects which were irrelevant to the case at hand. "I have been persecuted," she shouted, "and refused admission to hotels and my daughter refused at school!"

Sir Charles steered the testimony back to the case. Demosthenes interested him. He asked smoothly, with only the trace of a smile, if it were true that her spiritual adviser was Demosthenes. "There is an apparition appearing before me now," retorted Victoria, amid laughter in the courtroom. Sir Charles bowed in appreciation of the riposte, but he insisted on hearing more about the ancient Greek. He wanted to know if Demosthenes had dictated her speeches, or had merely suggested the general context. "I do not feel disposed to tell you," Victoria replied tartly, if lamely.

The counsel for the Museum wanted to know about The Woodhull's two divorces and of her intimacies with Theodore Tilton, which she herself had so proudly made public. Victoria said she had barely *known* Tilton, if that were his name. Free Love? "I never knew that love was anything but free," replied Victoria. Why had she written the article in WOODHULL & CLAFLIN'S WEEKLY, a sample copy of which the defense wished now to enter as evidence, that brought on the Beecher-Tilton scandal? Victoria said she had not written it. But it had appeared under her signature? Victoria said that when the article appeared she had been thousands of miles away lecturing. How many years had passed, Sir Charles wanted to know, before she publicly disowned that she had written the article? "Why am I so persecuted?" cried Victoria.

John Biddulph Martin, Esq., then took the stand. He testified that never in his life had he seen one word in Victoria's writings which endorsed the base and immoral views attributed to her. To the contrary, her real views on all issues were diametrically opposed to those she was said to hold by the venal press. It was evident to all in court that this was husband Martin's honest and sincere belief.

In his speech to the jury, Sir Charles Russell pointed out that the British Museum acquired considerably more than a quarter of a million new books each year, and that it was impossible to keep a staff of libel experts to comb through each volume for slanderous passages. The suit had been brought solely "to allow this lady to make statements in the box to contradict a number of publications offensive to her."

Sir Richard Webster in turn informed the jurors that all his client wanted was an apology: the trustees had made no expression of public regret.

Sir Charles interrupted his colleague. He said the trustees had sent a letter of regret to Mrs. Martin. Did the complainants want the Archbishop of Canterbury and other trustees "to stand forth in a penitential sheet?"

The jury returned a curiously worded verdict. It held the trustees to be at fault for allowing slanderous publications to be placed on the Museum shelves, but found that, strangely enough, "they were not guilty of negligence." Damages of one pound were awarded the complainants. For the Martins it was a Pyrrhic victory. They won a few shillings, and the fee of the expensive Sir Richard Webster, Q.C. was said to have been two thousand pounds.

It was but a matter of course that the case would be appealed, for, as the London TIMES remarked, soon another such action might be brought against the Museum by another such indignant husband and uxor, and the SPECTATOR pictured the distinguished trustees waiting in fear and trembling, "dreading the ten thousand libel actions lying dormant on the shelves of the Museums."

The case was appealed the following year, but before any testimony was heard Sir Richard Webster informed the court that the plaintiffs were satisfied, now that the pure character of Mrs. Victoria Woodhull Martin had been established, and that his clients would not oppose the appeal. That was the end of the matter. And the books have remained on the Museum shelves to this day.

Soon after the lawsuit the British Museum displayed still another volume on its shelves that horrified Martin. This was the official biography of the Reverend Henry Ward Beecher and its index contained the notation: *Woodhull, Victoria, blackmailed by*. The reference spelled out the "attempted" extortion by Vicky—the extortion that many people believed had taken place. Martin warned the Museum and booksellers that he was "taking time to consider how such libels could best be dealt with." No libel suit ever was filed.

. 13 .

There may have been another reason for the Martins' change of heart in fighting lawsuits, for now there was another suit, this time in the family. The searing iron of scandal often had touched, and even wrapped itself around, Vicky and Tennessee; but in this instance the principal was none other than Sir Francis Cook.

Tennessee's husband was sued for breach of promise and seduction, and for some reason the press seemed to think that the idea of the seventy-seven-year-old baronet defending himself against these goaty charges made for a good story.

The complainant, Mrs. Maidy Holland, who was not so young but still attractive, testified that she had lived with Cook as man and wife and had undergone a painful private operation at his behest, but only because Sir Francis had promised to marry her. But he had married the outlander, Tennessee Claflin. Mrs. Holland was asked on cross-examination if she had any documentary proof to support her charges. She said she did not. A sister of Lady Cook, Mrs. Victoria Woodhull Martin, had visited her and wheedled her out of old love letters after paying the sum of thirty pounds.

Sir Francis did not actually contest the case. When he took the stand he confessed to the liaison but denied he had ever promised to marry the lady. The jury returned a verdict in favor of Mrs. Holland, with nominal damages to be paid, and it was understood that the jilted woman was suitably rewarded by Sir Francis outside the court—this time with money.

. 14 .

In the summer of 1895 Victoria again visited New York, and for the last time. She made the trip, accompanied by her obedient husband, to straighten out another family squabble that of course had found its way into the newspapers. The many members of the Claflin clan were not happy unless they were quarreling. Victoria was not directly concerned in the dispute, but, as usually happened, she soon got into the news. AGAIN VICTORIA WOODHULL, wearily headlined THE NEW YORK TIMES. The story was occasioned by her "little girl," Zulu, who now was a spinster of thirty-five, and, reported the TIMES, "all the trouble, it is said, is caused by Cupid."

Victoria arrived in New York in June, just in time to be served with papers at the pier to appear in court, and the clustered reporters were curious to know what was causing all the fuss and what the suit was all about.

Victoria said she had not visited New York for some time and had heard the city was quite changed, now that the old reservoir had been taken down in Bryant Park and replaced by the library.

The reporters turned to Mr. Martin, who was standing uneasily by, and asked if he was satisfied with the damages of less than five American dollars in the British Museum suit.

Was it true, Victoria interrupted, that all the department stores had left Fourteenth Street and moved uptown?

Stern's and McCreary's had moved far uptown, to Twenty-third Street, but Macy's still was on Fourteenth, replied the reporters. Would she care to comment on daughter Zulu's troubles?

She would not.

Victoria undoubtedly regretted this decision, for sister Margaret Ann O'Halloran, eldest of the clan, soon afterward told the entire story to the press before Victoria could get her side of the controversy into the papers.

"All this trouble arose over Zulu falling in love," Mrs. O'Halloran told the TIMES. "Zulu, who is now thirty-five years old, promised her mother never to marry, and her mother left her in this country last year with Dr. and Mrs. Welles [Mrs. O'Halloran's daughter and son-in-law] to look after the HUMANITARIAN. Dr. Welles was to notify Mrs. Woodhull of any circumstances affecting Zulu.

"An old woman, whose name I do not know, persuaded Zulu to become engaged to a young man, who had taken a fancy to her, and Dr. Welles wrote of the affair to Mrs. Martin. Zulu afterwards went to London and I presume discredited Dr. Welles's statement. Then it was decided to turn him out."

The reporters already knew that Zulu had quarreled with her three relatives. Since she had signed the lease of their residence at 302 West Seventy-second Street she considered herself mistress of the place and had told them to get out. After many legal and not so legal arguments they were evicted, but Dr. Welles, the American agent for the HUMANITARIAN, had struck back and was now suing Victoria for $2,750 back pay for editorial work.

The reporters asked Mrs. O'Halloran what had happened when her sister had arrived in America. It appeared that The Woodhull had acted vigorously:

"She began to destroy and give away my daughter's dresses, she buried small articles, put the furniture in the furnace and gave away sofas and chairs, and then she burned seven trunks full of dresses belonging to my daughter. The work took eight days.

"Then she burned all the dresses belonging to her dead mother and sister, and her excuse was, 'Everything is cursed! I won't have any cursed property in my house.'"

Mrs. O'Halloran was asked how she felt toward her famous sister. Her answer was to the point:

"There is no language that can describe the rascality of Victoria Martin. Neither she nor her daughter have any friends in the family, while my other sister, Lady Cook, is honored and loved for her charitable work in London and Portugal. Why doesn't Victoria devote her remaining years to such work, instead of running from Europe to America and back again, and spending her husband's money to achieve notoriety?"

Dr. Welles summarized his opinion of the celebrated Victoria in these words:

"Mrs. Martin's mind is slightly affected, I believe. She thinks herself a second Christ."

In their stories the next day the reporters recalled that, years before in New York, Tennessee had defended herself and Victoria by declaring: *"He* was despised by the authorities in government, in philosophy and in religion, and His associates were Magdalens, sinners," but that she had added, modestly, "I would not have it understood from this reference that my sister and I presume to place ourselves as Christs of the present generation."

The newspapers visualized a long trial, with spicy details, but a few days later, on July 13, Victoria and Mr. Martin decided to forfeit the $3,500 bail she had posted to appear in court in the Dr. Welles suit. They quietly boarded the *Majestic,* but they were not to be let off so easily. Shortly before sailing time Victoria was served with papers secured by Mrs. Welles, demanding $1,500 damages for the furniture and dresses that Victoria had destroyed in her rage.

Mr. and Mrs. J. B. Martin took their luggage off the ship, went to the Sheriff's office and casually deposited a $1,000 bill for bail. They returned to the pier only to find that the *Majestic* had sailed. Accommodations were found on the *Lucania* and soon the party left American shores. The $1,000 bail was forfeited as the Martins did not defend the suit. Evidently for once they were utterly weary of all the family infighting. And never again was Victoria to see her native America.

Accompanying Victoria on the voyage was Zulu, who promised again never to marry. She never did.

. **15** .

John Biddulph Martin fell ill in November, 1898, and went to recuperate at his vacation home in Las Palmas in the Canary Islands. He failed to rally after an attack of pneumonia and died on March 20, 1899. The patrician was fifty-six years old and had been married to Victoria for eighteen years.

The death of Mr. Martin was mourned almost exclusively in financial circles. It was recalled that his papers, "Movements of Coins," "History, Functions, and Fluctuations of the Bank Note Circulation," and "The Evolution of Our Banking System," were valuable contributions to banking lore. "Those whom he assisted in the work of the [British Economic] Association will ever cherish the memory of that courteous colleague and kind friend," said the ECONOMIC JOURNAL. There was scant mention of the bereaved widow.

The obituary of Victoria's third husband as printed in the HUMANITARIAN much resembled that of her first, Dr. Canning Woodhull, which had been published in the WEEKLY. Each account gave a due measure of praise to the dead man, but each was mostly concerned with Victoria and her martyrdom:

"The last few months of his life were embittered by a fresh outbreak of the cruel persecution which he and his wife had faced together for years. In consequence of failing health his wife's enemies thought he was no longer able to defend her in the same way as formerly. In this they were mistaken for his vigilance never halted, but the mental wear told on him severely."

John Biddulph Martin, Esq., left an estate of 171,797 pounds sterling, net—about $835,000 after taxes had been paid—and his fifty-nine-year-old widow was his sole heir. In addition to stocks, bonds and cash, Martin left his beloved Vicky his London town house (the mansion survived the blitz and is standing today, having been converted into six separate flats) and his magnificent country estate, Norton Park. For Victoria, who had lived much of her early life in a tent, this must have been most gratifying.

This, as American newspapers pointed out, was a tidy sum to inherit, particularly for a person who not so many years before had been near bankruptcy, and who had been stone-broke many and many a time in her life.

. 16 .

Shortly before Christmas in 1898 Tennessee summoned the English journalists to Doughty House, served them champagne and announced that she was going to start off the New Year with a resolution—she was going to succeed once again in the business world. The firm she intended to establish would deal in stocks and bonds and would be known as Lady Cook & Co., Ltd. "When I and my sister, Vic, were bankers and brokers in Wall Street we often had the market in our hands," she informed the press. "We operated for Jay Gould, Vanderbilt and Fisk."

Nothing more was ever heard of this venture.

A few months later Lady Cook sailed for New York and on

her arrival told the newspapermen she would make her home in the United States (for some reason, every time the sisters returned to New York each would announce she planned to live there, permanently), and intended, once again in her life, to succeed in the business world. "She is thinking possibly to duplicate her successes of 1869 [sic] when she and Victoria Woodhull carried Wall Street by storm," reported the TIMES.

Nothing more was ever heard of this venture.

A few weeks later, the newspapers informed their readers that Tennessee meant to found in New York an institution similar to Alexandra House, the home for young women artists which she had founded—at least so said Lady Cook—in London. Tennessee said the cost of Alexandra House had been roughly about $1,250,000, or possibly a quarter of a million dollars more or less, but that she expected to allot a larger sum, say $2,000,000 as a starter, to get the American counterpart on its feet. Eventually, of course, she would contribute heavily to its upkeep. Had any of the reporters a good name for the place? Some of them thought Tennessee House would be a fine name. Tennessee said she was thinking of offering $5,000 to the person who came up with something perfect. She revealed she was buying a four-story house at 137 West One Hundred and Thirty-first Street, which would be completely remodeled and expanded. She had already started interviewing architects, and the new building would be one of the most magnificent ever built in the country.

Nothing more was ever heard of this venture.

A few days later, Lady Cook returned to Doughty House, Richmond, Surrey, outside London.

Tennessee had gone home for a purpose. Sir Francis, an octogenarian, was in his dotage and not far from death. Certain of his relatives (they were distant ones; Tennessee's ties with her husband's immediate family always had been, and would

continue to be, cordial) were convinced that, due to a legal
tangle, her marriage was not binding. There were rumors that
it would be contested after the old man's demise. (Fortunately
for Tennessee, no fuss was being made about her alleged marriage to John Bartels in Chicago thirty-three years before.)
Tennessee acted with characteristic dash. She took Sir Francis
Cook by the hand and in June, 1899, remarried him in a civil
ceremony, and her attorneys saw to it that the contract was
lawful. There is no reason to think this was a particularly tricky
maneuver. Their marriage of sixteen years was a happy one,
and Sir Francis was a fairly devoted husband, though at times
inclined to stray from the hearth. He never lost his faith in
Tennessee, even if he did not feel the compulsion to defend her
publicly with the vigor of a Mr. Martin. Sir Francis' children
always were on good terms with their stepmother and in general people usually became fond of Tennessee, once they knew
her.

At the same time Tennessee forestalled any possible litiga-
tion in the future. For an unannounced consideration (believed
to be, because of the estate she was eventually to leave, about
$750,000) she agreed to waive any further claims on the Cook
fortune, once its owner was in the grave.

It was generally agreed that Lady Cook had made a shrewd
move in remarrying and arranging for the widow's dower. Sir
Francis lived on but for eight months. Shortly after his eighty-
fourth birthday, on February 17, 1901, he died in Doughty
House.

In Cook's orbituary printed in the Thames Valley TIMES,
based on material supplied by Tennessee, it appeared that father Reuben Claflin had not been a lawyer and a famous judge
after all. Old one-eyed Buck had been a textile millionaire, just
like his son-in-law, Cook. The TIMES solemnly informed its
readers that "by what can hardly have been more than a pure

coincidence" it so happened that Buck "filled an almost similar position in the dry goods trade of New York to that which Sir Francis Cook occupied in London, his enormous store occupying the whole front of one block on Broadway between 11th and 12th Streets." The article was supposed to be an obituary of Cook, but he was overshadowed by the wealth of detail about Old Buck and Tennessee. Father Claflin's famed New York town house, nestling beneath the shadow of "Pauls," also was described. As for the grieving widow, Tennessee, the newspaper recalled "the exceedingly pleasant welcome extended by the Queen's daughter-in-law, the Duchess of Cornwall, when they met at a garden party at Lady Whittaker Ellis." Some facts of Cook's career also were mentioned.

Though he had taken care of his fifty-six-year-old widow in the bequest, Sir Francis left her outright the additional sum of 25,000 pounds (about $121,500), and the income for life on an investment of 50,000 pounds (about $243,000). Lady Cook, who had come to London twenty-four years before almost penniless, now was a millionairess in her own right.

Before he died, and because of his old age, Sir Francis had given the larger portion of his fortune to his children. He did not leave $60,000,000, as THE NEW YORK TIMES stated, coming to the awed conclusion that the wild and pretty Tennessee Claflin whom Americans had known had inherited it all, but his estate was respectable enough. Its net total, after taxes, duties, various fees and bequests to his children, was 1,600,000 pounds—about $8,776,000. His Montserrat castle in Portugal and two-thirds of all his other property were left to his eldest son, Sir Frederick Cook, a Member of Parliament and partner of Cook and Son, who was a year older than his stepmother, Tennessee. A daughter and her issue received 25,000 pounds outright, plus the income from an invested 100,000 pounds.

The remainder of the estate went to a younger son, Wyndham Francis Cook.

The main portion of the art collection, valued at about 2,000,000 pounds, was left to the eldest son. This heir died in 1920, the title falling to his son, Sir Herbert Frederick Cook. The fourth and present Baronet is Sir Francis Ferdinand Maurice Cook, who succeeded to the title on the death of his father in 1939.

The famed Cook art collection, held in the family for four generations, was partially dispersed in early World War II days. The portrait begun by Giorgione and finished by Titian was presented to the National Gallery in London. Forty pictures by Van Dyck were sold to a Dutch dealer in April, 1940. They fell into Nazi hands and some of the masterpieces have not been recovered to this day.

The remainder of the collection was sent to the Toledo Museum of Art in Ohio for safekeeping during the war, and in 1944-45 it was exhibited to hundreds of thousands of Americans. After the paintings were returned to Doughty House, Velasquez' "Old Woman Cooking Eggs" was sold in 1955 to the National Gallery of Scotland for £57,000, and fifty paintings were bequeathed on a long-time loan to the Iveagh Collection.

In 1958 at Sotheby's the "greatest assemblage of paintings formed in the country during the 19th century" brought to a close the dispersal of the collection. The auction realized £64,668 for 136 lots. The Metropolitan Museum of Art in New York, the National Gallery in Washington, and the National Gallery in London acquired many of the masterpieces.

. 17 .

No sooner had the body of Sir Francis Cook been laid to rest in West Norwood cemetery than "unpleasant rumors," as Tennessee put it, began to circulate. It was whispered that the old man had been poisoned. (For once, mother Roxy could not be blamed for the rumors: she was dead.)

Tennessee announced that the cause of her husband's death was senile decay, and applied to the thoroughly startled Home Secretary for an order to exhume Cook's body so that a postmortem examination could be made by five physicians. She then issued a public statement. She named no names, but in an aside to newspapermen she confided she was referring to John Henry Wallace, who had been Cook's secretary and who was described by Tennessee as ringleader of a blackmailing gang. The statement read:

> Since the death of my husband there has come to my knowledge a very thoroughly laid plan, concocted before his death, to blackmail his reputation. It was about to be put into execution when he died. Some parties to the conspiracy expected to secure large amounts of money during his life. His somewhat sudden end prevented a fulfillment of those hopes. The conspiracy reached a culmination by the circulation of rumors that Sir Francis Cook died an unnatural death and owed his demise to me, the conspirators hoping in this fashion to blackmail me.
>
> Had I not been a woman of world-wide reputation, I could have afforded to let these calumnies die. My own

health, alas, is extremely poor. [Tennessee was to live on for twenty-two more years.] Should I die these lies might go on forever. I have therefore resolved to refute them now.

I propose to go to the full limit of an autopsy, if necessary, in order that the world may know how baseless these stories are. Harrowing as it is, I shall not flinch. My husband was beloved by me and I by him, and these iniquitous slanders shall be stamped out if it costs me all the courage and wealth I have in the world. In this I have the full cooperation of all my step-children.

Years before in New York, when sister Utica, when Benjamin Sparr, and when Dr. Canning Woodhull had died, there had been "unpleasant rumors." The Claflins held autopsies and in all three instances they were cleared of the whispered charges. Tennessee undoubtedly remembered these occasions. But the horrified dignitaries in the Home Secretary's office informed her that exhumations were not lightly made in England, as perhaps they were in America, and that they "could not think of letting a sorrowing widow open a husband's grave to prove something that needed no proof."

This would have been the end of the matter if it had not been for John Henry Wallace. He sued Lady Cook, charging libel and slander. In the trial that followed, Wallace testified that, though he had been Cook's secretary, his allegiance had been divided between his master and his master's wife. He had watched the old man for Tennessee, to see if he "was carrying on." He had shadowed a certain unnamed lady whom Tennessee suspected was sleeping with Cook—who was in his eighties at the time.

Wallace's counsel seemed surprised that Lady Cook, who had more or less publicly charged that his client was an extortionist, had not realized she had committed slander. He thought

304 • *Vicky* •

that she, of all people, should be familiar with the ins and outs of blackmail, as she had been accused of the practice many times by the well-informed American press.

Tennessee's case was hopeless, and her counsel, the noted Sir Edward Clarke, knew it. He decided not to put Lady Cook on the stand, and he did not contest the fact that a slander had been committed, though he excused the act by explaining that his client had been in a state of nervous exhaustion following her beloved husband's death. Sir Edward Clarke's only hope was that the damages awarded to Wallace would be low.

The jury in the Court of the King's Bench brought in a verdict to award 670 pounds—about $3,250—to Wallace. Sir Edward beamed delightedly. Lady Cook, however, was in no such happy mood.

"Lord Alverstone, I am an American, and I want you to listen to me," Tennessee shouted at the judge as she sprang to her feet and brandished a sheaf of papers.

Lord Alverstone, it so happened, was the former Sir Richard Webster who had acted as counsel for the Martins in their suit against the British Museum. He calmly adjusted his wig and surveyed the gesticulating figure below him with distaste.

"I want this case reopened!" cried Tennessee, waving her arms wildly. "This has cost me thousands of pounds and I have trusted myself in the hands of an English judge and an English jury, and—"

Lord Alverstone eyed Tennessee coldly and beckoned to an usher.

"I have witnesses from America," Tennessee screamed hysterically. "I can bring hundreds of witnesses. I want to go in the witness box myself. That is all I ask."

"Usher, remove the Lady," the Lord Chief Justice commanded. Sir Edward Clarke attempted to soothe his client, taking her by the arm.

"I have been *had*—by counsel," shouted Tennessee, wrenching away from Clarke's grasp and glaring at him accusingly, "and by the jury!" She turned and stared fiercely at the standing jurors.

The court attendant pinioned her arms.

"Oh, don't pull me about!" Tennessee cried. The usher continued to push her to the courtroom door.

"I'll walk out," said Tennessee. "I have done more for England than anybody else. Oh, cruel, cruel, cruel!"

The melodramatic behavior of the American, so unusual in a staid English court, had not ended. Lady Cook's last words as she was being propelled bodily through the door culminated in the agonized shrieks:

"My reputation is ruined!"

· 18 ·

The sisters were getting old—at the turn of the century Victoria was sixty-two, Tennessee fifty-five—and, as the TRIBUNE noted approvingly in New York, were "agitating in a less obtrusive fashion lately." Each now decided to retire from the hurly-burly of the city and enjoy the quiet of the country. Victoria went to live on a historic estate in Worcestershire, while Tennessee settled down in the Montserrat castle in Portugal when she was not staying at Doughty House with her stepchildren. She announced she would spend thousands of pounds in Richmond to establish a Home for Unwed Mothers. The declaration was not greeted with enthusiasm—the good people of

Richmond seemed to think such a beneficence would encourage and even greatly increase the number of unwedded girls in their town. This was another project which fell through, and Tennessee began to live more and more in warm Cintra, where the Portuguese were appreciative of her qualities. There she founded and supported a number of free schools for the poor, and when her carriage appeared in the streets the humble folk took off their hats and bowed low.

Tennessee's reputation was not ruined, as she had predicted so violently. Instead it was enhanced. This came about after a visit to the Montserrat palace by a man in his early twenties named Thomas Beecham.

At the time of his stay in the castle, young Beecham had already made a fair-to-middling name for himself as a conductor of promise with a touring opera company, but he was more generally known as the son and heir of Sir Joseph Beecham, and thus a prize matrimonial catch. Sir Joseph had accumulated a fortune of some 30,000,000 pounds by concocting England's most popular laxative. Beecham's Pills sold at the rate of a million per day, and were advertised by a quatrain known throughout the British Empire:

> Hark the herald angels sing
> Beecham's Pills are just the thing.
> Peace on earth and mercy mild,
> Two for man, and one for child.

Beecham, in his autobiography, *A Mingled Chime,* said he obtained permission "through the lucky chance of an invitation to spend a few weeks in the Portuguese home of Sir Francis Cook, Montserrat, a few miles from Cintra, once the home of Beckford, author of *Vathek,* and noted by Byron in the first canto of his 'Childe Harold' . . . a splendid palace whose gardens are world-renowned for containing almost every tree, shrub and plant known to botany."

The youthful Thomas was not the first or last to be impressed by the picturesque beauty of Lady Cook's castle. As Byron described the scene:

> On sloping mounds, on in the vale beneath,
> Are domes where whilom kings did make repair;
> But now the wild flowers round them only breathe;
> Yet ruin'd splendour still is lingering there.
> And yonder towers the Prince's palace fair . . .

While vacationing at Montserrat, Thomas Beecham met, and was intrigued by, Tennessee's grandniece, Utica Celestia Welles, a beautiful girl who was studying medicine, and a special protégée of hostess Lady Cook. Utica (named after the Claflin sister who died in 1873) Celestia (patterned after Tennessee's middle name, Celeste) was the daughter of Dr. and Mrs. Charles Stuart Welles who had feuded with Victoria on her last visit to New York. The romance between Utica Celestia and young Thomas Beecham blossomed, and was abetted by Lady Cook.

Four decades later, in 1943 when Beecham wrote his autobiography, he was to say: "In planning this book I made the proper resolution to set down nothing that I had not seen or heard for myself." But Beecham, for reasons best known to himself, saw fit not to set down a great deal that he *had* seen and heard, for in this long account of his life there is no mention of the name of Lady Tennessee Cook, nor of Victoria C. Woodhull, nor even the name of Utica Celestia Welles, who was for forty years his wife.

The marriage of the patent-medicine prince and the grandniece of Tennessee and Victoria took place in London on July

26, 1903 (six days earlier, the destitute John Henry Wallace, whose award of 670 pounds had been set aside on appeal to a higher court, was found with his throat slashed, and was arrested for attempting suicide), and though it lasted the mentioned forty years it was not a success. There were two sons by the union, Adrian Welles Beecham, well known today as a composer, and Captain Thomas Welles Beecham of His Majesty's Navy, but the couple did not live together after 1909.

Sir Thomas Beecham, as he was to be known after he was knighted in 1916, went on to great fame. He became the revered symphonic conductor of the Royal Philharmonic Orchestra and appeared in all the capitals of the world, introduced the Russian Ballet to London, financed several seasons of opera at Covent Garden, and was to become celebrated in musical annals as the one member of the profession who went bankrupt to the tune of $14,000,000. In 1932 Sir Thomas contributed $1,250,000 to the upkeep of his wife and sons, and again in 1937 gave an additional $500,000, both by court orders. In 1943, when he was conductor of the Seattle Symphony Orchestra, he obtained a divorce in Boise, Idaho, from the grandniece of Tennessee and Victoria, asserting that from his spouse he had received "only carping criticism in my chosen work" and that she had "belittled the success which I continually attained." He later married Betty Humby, the child prodigy pianist who, when she grew up, was soloist at Beecham's concerts, and, after she died in 1958, he married Shirley Hudson, his twenty-seven-year-old secretary. Sir Thomas died in 1961, aged eighty-one.

· 19 ·

Victoria retired from the public arena to live privately and in great style. Her estate was named Norton Park, at Bredon's Norton in Worcestershire. She amused herself at first by establishing and supervising a free school on the grounds, but her interest waned and she turned again to her old, old love: the publication of pamphlets. She rewrote some of her early American speeches and had them printed as originals. In 1904 she put out "The Woodhull Family Genealogy," but no new details were added to that astonishing family tree. She arranged for the publication of "The Story of Norton Park, with Notes on Bredon Hill," by F. C. Champion and Rosa M. Barrett. It so happened that this was more precisely the story of Mrs. Victoria Woodhull Martin than of Norton Park. And at this time Victoria was pleased to learn that, for once, a book by a prominent person had mentioned her somewhat favorably. This rare event occurred when the correspondence of Charles Bradlaugh, the English social reformer and associate of Mrs. Annie Besant, was published by his daughter. In a letter written in October, 1873, Bradlaugh described meeting a "much-talked-of" individual in New York City:

"A slightly built lady entered, who was presented to me as Mrs. Victoria Woodhull, the present President of the American Spiritualists, and advocate of very advanced doctrines on social questions. The energy and enthusiasm manifested by this lady in our extremely brief conversation were marvellous; her eyes brightened, her whole face lit up, and she seemed all life, all fire. Many people here speak very bitterly against Victoria Woodhull; at present I prefer to take sides with none. It is enough to say that she is most certainly a marvellously audacious woman." Victoria at once turned out another booklet quoting Bradlaugh.

Zulu lived with Victoria at Bredon's Norton and, obedient to her mother's wish, never married. She aspired to become an actress, then an editor. She also attempted to write plays, and two of them, *Affinities* and *The Proposal*, were published at her own expense. They were ignored by theater producers. Her talent was limited, she had none of her mother's brains or looks, and it is likely that she will be remembered by posterity as being probably the only American woman ever named Zulu, if she is remembered at all. At the age of forty-five she started to dabble in psychical research, a field, incidentally, that once again stirred Victoria's interest too, though she was careful not to publicize it.

· 20 ·

The years drifted by, and the once renowned name of Victoria C. Woodhull was now seldom in the headlines. The newspapers did recall her to the public in February, 1914, when through the "Women's Aerial League of England," which Victoria had helped to found, she offered to give "a sculptured centerpiece, one of the heirlooms of my historic mansion, and $5,000 to the first man or woman to fly [alone] across the Atlantic." Mrs. Martin said she hoped the winner would be a fellow American —she never had relinquished her American citizenship—but there is nothing on the record to indicate that Lindbergh received the award thirteen years later.

Now it was Tennessee, almost always outshone by her sister, who received a greater share of the publicity. Lady Cook loved the attention of the newspapers—an attention which now was thoroughly respectful. Victoria never returned to America after her 1895 visit, but the energetic Tennessee continued to make many transatlantic trips. In 1908 she stumped the country for Bryan but—the Claflin family choices for the Presidency never had much luck—he lost. Repeating her stunt of thirty-six years before, Tennessee tried to register to vote. This time she, the distinguished titled British visitor, was not arrested. In 1913 Lady Cook toured the United States giving lectures which were, she claimed, the identical talks for which she had been so persecuted and so prosecuted for so many years.

The newspapermen now knew that Lady Cook would be good copy—good clean copy. She rode in the new subway in Manhattan and found it great fun. She announced she was going to build a string of clubhouses from New York to the West Coast, where women could meet to plan the fight for Suffrage, but this project never was started, let alone completed. She also announced she was starting a school to train perfect husbands, and that $400,000, and possibly more, would be expended to establish the largest and best art gallery in the world, right in New York City, but nothing more was heard about these schemes, once they had hit the headlines. Then, in July, 1913, Tennessee called the newspapermen together and, amidst the popping of champagne corks, she disclosed her latest notion:

"There is a dreadful scarcity of fine, honest and healthy men in England and France. I want to take two hundred fine young American men home with me and give them to my British and French lady friends—as husbands."

Some reporters thought she had added the words "as husbands" only in an afterthought; in any event, the publicity was splendid. Tennessee's hotel was besieged by hundreds of stalwart young Americans who were only too eager to stud in Britain and France. Lady Cook hurriedly sailed for England.

Tennessee took World War I in her stride. In August, 1915, she called a press conference of British and American correspondents, announcing that she intended "to raise armies of English women trained and armed like regular soldiers, ready to fight for their country." Tennessee reasoned that, when the men went overseas to fight, the women left home were the "logical defenders."

"I am going to rouse the women of England to defend their homes, to resist invaders, to fight for their honor!" Lady Cook spiritedly informed the reporters, anticipating Winston Churchill in patriotic fervor, if not in oratorical magnificence. After a few more cases of champagne had been lugged up from the wine cellar, Tennessee estimated that it would take about three months to organize, arm, and drill 150,000 women, but she was willing to spend some 200,000 pounds to halve the time. The regiments of her feminine fighters would be dressed in khaki uniforms, with knee-length skirts, and Tennessee said she already was being fitted in Bond Street for her Brigadier General's uniform.

Lady Cook revealed that that very afternoon she had visited Buckingham Palace ("and got in, too," THE NEW YORK TIMES noted, as if hard put to believe it) and had left a letter for Queen Mary. "I told her about Queen Boadicea, who called both men and women to follow her into battle," said Tennessee.

"Her scythed chariot mowed down her enemies like grass. Women have been brave in the past—we aren't all dolls."

The more the journalists thought about it, after additional rounds of drinks, the better they liked the idea of women sharing the burden of combat.

"I am going to see Queen Amélie of Portugal tomorrow," Tennessee said. "She'd make a splendid general. The Countess of Marlborough would make a splendid fighter, too. I'll also see Lady Jersey, Princess Louise, Lady Granard, and Mrs. John Ward."

After the casual mention of this dazzling array of names, Tennessee reminded the newspapers of incidents which had happened shortly before—incidents which, no matter how they tried, they could not recall:

"I have often stood in front of the Bank of England and told people that this war was coming. Wake up, England! I have been to the War Office several times since the war started. All I can do there is give them some information occasionally—and give my advice."

That was the last ever heard of Tennessee's army of British Amazons.

· 21 ·

Late in 1915 Tennessee made her last trip to the United States. The ship reporters noted that, though she was exquisitely gowned, she was not the beauty that had been Tennessee

Claflin. This was understandable enough, as Tennessee had just passed her seventieth birthday and forty-five years had elapsed since she had been known as the pretty Lady Broker. Tennessee said there were two reasons for her return to her native land: to visit the White House and confer with President Wilson on the progress of the war—it did not seem to matter that the Americans were still neutral—and to give a series of lectures on German atrocities in Belgium. As it happened, she did neither.

Tennessee was now older and wearier than she cared to admit, and she soon went back to England. As the years went by she moved restlessly from Doughty House to the castle in Montserrat, to a flat in South Kensington, and finally she went to live with Utica Celestia, now the Lady Beecham, at Sir Thomas Beecham's home in Upper Hamilton Terrace, London. There, on a Thursday night, January 18, 1923, she died, aged seventy-seven.

It had been a full life. Tennessee, who had seldom received "a good story" in the American press, did get one, once she was dead. The early history of the Claflin family was little known, THE NEW YORK TIMES discreetly remarked, though it was believed father Buck had been "a well-known lawyer." There followed a column-long obituary of the success story of Lady Cook, and every line of it was favorable.

Another TIMES, the famed TIMES of London, also was generous. There was no mention of scandal or strife. Instead, it appeared, "The Dowager Lady Cook" had spent her life in the United States "studying law in her father's office, then medicine and surgery, and then finance and banking." The TIMES scooped the entire world in revealing the presumed fact that Tennessee studied to be a lawyer, doctor, and surgeon.

Tennessee left a net estate of 149,540 pounds—about $727,-000. She died without making a will, and so, under English law, the fortune was divided among her nearest relatives, four of whom were residing in England (one being Victoria), and four in America, and letters of administration were granted her sister Mrs. Victoria Woodhull Martin. To one of the American heirs the fortune was welcome but unneeded. J. Euclid Miles, the son of Margaret Ann Miles O'Halloran, of Santa Monica, California, had become a millionaire through dealings in mining stocks. But the money left to Mrs. Polly Sparr in Brooklyn was a gift from heaven. Polly had been bedridden with a broken hip and penniless for four years, and during that time she had been unable to borrow a dollar from either of her sisters in England.

· 22 ·

Victoria's country residence at Bredon's Norton was recognized to be one of the most beautiful estates in England, and on its spacious grounds stood historic buildings and relics of bygone centuries. The property was located in a pretty wooded district in southwest central England near the Shakespeare shrines, and the lovely Avon ran through its fields, while nearby was the Severn.

Victoria lived in what was officially called the Mansion House, but she had her own name for it—Brainrest. It was a sixteenth-century structure of stone and half-timber, three stories high, a picturesque place with high-pitched gables, mullioned windows, and huge fireplaces. There was a private chapel on the grounds, as was the case at Tennessee's Doughty

House; but neither of the sisters used its facilities, leaving the task of worshiping to the villagers. The estate had long been in the hands of the Martin family, whose country seat was in the nearby village of Overbury, and upon the death of John Biddulph Martin had passed on to the woman many people still regarded as an American interloper.

The estate, situated on high ground in the Cotswolds, originally had been a vast 4,000-acre tract, but more than half of it had been sold for lots. Victoria still had elbow room, however, a private playground of her own of 1,500 acres. Aside from the numerous main buildings there were two guest cottages named Homer and Ohio in memory of Victoria's childhood days.

At first Victoria took an interest in the villagers. She supervised the staging of theatricals, gave a fine organ to the parish church and established and supported a school. Today many villagers recall their visits as schoolchildren to Victoria's demesne, where they were allowed to ride Shetland ponies and were shown the many heirlooms, such as the long carved table where Sir Walter Raleigh ate and the black oaken bed he had slept in. The school ran for two years and then Victoria withdrew as Lady Bountiful after a fiery argument with local officials. "She was always quick to change her mind," Edna Miles, who was Victoria's maid decades ago, recalled recently. "You were never quite sure what was coming up next." Victoria then switched her affections, making substantial donations to nearby Tewksbury Abbey.

Her great delight, as she grew older, was dashing around the countryside in fast cars, three of which she kept in stables of the estate. Cecil Creed, who came to the Martins as a fourteen-year-old pantry boy (and later became valet to Byron, Victoria's son who, retarded from infancy, died in his seventies) today recalls his mistress with affection. "Mrs. Martin and the Prince of Wales owned the first autos in England," stated Creed, and he remembers to this day how many times she threatened to sack him as chauffeur if he didn't drive with the throttle down. "Faster, faster!" she would cry.

In time she was regarded as a great lady of those parts. As the years drifted on she acquired respectability outside the community, too. The Prince of Wales, later Edward VII, was gracious enough to be entertained at Bredon's Norton, and the event was never forgotton in the village. The aged Earl of Coventry once stayed overnight (Victoria had herself photographed with him and sent the picture to all English and American newspapers; the Earl of Coventry was described as "Father of the House of Lords" and Victoria as "United States' Mother of Suffrage," which bewildered a new crop of leaders for women's rights in America who had never heard of her) and with such backing Victoria's good name was assured everywhere. It had taken forty-six years to establish this good name in England and, no doubt, it was worth it, at least to Victoria, for she gloried in entertaining solid and respectable people—Arthur Balfour the Prime Minister, the Lord Mayor of London, Nicholas Murray Butler, President of Columbia University in New York, and a slew of titled nonentities.

There even came the time when she deemed it unnecessary to put out pamphlets defending her past. A series of booklets were issued (titled "The Manor House Causeries"), but they tended more to concentrate on Victoria's train of royal ancestors, and what had once been called her checkered career was relegated to the background.

The aging Victoria spent most of her time on her new hobby, and it was not woman's suffrage, for in all the years she lived in England—exactly half a century—never did she show any in-

terest in the crusade. Once she was asked her opinion of Lady
Nancy Langhorne Astor, who, though American-born, was the
first woman elected to the House of Commons. Victoria merely
sniffed and said she was unimpressed. She did comment, however, when a remark of the suffragist, Jane Olcott, was repeated
to her. Miss Olcott had declared, "A man or a woman should be
free to give love whenever it is natural." Victoria said, rather
sharply, such a female should be hung on the gallows. She herself had always regarded Free Love as being what any decent,
upright citizen would describe it—"a pestilential mire of sen-
sual grossness."

Victoria's new hobby was to publicize in the United States
and Great Britain the historic properties on her Bredon's Norton estate, and to found and join various organizations set up to
foster Anglo-American friendship.

The Woodhull—for even to the day of her death was she so
known to Americans—did not need to call the estate to the attention of the English people, for its historic value had been
appreciated for centuries. On the grounds was an ancient Hermes Lodge, and an even more ancient Old Manor House, believed to be one of the earliest buildings of its kind in England.
The Old Manor House had been built long before Shakespeare's
day, and parts of it were believed to date as far back as the
eleventh century. Visitors from all England were welcomed by
Victoria to inspect it. There was also the Old Tithe Barn, which
had been used in the twelfth century to store produce given by
the parish people as their one-tenth to the church. The guests
were many and they were escorted by Victoria herself, just as
Tennessee had done when she showed her husband's art collection. Of course, the property could not be compared to the
Cook collection for value and drawing power, but the newspapers applauded Victoria's graciousness.

It was in the Old Manor House that Victoria formed the British Committee for the Promotion of Anglo-American Friendship, and here, at long last, Victoria became a President. She was unanimously elected to head the B.C.P. A-A.F., and she devoted much of her time to its activities until she discovered that the little organization was being overshadowed by the Sulgrave Committee of the Anglo-American Society. Many of the great names of the country were associated with this group— Mr. Asquith, the Duchess of Teck, the Archbishop of Canterbury, Viscount Bryce, Lord Rothschild, Lord Cowdray—and so Victoria quickly disbanded her organization and became one of the most fervent members of the Sulgrave Committee.

Sulgrave Manor was the estate where Lawrence Washington, an ancestor of George Washington, had lived from 1539 on, and his family had occupied the estate up to 1619. The Sulgrave Committee was formed to purchase the grounds and turn it into a Washington Shrine, and thus foster friendship between Britain and the United States. Victoria was an indefatigable worker for the cause. Her own property was but forty miles away, and so she visited Sulgrave Manor often, making the trip in the sidecar of a motorcycle. It undoubtedly was gratifying for her to read in the society columns of the aristocratic MORNING POST that among those working with their hands to restore the interior decorating of the place were such social bigwigs as Lady Lee of Fareham, the Countess of Sandwich, Lady Rathcreedon, Lady Arthur Herbert, Mrs. George Harvey—*and* Mrs. J. B. Martin and daughter, Z. Woodhull. Zulu was a little sensitive about her name and used the initial Z, which was a self-defeating effort because it prompted people to ask what the Z stood for.

Victoria at last, now in her eighties, had begun to circulate in high society. And it undoubtedly was comforting, too, for her to see in the subscription list announcing the purchase of the Manor and of its presentation to the British Peace Centenary Committee that, lo, her name led all the rest:

Mrs. J. B. Martin	$1,000
Lord Rothschild	500
Anglo-American Oil Co.	500
Lord Cowdray	500
Sir John Brunner	500

. . .

At the formal opening of Sulgrave Manor in June, 1921, the audience was delighted when a letter was read from Mrs. John Biddulph Martin in which she announced that the Old Manor House on her historic Bredon's Norton estate had been presented outright to the Sulgrave Committee to be used as a center for the work of the movement.

"The only condition which will be attached to this transfer," wrote Mrs. Martin, "will be that it shall always be devoted to the furtherance of Anglo-American amity."

Victoria's generosity was applauded by the newspapers on both sides of the Atlantic. There were reviews of her career in America showing her as the great exponent of Woman's Suffrage, and there was no snide mention of any dark episode in her life.

In the summer of 1922, Victoria announced to the newspapers that, to further the work of the Sulgrave Committee, she was presenting to the organization the Old Manor House on her historic estate, together with an adjacent property, Hermes Lodge. Again there were plaudits.

In February, 1923, Victoria announced that the Sulgrave Committee would receive from her the deeds to the Old Manor House on her historic Bredon's Norton estate, together with relics contained in the house valued at more than $80,000, and that no strings were attached to the gift. All people interested in Anglo-American friendship cheered.

In November, 1924, Victoria announced that it was her intention of giving, outright, the Old Manor House on her historic Bredon's Norton estate, together with Hermes Lodge and the Old Tithe Barn to the Sulgrave Committee. The Committee could do what it liked with the property—sell it, or use it as headquarters.

On September 23, 1925, in commemoration of her eighty-seventh birthday, Victoria announced, as printed by THE NEW YORK TIMES:

"Mrs. Victoria Woodhull Martin, who enters her 89th year [sic] today, has presented beautiful Old Manor House on her estate at Bredon's Norton, together with its historical contents, charming grounds and twelfth century Tithe Barn to the Sulgrave Committee of the Anglo-American Society." Victoria was getting plenty of mileage out of her old buildings.

The patience of the Society members was exhausted. A delegation visited Mrs. J. B. Martin and talked to her sternly. At the conclusion of the meeting it was announced that it was but a matter of days before the deeds of the historic structures on historic Norton Park would be transferred to the Sulgrave Committee.

· 23 ·

Few people in the world, outside of Winston Churchill, stayed in the public eye as long as Victoria Woodhull. For almost sev-

enty years she had been tirelessly interviewed by journalists.
Sometimes she had been able to use the newspapers to promote
her beliefs or to defend herself; usually they used her because
she was colorful copy. Now, in May, 1927, Victoria saw in the
flesh her last reporter, gave her last interview. And by that time
the word "audience" might have been more appropriate.

The London correspondent of THE NEW YORK TIMES talked
to her in Brighton. Victoria's daughter, Zulu, an old lady herself, was present and it was evident that she was not even a pale
carbon copy of her famous mother.

The TIMES man tactfully acknowledged that since 1920 the
women of the United States had been allowed to vote, thanks to
Victoria's crusades.

Victoria conceded that the fact that she had brought
Women's Suffrage to the Americans was history. Alone and
single-handedly, she added, a trifle redundantly.

The reporter asked how he could quote her to support the
current campaign to bring suffrage to the twenty-one-year-old
women of Britain. (It was not until 1928 that Englishwomen
between the ages of twenty-one and thirty were allowed the ballot.) He was surprised to hear that she had changed her views,
even though they were no longer considered wildly radical.

"I want women to have the vote as soon as they are fit for it,"
said Victoria firmly, "but I do not believe in forced maturity.
Twenty-five is young enough for persons of both sexes to exercise the franchise."

What about Victoria Woodhull at twenty-one? Surely she
had been qualified to vote at that age.

"My case was exceptional," replied Victoria with characteristic modesty. "I was making history at twenty-one."

This was somewhat of an exaggeration, as Victoria at twenty-
one was touring the Midwest, telling fortunes in a medicine
show.

"What about your daughter?" asked the newspaperman.

Zulu cleared her throat and said, "Well, yes . . ."

Victoria raised a forefinger and shushed Zulu, as if she were a child.

"Certainly not," she said, answering the question herself.

"Mama is right," chimed in the sixty-six-year-old Zulu. "I knew nothing when I was twenty-one, though I was studious and had read a great deal. I . . . "

Victoria waved the admonitory finger again to silence her daughter. She had the last word before dismissing the newspaperman:

"My sister, Tennessee, and I were mercilessly slandered fifty years ago when we dared advocate women's emancipation and discussed eugenics in America, but time has proven that we were right."

· 24 ·

Mrs. Victoria Woodhull Martin announced early in May, 1927, that on September 23, when her eighty-ninth birthday arrived, she intended to celebrate the historic occasion by deeding various properties and a large sum of money to the Sulgrave Committee. This could be regarded as a definite promise—the lawyers were busy drawing up the papers. The Sulgrave Committee members, who all too long had seen this particular carrot dangling from a stick, figuratively held their breath.

It was believed that The Woodhull would reach the goal, as she was in fairly good health considering her age, but, shortly before midnight on June 9 she died quietly in her sleep at her Norton Park mansion. She was cremated and there was no service. Following the instructions of her will, her ashes were scattered midway in the Atlantic "as a link between my two countries."

In life Victoria had always surpassed Tennessee, and in death the pattern continued. Eight years older than Tennessee, she survived her by four years. Tennessee married the richer man, but Victoria left the most money. After taxes, her estate in England alone (she also left property in New York) was valued at 181,722 pounds, about $883,000. Zulu was her sole heir. If Zulu had not survived her, the greater part of her fortune would have gone to one of her earlier loves: The Society for Psychical Research.

Zulu, always a strange, eerie woman, became even more eccentric after her mother died. Now she turned into a recluse, living in darkened rooms, spending most of her time reading, and seeing no one except servants who brought her meals. Occasionally, late at night, she would venture out on the grounds of the estate and when she came to one of the many rose beds she would quickly turn away—flowers held a special terror for her. The servants ran her and ran the house; they would give parties which she never attended.

Zulu Maud Blood, who fell in love for the first time at thirty-five and promptly fell out of it when Victoria heard the news, died in 1940, aged seventy-nine. She never married so the lines of Victoria and Tennessee became extinct. On the death certificate she was described as "Spinster of independent means, daughter of —— Woodhull, a medical practitioner, deceased." True to the traditional disregard of the Claflin clan of the facts, she went to her grave bearing the wrong name. The entry of death filed in Somerset House, London, lists her name not as Zulu Maud Blood but as Zulu Maud Woodhull.

· 25 ·

In the early years of her life The Woodhull sought fame, but usually was forced to settle for notoriety. In her twilight years she sought, and sought desperately, for Respectability.

In our modern era, the surest way to achieve Respectability, and for that matter, fame too, is to live to be eighty-nine. By then your backbiting contemporaries are dead. By then your peccadillos are forgotten, and the more disreputable aspects of your career have been blanked out of your own memory. By then the members of younger generations have taken over and you are regarded with a certain awe by these younger people because of your venerable age alone. It is hard for the present generation to visualize an old lady of eighty-nine causing such furore by promoting social measures which, radical in a previous age, had been adopted in another. And they are also indulgent in considering sexual escapades that outraged the dreary bourgeois of a remote era. Fornication of a half-century ago is now irrelevant.

And so, when the one-time feminine firebrand died at eighty-nine she was known and accepted as the respectable Mrs. Martin. Victoria would have been delighted to know that finally she was admitted to *Who's Who in America,* but unfortunately she died before seeing her name in those ultra-respectable pages. *Who's Who* discreetly summed up her career with the notation that she had been "a banker in New York." That was all. She would have liked to know, too, that she was honored by a memorial plaque placed in Tewksbury Abbey. At the dedication ceremony the Bishop of Gloucester eulogized her as "a distinguished and remarkable American woman."

Longevity brought the prize, Respectability. Victoria Woodhull died only forty years ago and, incredible as it may seem, she was born when Martin Van Buren was President, and she lived into the reign of Calvin Coolidge. When she was born in 1838, Lincoln was a struggling young lawyer in Springfield, Illinois. Between the birth of her father, old Buck—when Washington was President—and her death there was a span of one hundred and fifty years. Longevity meant that Victoria outlived all her contemporaries, with the exception of Bennie Tucker, who was half her age when he met her. She survived Comstock, Tilton and his Lib, Train, Andrews, Blood, Tennessee, Vanderbilt, Henry James, Mrs. Stanton and Miss Anthony, Laura Cuppy Smith, Howe & Hummel, the Reverend Henry Ward Beecher, and all the rest of the cast.

. 26 .

It would have pleased her to have known that the death of Victoria C. Woodhull was mourned in long columns of type, although, because New York was preparing for a huge reception for Lindbergh, who had flown the Atlantic alone, the news tended to be placed deep inside the newspapers. As practically all of her contemporaries were dead, editors were forced to consult the clippings. The stories were charitable. Victoria was hailed as "Mother of Suffrage" and the scandals were skimmed over.

She would have liked to have read the encomium paid her by the MORNING POST of London, that socially correct paper favored by the upper classes:

"There goes to her long rest a veteran who lived to see the triumph of a cause for which she was one of the first to contend. Mrs. Martin cleared the way for leaders of agitation for equal political rights alike in America, this country and elsewhere. The younger generation knows not the indomitable leader to whom their enfranchisement owes so much. It was she who blazed the trail for those more insurgent leaders who finally won the victory."

The TIMES of London was generous with her, as was the case when Tennessee died. There was no hint of scandal in her life. In the United States "Miss Victoria contented herself with banking which she carried on in New York and scientific agriculture." The authoritative TIMES found, strangely, that Victoria had studied law, medicine, and surgery, just as Tennessee had. There was no mention of Spiritualism or other raffish pursuits.

Victoria had lived so long that some of the incidents in her colorful career had passed into the realm of legend. The Worcester DAILY TIMES recalled in its obituary that she had all but caused a revolution in the United States. The newspaper explained:

"Their sufferings while awaiting trial told on their health, and Mrs. Martin was, on one occasion, reported to be dead. The masses were stirred for they believed in the mission of Mrs. Martin and her sister, and they threatened to pull down or burn the Government buildings, but after a few days she recovered and the fury abated."

In the United States the newspapers could find only one person who had known Victoria in her heyday. Bennie Tucker, who had blown hot and cold on Victoria, now blew cold. "She

would have been glorious, if she hadn't been infamous," declared Bennie. But the *Nation*, the distinguished journal with a
long memory, recalled: "Fifty-five years ago Victoria Woodhull's name was on every tongue and in every newspaper. She
and her sister were not merely famous—they were notorious."

Why were they notorious?

For no good reason, the *Nation* found. When the Claflin sisters were crusading for their sex no respectable office would
hire women to act as secretaries, or to answer the telephone, or
to do anything except scrub floors. So the tag, notorious, was
applied to the sisters. "Almost every reform for the advocacy of
which Victoria Woodhull and her sister were so bitterly attacked has long since become a commonplace," noted the magazine.

Many a modern writer has pondered over the curious personalities of Victoria and Tennessee, and the appraisals have been
generally sympathetic. Emanie Sachs, who in 1928 wrote a
masterful biography of Victoria, saw her as "a woman who
dared to do anything she wanted to do." Herbert Asbury
thought the sisters ". . . probably deserve the crown as
America's shrewdest and most bizarre adventuresses, as well as
the most successful." The verdict of Heywood Broun and Margaret Leech in their biography of Comstock was: "The two
wild sisters were undoubtedly reprehensible in their conduct
. . . but, as we read their stories, they are touched by a mad
and reckless gallantry." Gerald W. Johnson paid tribute to Victoria as the spirited woman who "jarred this nation right down
to its heels and laid prostrate a number of swelling reputations
and a larger number of swollen conventions and punctilios."
He pointed out that the rights for which she fought, for a
woman to be accepted on her merits as a human being, are no
longer questioned. Johnson concluded: "She spoke the truth

courageously, and no man or woman has ever yet defied peril to speak the truth without producing a profound and lasting effect."

Whatever the truth, whatever the persecution complex that triggered Victoria's explosive aggressiveness, whatever the drive that made her seek for acceptance in high social circles, whatever her insatiable love for publicity, whatever the ambition that drove her to seemingly unobtainable goals, goals which in the end she usually reached—when the histories came to be written about woman's suffrage, about Socialism and Communism, about Free Love, about eccentrics, about the excesses of the press, about Wall Street and finance, about Spiritualism, about the great American orators, about Anglo-American friendship, about a host of other subjects, there is the name of Victoria C. Woodhull. What the ultimate judgment of posterity on Victoria C. Woodhull will be, no one knows. Yet surely few people today will deny that she was *sui generis*.

A SELECTED BIBLIOGRAPHY

BOOKS

Abbott, Austin. *Official Report of the Trial of Henry Ward Beecher*. 2 vols. New York, 1875.

Altrocchi, Julia Cooley. *The Spectacular San Franciscans*. New York, 1949.

Andrews, Wayne. *The Vanderbilt Legend*. New York. [1941]

Anonymous. *The Beecher-Tilton Scandal, a Complete History of the Case, with Mrs. Woodhull's Original Statement*. Brooklyn, 1874.

Bach, Marcus. *They Have Found a Faith*. Indianapolis, 1946.

Barrows, Chester L. *William M. Evarts*. Chapel Hill, N.C., 1941.

Beecham, Sir Thomas. *A Mingled Chime*. New York, 1943.

Bonner, Hypatia Bradlaugh. *Charles Bradlaugh*. London, 1908.

Brooks, Van Wyck. *The Pilgrimage of Henry James*. New York, 1925.

——— *The Times of Melville and Whitman*. New York, 1927.

Broun, Heywood, and Leech, Margaret. *Anthony Comstock*. New York, 1927.

Butterfield, Roger. *The American Past*. New York, 1947.

Catt, Carrie Chapman, and Shuler, Nettie Rogers. *Women's Suffrage and Politics*. New York, 1923.

Claflin, Tennessee. *Constitutional Equality, a Right of Women*. Woodhull, Claflin & Co., New York, 1871.

——— *Essays on Social Topics*, by Lady Cook. Four volumes bound as

two. Roxburghe Press [London]. n.d. [1897] [Later reissued under title, *Talks and Essays.*]

Clews, Henry. *Twenty Eight Years in Wall Street.* New York, n.d. [1887].

Commons, John R., and associates. *History of Labour in the United States.* Vol. 2. New York, 1926.

Crockett, Albert Stevens. *Peacocks on Parade.* New York, 1931.

Davis, Paulina Wright. *History of the National Woman's Rights Movement for Twenty Years.* Woodhull, Claflin & Co., New York, 1871.

Dorr, Rheta Childe. *Susan B. Anthony.* New York, 1928.

Doyle, John P. *The Romance of Plymouth Church.* Hartford, 1874.

Fowler, William Worthington. *Ten Years in Wall Street.* Hartford, 1870.

Harper, Ida Husted. *The Life and Works of Susan B. Anthony,* 3 vols. Vol. 1 & 2, Indianapolis, 1898. Vol. 3, Kansas City, 1908.

Hibben, Paxton. *Henry W. Beecher, An American Portrait.* New York, 1927.

Hillquit, Morris. *History of Socialism in the United States.* New York, 1903.

Holbrook, Stewart. *Dreamers of the American Dream.* New York, 1957.

Hudson, Frederic. *Journalism in the U.S. from 1690 to 1872.* New York, 1873.

James, Henry. *The Siege of London.* New York, 1883.

Josephson, Matthew. *The Robber Barons.* New York, 1934.

Kramer, Dale. *Heywood Broun.* New York, 1949.

Lutz, Alma. *Created Equal, a Biography of Elizabeth Cady Stanton.* New York, n.d. [1940].

Lynch, Denis Tilden. *"Boss" Tweed.* New York, 1927.

—— *The Wild Seventies,* New York, 1941.

McGurrin, John. *Bourke Cockran.* New York, 1948.

Madison, Charles A. *Critics and Crusaders.* New York, 1947.

Marberry, M. M. *The Golden Voice.* New York, 1947.

Mott, Frank Luther. *A History of American Magazines, 1865-1885.* Cambridge, Mass., 1938.

Mulholland, John. *Beware Familiar Spirits.* New York, 1938.

Oliver, Leon. *The Great Sensation.* Chicago, 1873.

Pearson, Hesketh. *Marrying Americans.* New York, 1961.

Rourke, Constance Hayfield. *Trumpets of Jubilee.* New York, 1937.

Sachs, Emanie. *The Terrible Siren.* New York, 1928.

Seitz, Don. *The Dreadful Decade.* Indianapolis, 1926.

—— *Uncommon Americans.* Indianapolis, 1927.

Smith, Arthur D. Howden. *Commodore Vanderbilt.* New York, 1927.

Smith, Matthew Hale. *Twenty Years Among the Bulls and Bears of Wall Street.* New York, 1871.

Sprague, Homer B. *Recollections of Henry W. Beecher.* Newton, Mass., 1905.

Stowe, Lyman Beecher. *Saints, Sinners and Beecher.* New York, c. 1934.

Symes, Lillian, and Clement, Travers. *Rebel America.* New York, 1934.

Thornton, Willis. *The Nine Lives of Citizen Train.* New York, 1948.
Tilton, Theodore. *Tempest Tossed.* New York, 1874.
Train, George Francis. *My Life in Many States and Foreign Lands.* New York, 1902.
Tucker, Benjamin Ricketson. *Individual Liberty.* New York, 1926.
Verbatim Report of the Action of Theodore Tilton against Henry W. Beecher, 3 vols. New York, 1875.
"Verdendorp, Basil." [pseud.] *The Verdendorps.* New York, n.d. [1880?].
Wallace, Irving. *The Square Pegs.* New York, 1957.
Who's Who in America, 1927.
Williamson, Francis P. *Beecher and His Accusers.* Philadelphia, n.d. [1874].
Woodhull, Victoria C. Foreword by, in *Elective Affinities,* by Goethe. Boston, 1872.
———— *One Moral Standard for All.* New York, n.d. [1895?].
———— *Origins, Tendencies and Principles of Government.* Woodhull, Claflin & Co., New York, 1871.
Wyck, Frederic Van. *Recollections of an Old New Yorker.* New York, 1932.

PAMPHLETS, SCRAPBOOKS, ETC.

Anonymous. "Brief Sketches of the Life of Victoria C. Woodhull [Mrs. J. B. Martin]." [London] n.d. [1893].
———— "Life and History of T. C. Claflin, now Lady Cook." London, 1892.
Bell, Clark. "Speech of Clark Bell, Esq., upon the inquiry as to the sanity or insanity of George Francis Train." New York, 1873.
Bowen, Henry C. "Scrapbook compiled in the Office of the INDEPENDENT." 5 vols. n.d. At the New York Public Library.
Claflin, Tennessee. "The Ethics of Sexual Equality, a Lecture delivered at the New York Academy of Music, March 29, 1872." Woodhull, Claflin & Co., New York, 1873.
———— "Illegitimacy." London, n.d. [188-].
———— "Who Rules?" [London] n.d. [191-].
Darewin, G. S. "Synopsis of the Lives of Victoria C. Woodhull and Tennessee Claflin." London, 1891.
Darwin, M. F. "One Moral Standard for All." New York, n.d. [1895?].
Fairfield, Rev. Edmund B. "Wickedness in High Places." Mansfield, Ohio, 1874.
Legge, Madeleine. "Two Noble Women, Nobly Planned." London, 1893.
Miscellaneous Biographical Material on Victoria C. Woodhull. At the New York Public Library.
Raymond, Robert R. "Malice in High Places." n.d. [1874].

"Scrapbook of clippings relating to the Beecher-Tilton Trial." Presented to to the New York Public Library by Hamilton Holt, Esq., April 15, 1915.

"Scrapbook of clippings relating to the Vanderbilt Will Case." At the New York Public Library.

Stedman, Charles J. "Ye Tilt-on Beecher; or, Ye Muddle of Ye Mutual Friends." Anonymous. By the author of "Ye Russian Ball." New York, n.d. [1874].

Tilton, Theodore. "Golden Age Tracts, No. 3": Victoria C. Woodhull. New York, 1871.

Treat, Dr. Joseph. "Beecher, Tilton, Woodhull, the Creation of Society." New York, 1874.

Woodhull, Victoria C. "A Fragmentary Record of Public Work Done in America, 1871-2." London, 1887.

—— "A Lecture on Constitutional Equality, being a lecture delivered in Lincoln Hall, Washington, D.C., also in Cooper Institute, New York, Academy of Music, Brooklyn, Academy of Music, Philadelphia, Opera House, Syracuse, together with her secession speech delivered in Apollo Hall, New York, May 12, 1871." Woodhull, Claflin & Co., New York, 1871.

—— "Origin, Tendencies, and Principles of Government." New York, 1871.

—— "And the Truth Shall Make You Free, being a speech given at Steinway Hall, New York." Woodhull, Claflin & Co., New York, 1871.

—— "A Page of American History, 1870-76." London, n.d. [1888?].

—— "A Speech on Labor & Capital." n.d.

—— "A Speech on the Garden of Eden." "Revised" edition, London, 1890.

—— "A Speech on the Principles of Finance." Woodhull, Claflin & Co., New York, 1871.

—— "Breaking the Seals." n.d. [1875?].

—— "Campaign Document, No. 2, of the Equal Rights Party." Woodhull, Claflin & Co., New York, 1872.

—— "Carpenter and Cartter Reviewed." A Speech delivered before the Woman's Suffrage Convention, Lincoln Hall, Washington, D.C., Jan. 19, 1872. New York, 1872.

—— "Freedom! Equality!! Justice!!! A Speech on the impending Revolution, delivered in the Music Hall, Boston, Thursday, February 1, 1872, and in the Academy of Music, New York, Feb. 20, 1872." Woodhull, Claflin & Co., New York, 1872.

—— "Humanitarian Government." Published by the British Association, London, 1890.

—— "Humanitarian Money." London, n.d. [1892].

—— "Paradise Found." London, n.d. [189?].

—— "Stirpiculture." London, n.d. [1888].

———— "The Talebearer." London, n.d.
———— "The Alchemy of Maternity." London, n.d. [1889?].
———— "The Arguments for Woman's Electoral Rights, a Review of my Work at Washington, D.C., 1870-1." London, 1887.
———— "The Elixir of Life." New York, 1873.
———— "The Human Body as the Temple of God." London, 1890. [Tennessee Claflin listed as co-author.]
———— "The Rapid Multiplication of the Unfit." London, 1891.
———— "Tried as by Fire, or, the True and the False Society, an Oration delivered 150 consecutive nights." New York, 1874.
Woodhull, Zulu Maud. *Affinities, a Play*. [London] 1896.
———— "The Proposal, a Dialogue." [London] [1899?].

MAGAZINES

American Heritage, June, 1956. "Dynamic Victoria," by Gerald W. Johnson.
Annals of the American Academy of Political Science. [Philadelphia] July, 1897, for sketch of John Biddulph Martin.
Chambers's Journal, Vol. 48, July 15, 1871. "A Specimen of Feminine Journalism."
Christian Union.
Cosmopolitan, Dec., 1936. "Six Sinful Sinners," by Herbert Asbury.
Economic Journal, June, 1897. [London] For sketch of John Biddulph Martin.
Harper's Weekly.
Humanitarian. 3 vols. New York, n.d.
Independent Woman, Oct., 1956. "No New Thing Under the Sun," by E. H. Trepte.
Leslie's Illustrated Weekly.
Liberty [Boston].
Modern Review, April, 1893. [London].
New York Times Magazine. May 27, 1956. "Woman for President?" By H. Cheshire and M. Cheshire.
New Yorker, June 12, 1954. "That Was New York; Beecher-Tilton Case." By Robert Shaplen.
Nation, June 29, 1927. On death of Victoria C. Woodhull.
Puck [New York].
Westminster Review [London], April, 1899. Review of Zulu Maud Woodhull's play, *Affinities*.
Vineland [New Jersey] *Historical Magazine*.

NEWSPAPERS

New York HERALD TRIBUNE, THE NEW YORK TIMES, WORLD, DAILY GRAPHIC, SUN, EVENING POST; Chicago MAIL, INTER-OCEAN; Brooklyn EAGLE; Hartford TIMES, DAILY COURANT; Newark, Ohio, ADVOCATE; WOODHULL & CLAFLIN'S WEEKLY; POMEROY'S DEMOCRAT; London TIMES.

Index

Albany *Post*, 186.
Alexandra House, 243–4, 271, 298.
Alta California, 89.
Andrews, Stephen Pearl, 13, 26, 58, 93, arrested, 114; 185–6, 217, 326.
Anthony, Susan B., suffragette, on V., 18; on V., 19–20; on V., 23; 85, on V., 86–7; 123, 326.
Asbury, Herbert, 328.
Astor House, N.Y., 11.
Astor, William B., 83.
"Aurora" (painting), 9, 191, 236.

Bartels, John, 269, 299.
Beecham, Adrian Welles, 308.
Beecham, Sir Thomas, background, 306; marries Utica Welles, 307; career, death, 308.
Beecham, Capt. Thomas Welles, 308.
Beecham, Lady Utica (Tennessee's

grandniece), marries Beecham, 307; 314.
Beecher, Catherine, and V., 26–7.
Beecher, Rev. Henry Ward, 19, 27, 34–5, scandal starts, 38–41; writes *Life of Christ*, 39; V.'s letter to, 64–5; his reaction, 65–6; 81; V. appeals to, 97; 98, "exposed" by V., 99–105; accused by V., 109–11; 118, 123–5, 127–8, 129, 137, attacked by *Thunderbolt*, 142–3; 144–6, 162–3, 167, "investigated," 168–71; whitewashed, 173; on trial, 173–9; V. defends, 180–1; 205, death, 248–9; 326.
Beecher, Lyman, 125.
Beechem, Rev. Thomas, 124–5.
Benjamin, Park, 39.
Bennett, James Gordon, 14.
Blood, Col. James H. (V.'s 2d hus-

338 • *Index* •

band), 12–13, 26, 28, family
squabble, 29–32; 38, 45, another
family row, 55–7; 93, 95, arrested,
114; 130–1, arrested, 135; 139,
wins trial, 147–8; 150–1, 155–7,
wins Challis trial, 158–60; 164,
European trip, 167; 172–3, 183–4,
V. divorces, 188; 206, 215, 217–19,
223, death, 239; 242, 326.
Blood, Zulu Maud—see Zulu Woodhull.
Boston *Journal*, 101.
Bowen, Henry C., 33, 39–41, 145.
Bradlaugh, Charles, von V., 309–10.
Bredon's Norton, Worc., 309–10,
315–18, 320–1.
British Museum, Martin warns, 283;
sued by Martins, 287–91; 304.
Brooke, Charles W., 158–60.
Brooker, Utica (V.'s sister), 13, 69,
84, 146, family row, 148; death,
149; 206, 240.
Brooklyn *Eagle*, 44–5, on V., 51;
125, 140–2, 147, 162–3, 170–1, at-
tacks sisters, 264.
Brooklyn *Sunday Press*, Tilton's
notes to V., 51–2; 163.
Brooklyn *Union*, 39–40.
Broun, Heywood, 328.
Bryant, William Cullen, 257.
Bullard, Laura Curtis, 19.
Burns, Rosa, 245–7.
Burns, Ross, 244–8.
Butler, Gen. Benjamin F., 20, 23,
139–40, 152, 231.
Byrnes, Inspector Thomas E., 264–5.

Campbell, Lord Colin, 220–1, 234.
Carpenter, Matthew Hale, 20.
Carter, Judge, 87–8.
Challis, Luther C., in scandal, 105–7;
causes sisters' arrest, 113–14;

117–19, 125, 137, loses trial,
158–60.
Chicago *Journal*, 171.
Chicago *Mail*, 181–2, 284.
Chicago *Times*, interviews V., 91–2;
ditto, 94–5; ditto, 109–11; 125–6,
interviews Tilton, 128; 143, 163.
Chicago *Tribune*, 153.
Cleveland *Leader*, on V., 269–70.
Christian Union (weekly), 39, 81.
Claflin, Governor, on Tennessee,
129–30.
Claflin, H. B., 145.
Claflin, Hebern (V.'s brother), 37,
243.
Claflin, Reuben "Buck" Buckman
(V.'s father), 11, 37, 44, 202, sails
for England, 203; 229, death,
239–41; 256, 266–69, 299–300, 314,
326.
Claflin, "Roxy" Roxanna Hummel
(V.'s mother), 11, family row,
29–32; 44, another row, 55–7; 119,
149, 151, 154–5, 167, 183, 185, 193,
202, sails for England, 203; 219,
229–30, death, 241; 256, 266–69.
Claflin, Tennessee (Tennie C.), description of, 5–6; quoted, 6; and
Vanderbilt, 7–10; founds *Woodhull
& Claflin's Weekly*, 15–17; family
row, 29–32; background rumors,
37–8; another row, 55–7; runs for
Congress, 57–60; publishes "Constitutional Equality . . . ," 58; at
Steinway Hall lecture, 67; lecture
tour, 73–4; 84, *N.Y. Times* attacks,
90–1; as "Colonel," 92–3; Comstock causes arrest, 112–14; jailed,
115–16; in court, rejailed, 118–19;
out on bail, 127; Governor attacks,
129–30; in and out of jail, 138–9;
144, meets Beecher's friends,
145–6; wins trial, 147–8; Challis

trial, not guilty, 158–60; silent on Beecher scandal, 162–3; meets Tucker, 164–6; European trip, 167, 172–3; discards Spiritualism, Free Love, 187–8; indictments quashed, 189; *Weekly* folds, 190; Vanderbilt dies, will probated, 191–5; sails for England, 196; meets Francis Cook, 212–14; sails for U.S., 219; wooed by Cook, 232–3; family row, 236; marries Cook, 237; becomes Lady Cook, 243; snubbed, 254; respectability campaign, 255–8, 260; Ottawa (Ill.) exposé, 262, 266–70; N.Y. visit, 262–4; return to England, 270; back to U.S., 1892, 274; husband sued, 291–2; returns to London, 295; visits N.Y., 297–8; remarries Cook in civil ceremony, 299; in lawsuit, 305–6; visits to U.S., 311; and W.W.I, 312–13; last U.S. trip, 313; dies 1923, 314; her estate, 314–15; 324, 326, 327.

Clark, Edward H. G., 142–3.
Clarke, Sir Edward, 304–5.
Clewes, Henry, 10, 118, 176.
Cogswell, Anna, actress, 46–7, 161.
Committee for the Suppression of Vice, 112.
Communism, 53–4.
Comstock, Anthony J., causes sisters' arrest, 112–13; 120–1, 125–6, 135, 137–9, 142, 147, 263, 326, 328.
Cook art collection—see Sir Francis Cook.
Cook, Sir Francis, meets Tennessee, 212–14; woos her; 232–3, 235–6, marries her, 237; background, 237–8; art collection, 238–9; made baronet, 243; offers reward, 261–2; art collection, 271–3; sued, 291–2; remarries T. in civil ceremony,

299; death, 299; his will, 300, art collection to U.S., 301; 302–3.
Cook, Sir Francis Ferdinand, 301.
Cooper Institute, N.Y., 24, V. lectures at, 135–7.
Cornhill Magazine, 226, 228.
"Corsican Brothers, The" (play), 47.
Creed, Cecil (V.'s chauffeur), 316–17.
Cuckoo magazine, 215–18.

Davis, Noah, U.S. District Atty., 113–14.
Davis, Pauline, 19.
Delmonico's Restaurant, N.Y., 6, 9.
Demosthenes, visits V., 49–50; 202.
Dickenson, Anna, 24.
Doughty House (Cook's mansion), 213, 237–9, 271–3, 297–9, 301, 305, 314.
Douglass, Frederick, 88.
Dubuque, Iowa *Herald*, 154.

Economic Journal (London), 296.
Ellery, George H., 145.
Equal Rights Party, 87–8, 94, 96, 126.
Evarts, William M., 174–9.

Fisk, Jim, 8, 92, 118, 174.
Frank Leslie's Budget of Fun, 52.
Frank Leslie's Magazine, 54.
Free Love, 42, 76, 82, 89–90, 118, 128–9, V. espouses, 150; 181, 183, 256.
Frothingham, Rev. Octavius Brooks, 130, 176.
Fullerton, William, Beecher trial, 174–9.

Galesburg, Ill. *Republican*, 154.
Golden Age (ed. by Tilton), 40–2, "Biography" of V., 43–50; 94, 240, 261.

Golden City, 89.
Grant, Pres. Ulysses S., 14, 21, 38, 93, 126.
Greeley, Horace, 28, 94, 126, 180.
Green, Johnnie, 148–9, 205.

Harper's Weekly, on V., 52; calls V. "Mrs. Satan," 89–90.
Harris, Senator, 18.
Hartford *Courant*, on V., 63.
Hartford *Post*, 78.
Hartford *Times*, 125.
Harvey, Dr. J. H.—see Col. James H. Blood.
Hawley, Governor, on V., 63.
Heywood, Ezra Hervey, 140–1.
Hoffman House, N.Y., 6, 11.
Homer, Ohio, 37, 43, 243, 316.
Hooker, Isabella Beecher, on V., 19; 20, 26, 85–6, 124–5, 170–1.
Howe & Hummel, 116, 273, 326.
Howe, Julia Ward, suffragette, 23.
Howe, William F. (V.'s counsel), 117–19, 138–9, 273–4.
Hugo, Victor, 225, 234.
Humanitarian, 278–81, 293–4, 296.
Humby, Betty, 308.
Hummel, Abe (V.'s counsel), 116–17, 138.

Independent (weekly), 33, 39–40, 112.

James, Henry, 226–8, 326.
Johnson, Gerald W., on V., 259; on V., 328–9.
Julian, Representative George W., 18, 20.

Kalloch, Isaac S., on V., 71; 174.
Kiernan, James, 127, 205.
Kokomo (Ind.) *Dispatch*, 186.

Lady Cook—see Tennessee Claflin.
Leech, Margaret, 328.
Livermore, Mrs. Mary, suffragette, 23–4, 78.
Lookwood, Mrs. Belva A., 231.
London Court Journal, 208–10, 214.
London *Traveller*, 208.
London *World*, 228.

MacKinley, Edward, 127, 138, sues V., 273–6.
Martin, Fernando de Francisco, 212–13, 244–6.
Martin, Mrs. J. B.—see Victoria C. Woodhull.
Martin, John Biddulph, meets V., 201–2; 207, 210, 216, 218, background, 212–4; marries V., 228; 230, 232, visits U.S. 1885, 233–4; honored, 244; letter to N.Y. *Herald*, 247–8; 254, offers reward, 261–2; N.Y. visit, 262–4; defends V., 264–5; returns to England, 270; back to U.S. 1892, 273; 280, visits Chicago, 281–2; returns to Chicago, 284–5; sues Brit. Museum, 287–91; returns to London, 295; death, 296; his estate, 297; 299.
Martin, Mrs. Margaret Ann, 210–11, 224, 226, death, 228.
Marx, Karl, 28, 53–4.
McDermott, James M., 142, 163.
Memphis *Appeal*, 99–100.
Meriweather, Mrs. E. A., on V., 99–100.
Miles, D. C. (V.'s brother-in-law), arrested, 114.
Miles, D. W., 130.
Miles, Edna (V.'s maid), 316.
Miles, J. Euclid, 315.
Miles, Mrs. Margaret Ann (V.'s sis-

ter), 13, 154–5, 192–3, 206, 236, remarries, 263; 274–6, 293–4, 315.
Montserrat, Viscount of—see Sir Francis Cook.
Morning Post (London), obit on V., 327.
Mott, Lucretia, suffragette, 27, death, 219.

Nast, Thomas, caricatures V., 89.
Nation, The (N.Y.), obit on V., 328.
Newark (N.J.) *Call*, 180.
New York *Dispatch*, 117.
New York *Graphic*, on V., 144; 239.
New York *Herald*, 6, 14, interviews V., 109–11; 116, 118, 137, 141, 149, on V., 150; 180–2, 247–8.
New York *Sun*, 5, 104, 139, 148, 234, 240, 256.
New York *Sunday Mercury*, 116, 125.
New York *Telegraph*, 98–9.
New York Times, 20–21, 30, 34–5, attacks V., 83–4; on V., 90; 91–3, 116, 125, 139, 174–6, 179, interviews sisters, 192–5; on V.'s London debut, 200–1; 220, 236–7, 243, 263, 285, 292–3, 314, 322–3.
New York *Tribune*, on V., 28; 176, 263.
New York *World*, 34, 153, 227–8, on V., 234–5; 240.
Norton Park (V.'s estate), 297, 309, description of, 315–16; 321, 324.

O'Halloran, Mrs. Margaret—see Margaret Ann Miles.
Osborn, U.S. Commissioner, 113–14, 117.

Pall Mall Gazette, 215.
Panarchy, 13.

Paris *Call*, 225.
Philadelphia *Record*, 155.
Philadelphia *Press*, on V., 21.
Philadelphia *Star*, 126.
Pillsbury, Parker, on V., 107–8; 151.
Pittsburgh *Leader*, on V., 144.
Plymouth Church (Brooklyn), on sisters, 27; 38–9, 111, 162.
Pomeroy's Democrat, on V., 52; 128–9, 144–5.
Pomeroy, Samuel C., on V., 18–19.
Psyche Club (N.Y.), 23, 246.

Reid, Jacob Whitelaw, 176.
Reymart, Judge J. D., 87, 114, 116, 145.
Ruggles, Emily B., 153–4.
Russell, Sir Charles (Lord Russell), 288-90.
Russell, Lillian, 221.

Sachs, Emanie (V.'s biographer), 157, 328.
Salomon, Editha, actress, 36.
San Francisco *Chronicle*, 154.
Seitz, Don, on V., 24–5.
Shearman, "Tearful Tommy," Beecher trial, 174–9.
Sherry's Restaurant (N.Y.), 6.
Siege of Paris, The, 226–8.
Smith, Laura Cuppy, suffragette, 119, 136, 326.
Sparr, Dr. Benjamin, 13, death, 55–6; 240–1, 245.
Sparr, Millard F., 274.
Sparr, Mrs. Polly (V.'s sister), 13, family row, 30; ditto, 55–7; 206, 236, in scandal, 244–8; 315.
Spirit of Kansas, on V., 71.
Spiritualism, meeting, 60; 98–100, meeting, 154–5; 181, 183, 213, 269, 327.

342 • *Index* •

Springfield *Republican,* 78, 132.
Stanton, Elizabeth Cady, suffragette, on V., 23; 24, 27, 41, 85–6, 103, 123–4, 180, 187, 326.
Stedman, Charles J., poem on scandal, 108.
Steinway Hall (N.Y.), 64–71.
Stewart, A. T., 83.
Stirpiculture, 256, 284.
Stowe, Harriet Beecher, attacks V., 81.
Sulgrave Committee, 319–21, 323.
Sutherland, N.Y. Judge, 158–60.
Swindell, Anne L., sues V., 37.

Tewksbury Abbey, 316, 325–6.
Thunderbolt, exposes Beecher, 142–3.
Thurman, Mrs. A. M., 166–7.
Tilton, "Lib" Elizabeth, 40–1, 66, in Beecher scandal, 103–5; 128–9, 162, Beecher "investigation," 168–71; Beecher trial, 174–9; 326.
Tilton, Theodore, and Beecher scandal, 39–41; meets V., 41–2; "Biography" of V., 43–50; 55, at Steinway Hall lecture, 67–71; rift with V., 94–6; in Beecher scandal, 103–5; V.'s betrayal, 109–11; 115, 128–9, 142, 146, Beecher "investigation," 168–71; at Beecher trial, 173–9; 180, 205, 240, 261, 326.
Times (London), 314, obit on V., 327.
Tracy, Gen. Benjamin F. (Beecher's counsel), 168–9, Beecher trial, 174–9.
Train, Charles Francis, puts up bail, 114–15; arrested, 120–2; 326.
Treat, Dr. Joseph, 58, 186, libelous pamphlet, 190; 204–6, 215, 219.
Troy *Daily Press,* 125.

Tucker, "Bennie" Benjamin R., meets V., 156–7; sees V. again, 164–6; European tour, 167, 172–3; 204, 241, 326, 327–8.

Vanderbilt, Commodore Cornelius, 7, and Claflin sisters, 7–10; 185, death, 190; will of, 191–5; 236, 270, 326.
Vanderbilt, Mrs. Sophia, 8.
Vanderbilt, William Henry, 191–5.

Wallace, John Henry, 302–4, 308.
Washington *Daily Patriot,* on sisters, 20–1.
Washington *Gazette,* 186.
Watertown (N.Y.) *Dispatch,* 186.
Webster, Sir Richard (Lord Alverstone), 288, 290–1, 304.
Welles, Charles Stuart, 280, 293–5, 307.
Welles, Utica Celestia—see Beecham, Lady Utica.
Wilde, Oscar, 216, 218.
Woman's Suffrage, 18–23, 1871 meeting, 27–8; 1872 convention, 85–9; 181.
Woodhull, Byron (V.'s son), 13, 316–17.
Woodhull, Dr. Canning (V.s 1st husband), 12–13, 31, marries V., 45–6; 47–8, death, 84; 223, 241.
Woodhull, Victoria (Vicky) C., description of, 5–6; and Vanderbilt, 7–10; writes for N.Y. *Herald,* 14; founds *Woodhull & Claflin's Weekly,* 15–17; comment on, 17; Washington Memorial, 18–22; called Free Lover, 23; on lecture tour, 24–6; 1871 suffragette speech, 27–8; family row, 28–32; Open Letter, 34–6;

sued twice, 36–7; background
rumors, 37–8; Beecher scandal
starts, 38–41; meets Tilton,
41–2; friendship with Tilton,
42; Tilton's "Biography" of,
43–50; and Marxism, 53–4;
family squabble, 55–7; nominated
for pres., 60–1; V.'s reply, 61–2;
publishes "Origins . . . ," 61;
lecture tour, 62–3; lectures in
Steinway Hall, 64–71; letter to
Beecher, 64–5; for Free Love,
69–71; family evicted, 71;
lecture tour, 73–4; *Weekly*
accused, 78–80; Acad. of Music
lecture, 82–4; Canning Woodhull
dies, 84; 1872 Suffrage
Convention, 85–9; founds Equal
Rights Party, 87–8; nom. for
pres., 88–9; *Harper's Weekly*
attacks, 89–90; admits to Free
Love, 90; family evicted, 94,
97–8; rift with Tilton, 94–6;
appeals to Beecher, 97; in court,
98; exposes Beecher scandal,
99–105; Challis scandal, 105–7;
tells all on Tilton, 109–11;
Comstock causes arrest of,
112–14; jailed, 115–16; in court,
rejailed, 118–19; Open Letter to
N.Y. *Herald*, 122–3; support for,
123–6; loses Pres. election, 126;
out on bail, 127; more
publications, 130; Cooper Inst.
lecture, 135–7; in and out of
jail, 138–9; *Thunderbolt* on,
142–3; illness and recovery,
144–5; wins trial, 147–8; sister
Utica dies, 149; espouses Free
Love, 150; Western tour, 151–7;
meets Bennie Tucker, 156–7;
Challis trial, 158–9; not guilty,
160; West Coast tour, 161; silent

on Beecher scandal, 162–3; sees
Tucker again, 164–6; European
trip, 167, 172–3; Beecher
"investigation," 168–72; role in
Beecher trial, 174–9; turns on
Tilton, 180–1; Open Letter to
N.Y. *Herald*, 181–2; lecture tour
fails, 184–6; discards
Spiritualism, Free Love, 187–8;
divorces Blood, 188; indictments
quashed, 189; *Weekly* folds, 190;
Vanderbilt dies, will probated,
191–5; sails for England, 196;
London lecture debut, 200–2;
meets Martin, 201–2; letter to
London Court Journal, 208–10;
2d bid for Presidency, 211–12;
explains away Free Love, 216–17;
sails for U.S., 218–19; Woodhull
Manifesto, 224–6; Henry James'
Siege of Paris published, 226–8;
marries J. B. Martin, 228;
Claflin "pedigree," 228–30; 1884
election results, 231; visits U.S.
1885, 233–4; father Claflin dies,
239–41; ex-husband Blood dies,
239, 242; family scandal, 244–8;
snubbed, 254; respectability
campaign, 255–8; 1888 election
results, 258; Ottawa (Ill.) exposé,
262, 266–70; N.Y. visit, 262–4,
returns to England, 270; back
to U.S., 1892, 274; U.S.
election results, 277; founds
Humanitarian, 279; visits
Chicago, 281–2; lecture tour
canceled, 283–4; returns to
Chicago, 284–5; various
publications, 285–7; sues Brit.
Museum, 287–91; last U.S. visit,
292–5; family row, 293–5; returns
to London, 295; and Sulgrave
Committee, 319–21; last

interview, 322–3; death, 1927, 324; her estate, 324; appraisals of, 325–29.

Woodhull, Zulu Maud (V.'s daughter), 13, birth, 48; 76–7, 151, at Challis trial, 158–60; European tour, 167, 172–3; 185, 219, "engagement," 220–1; visits U.S. 1885, 233–4; N.Y. visit, 262–5; 280, 292–5, 310, 319, 323, V.'s heir, 324; death, 1940, 324.

Woodhull & Claflin's Journal, 214–15.

Woodhull & Claflin's Weekly, sisters found, 15–17; 24, 26, on V., 33–4; 41, 51, 54, 71, accused of blackmail, 78–80; 82, 85, suspends publication, 97; 98, prints Beecher exposé, 101–5; Challis scandal, 105–7; first-run sellout, 107; and Comstock, 112; confiscated, 113, 116; editors arrested, 114; 118, 129, 137, 141, 147, 149, 162–4, 183–5, 187–8, 204, 206, 209, 256–7, 260, 275–6, 281, 289, 296.

Worcester (England) *Daily Times,* obit on V., 327.

Worcester *Spy,* 78.